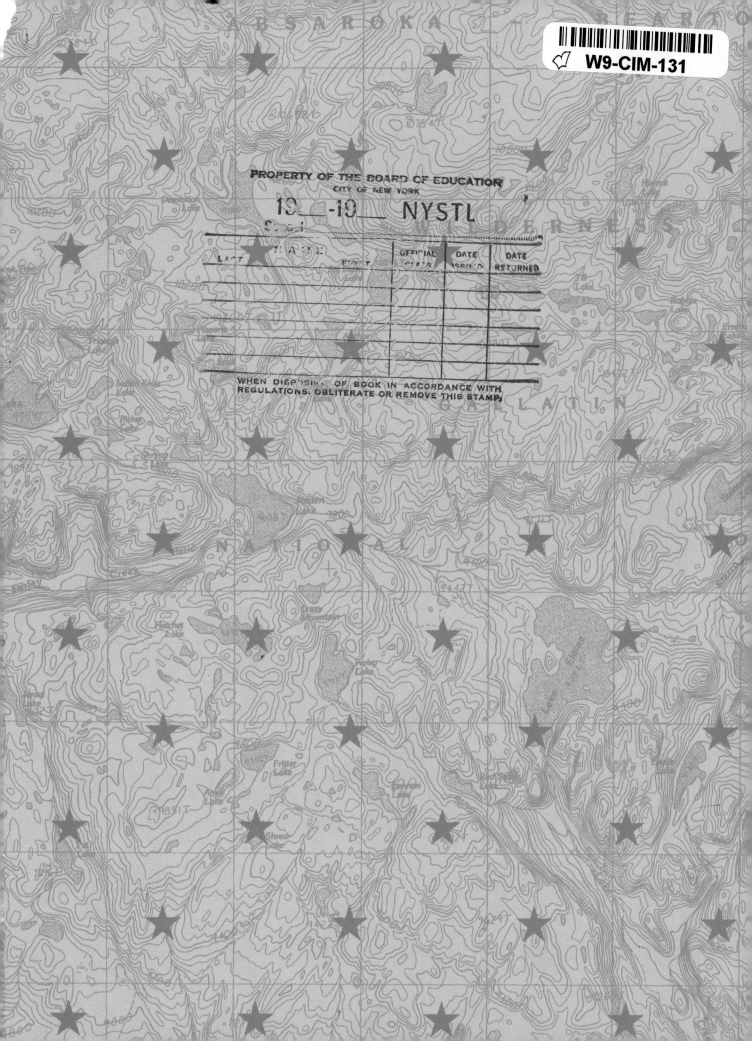

W9-CIM-131

HOUGHTON MIFFLIN HARCOURT

SOCIAL STUDIES

NEW YORK CITY

NEW YORK HISTORY AND GOVERNMENT

Program Authors

Dr. Herman J. Viola
Dr. Sarah Witham Bednarz
Dr. Carlos E. Cortés

Dr. Cheryl Jennings
Dr. Mark C. Schug
Dr. Charles S. White

Visit **Education Place**®
www.eduplace.com/kids

 HOUGHTON MIFFLIN HARCOURT

Authors

Senior Author
Dr. Herman J. Viola
Curator Emeritus
Smithsonian Institution

Dr. Cheryl Jennings
Project Director
Florida Institute of Education
University of North Florida

Dr. Sarah Witham Bednarz
Associate Professor, Geography
Texas A&M University

Dr. Mark C. Schug
Professor and Director
Center for Economic Education
University of Wisconsin, Milwaukee

Dr. Carlos E. Cortés
Professor Emertius, History
University of California, Riverside

Dr. Charles S. White
Associate Professor
School of Education
Boston University

Program Consultants

Philip J. Deloria
Associate Professor
Department of History and
Program in American Studies
University of Michigan

Lucien Ellington
UC Professor of Education and Asia
Program Co-Director
University of Tennessee, Chattanooga

Thelma Wills Foote
Associate Professor
University of California

Stephen J. Fugita
Distinguished Professor
Psychology and Ethnic Studies
Santa Clara University

Charles C. Haynes
Senior Scholar
First Amendment Center

Ted Hemmingway
Professor of History
The Florida Agricultural &
Mechanical University

Douglas Monroy
Professor of History
The Colorado College

Lynette K. Oshima
Assistant Professor
Department of Language, Literacy
and Sociocultural Studies and Social
Studies Program Coordinator
University of New Mexico

Jeffrey Strickland
Assistant Professor, History
University of Texas Pan American

Clifford E. Trafzer
Professor of History and
American Indian Studies
University of California

New York State Social Studies Standards
Elementary School

STANDARD 1

HISTORY OF THE UNITED STATES AND NEW YORK

Students will use a variety of intellectual skills to demonstrate their understanding of major ideas, eras, themes, developments, and turning points in the history of the United States and New York.

1.1 The study of New York State and United States history requires an analysis of the development of American culture, its diversity and multicultural context, and the ways people are unified by many values, practices, and traditions.

1.2 Important ideas, social and cultural values, beliefs, and traditions from New York State and United States history illustrate the connections and interactions of people and events across time and from a variety of perspectives.

1.3 The study about the major social, political, economic, cultural, and religious developments in New York State and United States history involves learning about the important roles and contributions of individuals and groups.

1.4 The skills of historical analysis include the ability to: explain the significance of historical evidence, weigh the importance, reliability, and validity of evidence, understand the concept of multiple causation, and understand the importance of changing and competing interpretations of different historical developments.

STANDARD 2

WORLD HISTORY

Students will use a variety of intellectual skills to demonstrate their understanding of major ideas, eras, themes, developments, and turning points in world history and examine the broad sweep of history from a variety of perspectives.

2.1 The study of world history requires an understanding of world cultures and civilizations, including an analysis of important ideas, social and cultural values, beliefs, and traditions. This study also examines the human condition and the connections and interactions of people across time and space and the ways different people view the same event or issue from a variety of perspectives.

2.2 Establishing timeframes, exploring different periodizations, examining themes across time and within cultures, and focusing on important turning points in world history help organize the study of world cultures and civilizations.

2.3 The study of the major social, political, cultural, and religious developments in world history involves learning about the important roles and contributions of individuals and groups.

2.4 The skills of historical analysis include the ability to investigate differing and competing interpretations of the theories of history, hypothesize about why interpretations change over time, explain the importance of historical evidence, and understand the concepts of change and continuity over time.

STANDARD 3

GEOGRAPHY

Students will use a variety of intellectual skills to demonstrate their understanding of the geography of the interdependent world in which we live — local, national, and global — including the distribution of people, places, and environments over the Earth's surface.

3.1 Geography can be divided into six essential elements, which can be used to analyze important historic, geographic, economic, and environmental questions and issues. These six elements include: the world in spatial terms, places and regions, physical settings (including natural resources), human systems, environment and society, and the use of geography.

3.2 Geography requires the development and application of the skills of asking and answering geography questions, analyzing theories of geography, and acquiring and organizing geographic information.

STANDARD 4

ECONOMICS

Students will use a variety of intellectual skills to demonstrate their understanding of how the United States and other societies develop economic systems and associated institutions to allocate scarce resources, how major decision-making units function in the U.S. and other national economies, and how an economy solves the scarcity problem through market and non-market mechanisms.

4.1 The study of economics requires an understanding of major economic concepts and systems, the principles of economic decision making, and the interdependence of economies and economic systems throughout the world.

4.2 Economics requires the development and application of the skills needed to make informed and well-reasoned economic decisions in daily and national life.

STANDARD 5

CIVICS, CITIZENSHIP, AND GOVERNMENT

Students will use a variety of intellectual skills to demonstrate their understanding of the necessity for establishing governments, the governmental system of the United States and other nations, the United States Constitution, the basic civic values of American constitutional democracy, and the roles, rights, and responsibilities of citizenship, including avenues of participation.

5.1 The study of civics, citizenship, and government involves learning about political systems; the purposes of government and civic life; and the differing assumptions held by people across time and place regarding power, authority, governance, and law.

5.2 The state and federal governments established by the Constitutions of the United States and the State of New York embody basic civic values (such as justice, honesty, self-discipline, due process, equality, majority rule with respect for minority rights, and respect for self, others, and property), principles, and practices and establish a system of shared and limited government.

5.3 Central to civics and citizenship is an understanding of the roles of the citizen within American constitutional democracy and the scope of a citizen's rights and responsibilities.

5.4 The study of civics and citizenship requires the ability to probe ideas and assumptions, ask and answer analytical questions, take a skeptical attitude toward questionable arguments, evaluate evidence, formulate rational conclusions, and develop and refine participatory skills.

New York's Land and First People

NYC UNIT 1

1

🌐 Unit Almanac **Physical Features of New York State** **2**

Reading Social Studies **4**

CHAPTER 1 **New York's Geography** **6**

Study Skills **7**
Vocabulary Preview **8**

Lesson 1 │ New York's Location **10**

Lesson 2 │ Geography of New York **14**

Infographics
New York from Space **18**

Skillbuilder
Review Map Skills **20**

Chapter 1 Review **22**

CHAPTER 2 **New York's First People** **24**

Study Skills **25**
Vocabulary Preview **26**

Lesson 1 │ Algonquians and Haudenosaunee **28**

Primary Sources
Native American Artifacts **32**

Skillbuilder
Make a Map **34**

Lesson 2 │ Case Study
The Lenape **36**

Biography
Native Americans Past and Present **42**

Chapter 2 Review **44**

Fun with Social Studies **46**
Unit 1 Review for Understanding **48**
Unit 1 Activities **50**

🌐 Unit Almanac **European Explorers Around New York**............ 52

Reading Social Studies................ 54

CHAPTER 3 **Early New York City**.................... 56

Study Skills.................... 57

Vocabulary Preview.................... 58

Lesson 1 First Explorers.................... 60

Biography
Explorers of New York.................... 64

Skillbuilder
Use Latitude and Longitude.................... 66

Lesson 2 Case Study
New Amsterdam.................... 68

Infographics
Dutch Style in New Amsterdam.................... 74

Lesson 3 Case Study
English Rule in New York.................... 76

Primary Sources
African Americans in New York City.................... 80

Skillbuilder
Read a Circle Graph.................... 82

Chapter 3 Review.................... 84

Fun with Social Studies.................... 86
Unit 2 Review for Understanding.................... 88
Unit 2 Activities.................... 90

NYC UNIT 3

The Revolution in New York

91

🌐 Unit Almanac **North America, 1740s**............................ 92

Reading Social Studies 94

| CHAPTER 4 | **The Thirteen Colonies** | 96 |

Study Skills 97

Vocabulary Preview 98

Lesson 1 | Starting the Colonies 100

Lesson 2 | Characteristics of the Colonies 104

Infographics
Trade with England 110

Lesson 3 | The New York Colony 112

Skillbuilder
Write a Report 116

Chapter 4 Review 118

| CHAPTER 5 | **The American Revolution** | 120 |

Study Skills 121

Vocabulary Preview 122

Lesson 1 | Colonists Resist 124

Primary Sources
The Declaration of Independence 128

Skillbuilder
Understand Point of View 130

Lesson 2 | Role of New York in the War 132

Biography
New York's Revolutionary Leaders 138

Chapter 5 Review 140

Fun with Social Studies 142

Unit 3 Review for Understanding 144

Unit 3 Activities 146

The New Nation

147

🌐 **Unit Almanac** Westward Expansion.................................. 148

Reading Social Studies 150

CHAPTER 6 **The Challenge of Independence** 152

Study Skills.. 153

Vocabulary Preview 154

Lesson 1 | The Constitution............................... 156

Primary Sources

Foundations of Our Government........................... 160

Skillbuilder

Make a Timeline 162

Lesson 2 | The Bill of Rights............................... 164

Biography

Strengthening Democracy 168

Infographics

Values and Traditions 170

Skillbuilder

Interpret Historical Images 172

Chapter 6 Review 174

Fun with Social Studies................................... 176

Unit 4 Review for Understanding...................... 178

Unit 4 Activities 180

Growth of New York 181

NYC UNIT 5

🌐 Unit Almanac Railroads in New York, mid-1800s................. 182
Reading Social Studies 184

CHAPTER 7 The United States in the Early 1800s 186

Study Skills.. 187
Vocabulary Preview 188

Lesson 1 | The Industrial Revolution 190
Lesson 2 | The Struggle for Rights 196
Lesson 3 | The Civil War 200
Primary Sources
Civil War Photographs 204
Skillbuilder
Resolve Conflicts 206

Chapter 7 Review 208

CHAPTER 8 Immigration and Migration 210

Study Skills.. 211
Vocabulary Preview 212

Lesson 1 | Case Study
The Melting Pot 214
Skillbuilder
Identify Primary and Secondary Sources............. 220

Lesson 2 | Case Study
Living in New York..................................... 222
Infographics
New York City Neighborhoods 228

Lesson 3 | Case Study
New York City Expands 230
Biography
Labor Union Leaders 236

Chapter 8 Review 238

Fun with Social Studies 240
Unit 5 Review for Understanding 242
Unit 5 Activities 244

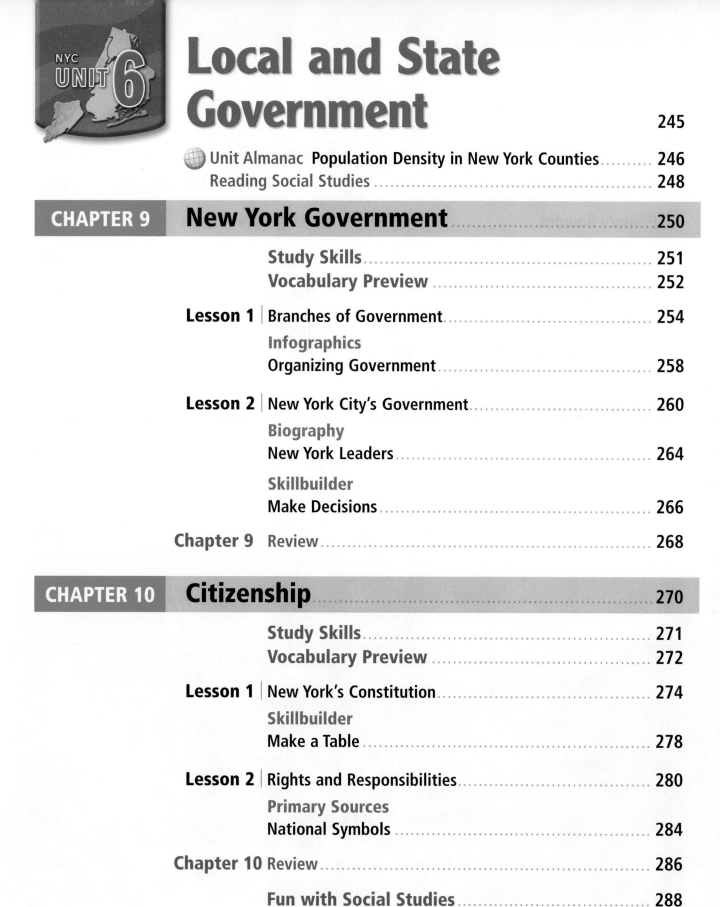

NYC UNIT 6

Local and State Government

245

🌐 Unit Almanac **Population Density in New York Counties** 246
Reading Social Studies 248

CHAPTER 9 | **New York Government** 250

Study Skills 251
Vocabulary Preview 252

Lesson 1 | Branches of Government 254
Infographics
Organizing Government 258

Lesson 2 | New York City's Government 260
Biography
New York Leaders 264

Skillbuilder
Make Decisions 266

Chapter 9 Review 268

CHAPTER 10 | **Citizenship** 270

Study Skills 271
Vocabulary Preview 272

Lesson 1 | New York's Constitution 274
Skillbuilder
Make a Table 278

Lesson 2 | Rights and Responsibilities 280
Primary Sources
National Symbols 284

Chapter 10 Review 286

Fun with Social Studies 288
Unit 6 Review for Understanding 290
Unit 6 Activities 292

References

Citizenship Handbook R2

New York Governors R2

Primary Sources R3

The Declaration of Independence R3

The Constitution of
    the United States, 1789 .... R6

New York Constitution Excerpts R24

Resources R26

Five Themes of Geography R26

Geographic Terms R28

Atlas R30

Glossary R46

Index R50

Acknowledgments R62

Features

Infographics

New York from Space	18
Dutch Style in New Amsterdam	74
Trade with England	110
Values and Traditions	170
New York City Neighborhoods	228
Organizing Government	258

Primary Sources

Native American Artifacts	32
African Americans in New York City	80
The Declaration of Independence	128
Foundations of Our Government	160
Civil War Photographs	204
National Symbols	284

Biographies

Ely S. Parker	42
Joanne Shenandoah	43
The Mohawk Ironworkers	43
Giovanni da Verrazano	64
Henry Hudson	65
Samuel de Champlain	65
Cornplanter	138
George Clinton	139
John Jay	139
Alexander Hamilton	168
Samuel Eli Cornish	169
Rose Schneiderman	236
Kate Mullany	237
Asa Philip Randolph	237
Herman Badillo	264
Betty W. Ellerin	264
Fiorello La Guardia	265
Constance Baker Motley	265

Skill Lessons

Take a step-by-step approach to learning and practicing key social studies skills.

Map and Globe Skills

Review Map Skills	20
Make a Map	34
Use Latitude and Longitude	66

Skill Practice: Reading Maps
12, 15, 16, 30, 37, 69, 101, 104, 126, 133, 201

Chart and Graph Skills

Read a Circle Graph	82
Make a Timeline	162
Make a Table	278

Skill Practice: Reading Charts
105, 106, 107

Skill Practice: Reading Graphs
78

Study Skills

Write a Report	116
Identify Primary and Secondary Sources	220

Citizenship Skills

Understand Point of View	130
Resolve Conflicts	206
Make Decisions	266

Reading and Thinking Skills

Interpret Historical Images	172

Reading Skills/Graphic Organizer

Categorize
76, 260

Cause and Effect
124, 190, 214, 222

Classify
132

Compare and Contrast
28, 104, 200, 274

Draw Conclusions
60, 100, 230

Generalize
10

Main Idea and Details
14, 36, 68, 112, 156, 280

Problem and Solution
164

Sequence
196

Summarize
254

Reading Social Studies Skills

Generalize	4
Draw Conclusions	54
Compare and Contrast	94
Main Ideas and Details	150
Cause and Effect	184
Summarize	248

Chapter Study Skills

Preview and Question	7
Anticipation Guide	25
Pose Questions	57
Use a K-W-L Chart	97

Connect Ideas	121
Use Visuals	153
Organize Information	187
Vocabulary	211
Skim and Scan	251
Make an Outline	271

Visual Learning

Become skilled at reading visuals. Graphs, maps, and fine art help you put all of the information together.

Maps

Physical Features of New York State	2
Location of New York State: Continental United States	12
Location of New York State: North America	12
Location of New York State: Western Hemisphere	12
New York Land Regions	15
New York's Lakes and Rivers	16
New York State	20
New York	23
New York Native Americans, 1100	30
Lenape Lands	37
Eastern United States Resources	49
European Exploration Around New York	52
Dutch Settlement, 1611–1640	62
Latitude Globe	66
Longitude Globe	66
The Northeast	67
New Netherland	69
New York: Latitude and Longitude	85
Henry Hudson's Voyage	89
North America, 1740s	92
The Thirteen Colonies	101
Triangular Trade Routes	108
Cannon Route from Fort Ticonderoga	126
New York American Revolution Battles	133
Westward Expansion	148
Railroads in New York, mid-1800s	182
Traveling the Erie Canal	192

Union and Confederate States, 1861   201
New York City Neighborhoods, 1920   229
Population Density in New York Counties   246
New York Counties   256
The World: Political   R30
The World: Physical   R32
Western Hemisphere: Political   R34
Western Hemisphere: Physical   R35
United States: Political   R36
United States: Physical   R38
New York: Political   R40
New York: Physical   R41
New York: Precipitation   R42
New York: Temperature   R42
New York: Major Roads and Airports   R43
New York: State Parks   R43
Albany, New York   R44
Buffalo, New York   R44
New York City Boroughs   R45

Charts and Graphs

Mountains in New York   3
Rivers in New York   3
New York by the Numbers   19
Seasonal Ceremonies   40
Crossing the Atlantic Through the Years   53
Population Growth of New York City   78
Workers in New York, 1700s   83
City Populations, 1740s   93
City Populations Today   93
New England Colonies   105
Middle Colonies   106
Southern Colonies   107
New York–England Trade   110
Traded Goods   111
Population Growth, 1800s   149
Population Growth Today   149
Immigration to New York State, 1860   183
Immigration to New York State Today   183
Changes in Immigration, 1880–1920   215
Population of New York City, 1900   222
Immigrants in Manhattan, 1900–1950   228
Famous New York City Skyscrapers   231
New York City Land Area   247
New York City Population, 2006   247

National and State Governments   258
Make Decisions   266
Amendments to New York's Constitution   276
Amendments to the
     New York State Constitution   278
Federal Holidays   283
Citizens Take Responsibility in New York City   287

Timelines

English Rule in New York   76
Moving Toward Independence   128
History of the Constitution   162
Chapter Preview Timelines
26, 58, 98, 122, 154, 188, 212
Lesson Timelines
60, 100, 104, 112, 124, 132, 156, 164, 190, 196, 200, 274
Lesson Review Timelines
63, 103, 127, 137, 159, 195, 199, 203, 277
Chapter Review Timelines
85, 119, 141, 175, 209, 239, 287
Skillbuilder Timeline   162

Diagrams and Infographics

New York from Space   18
Three Sisters   31
Lenape Village   38
New Amsterdam in the 1600s   70
Dutch Style in New Amsterdam   74
Trade with England   110
Values and Traditions   170
Traveling the Erie Canal   192
New York City Neighborhoods   228
New York's Three Branches of Government   255
Organizing Government   258
Checks and Balances   259

New York City Databank

CITY OF NEW YORK

Windmill sails

Beaver

American Eagle

Latin for "Seal of New York City"

Year of city's founding

New York City Facts

Population, 2006	8,214,426
Land Area	322 square miles
Economy	**Leading Industries:** Finance, transportation, communications, construction, tourism, publishing, entertainment
City Nicknames	The Big Apple, Gotham City, Empire City, The City That Never Sleeps

▶ Empire State Building

When it was built in 1931, the Empire State Building was the tallest building in the world.

▲ Peregrine Falcons

New York City is home to the largest population of peregrine falcons of any city in the world.

▲ New York City Subway

There are over 722 miles of subway tracks running through New York City.

▲ Pelham Bay Park

Pelham Bay is the largest park in New York City. Over 400 species of animals live in the 2,764 acres of the park.

◀ St. Paul's Chapel

Built in 1766, St. Paul's Chapel is the oldest public building in New York City. George Washington attended church here on the day he became President.

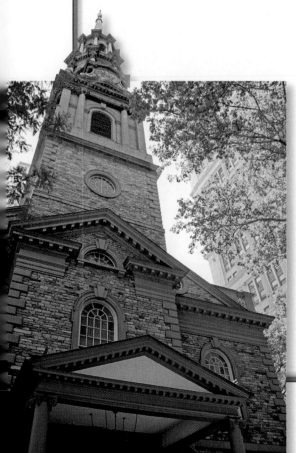

Constitution Day

★★★★★★★★★★★★★★★★★★★★★★★★

What are all the things a government should do? That's a big question. Leaders of our new nation, over 200 years ago, had to decide the answer. Their goal was to create a plan for the United States government. They wanted a government that could protect the common good and serve the people. The plan they created was called the Constitution of the United States. They signed it on September 17, 1787. A special part of the Constitution, called the Bill of Rights, listed rights the Constitution would protect.

Today, the Constitution still organizes our government and protects our rights. We celebrate Constitution Day and Citizenship Day during the week of September 17.

Visitors can view the original Constitution at the National Archives Building in Washington, D.C.

The Constitution begins with the words "We the People," which shows that it was written by and for the people of the United States.

Today, the Constitution has 4,440 words. It is the oldest and shortest written constitution in the world.

Two of the people who worked on the Constitution, George Washington and James Madison, later became Presidents of the new country.

Activity

WHAT ARE YOUR RIGHTS? The Bill of Rights protects many important rights including freedom of religion, freedom of speech, and freedom of the press. Choose one of these rights and create a display. Use images and captions to show how people enjoy this freedom.

New York's Land and First People

The Big Idea

How did the early Native Americans in New York use the resources around them?

WHAT TO KNOW

✔ What are the different ways to describe the location of New York?

✔ What are New York's major landforms and bodies of water?

✔ What was the Haudenosaunee League?

✔ What natural resources did the Lenape use for food and shelter?

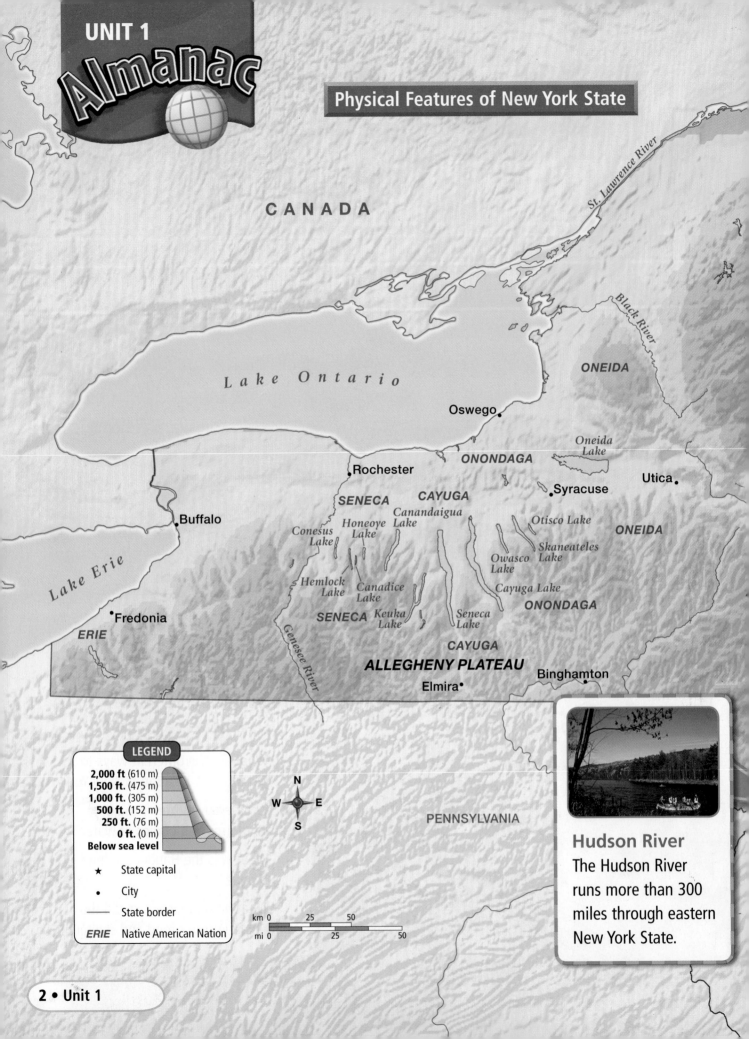

Physical Features of New York State

CANADA

St. Lawrence River

Black River

Lake Ontario

ONEIDA

Oswego

Oneida Lake

ONONDAGA

Rochester

Syracuse

Utica

SENECA

CAYUGA

Canandaigua Lake

Otisco Lake

ONEIDA

Buffalo

Honeoye Lake

Conesus Lake

Skaneateles Lake

Owasco Lake

Cayuga Lake

ONONDAGA

Hemlock Lake

Canadice Lake

Lake Erie

SENECA

Keuka Lake

Seneca Lake

Fredonia

CAYUGA

ERIE

Genesee River

ALLEGHENY PLATEAU

Binghamton

Elmira

PENNSYLVANIA

LEGEND

2,000 ft (610 m)
1,500 ft. (475 m)
1,000 ft. (305 m)
500 ft. (152 m)
250 ft. (76 m)
0 ft. (0 m)
Below sea level

★   State capital

•   City

—   State border

ERIE   Native American Nation

N W E S

km 0   25   50
mi 0   25   50

Hudson River

The Hudson River runs more than 300 miles through eastern New York State.

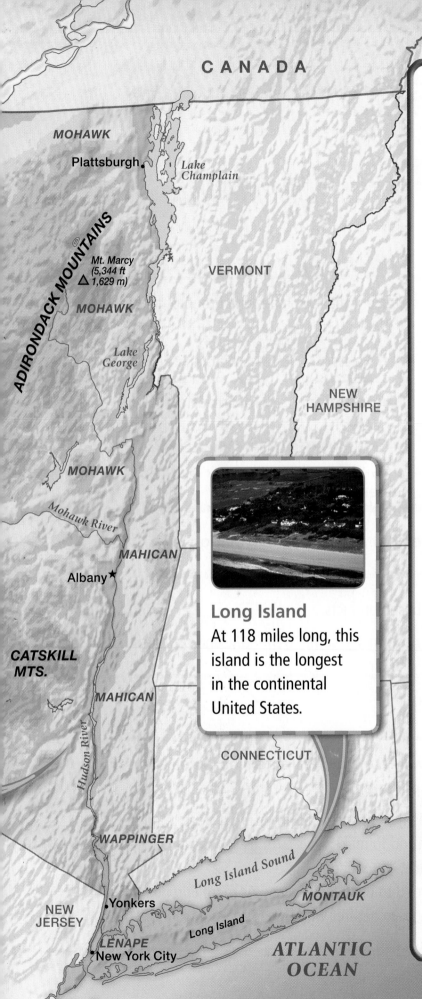

CANADA

MOHAWK

Plattsburgh

Lake Champlain

ADIRONDACK MOUNTAINS

Mt. Marcy
(5,344 ft
△ 1,629 m)

VERMONT

MOHAWK

Lake George

NEW HAMPSHIRE

MOHAWK

Mohawk River

MAHICAN

Albany ★

CATSKILL MTS.

MAHICAN

Hudson River

WAPPINGER

Long Island Sound

MONTAUK

NEW JERSEY

Yonkers

LENAPE
New York City

Long Island

ATLANTIC OCEAN

Long Island
At 118 miles long, this island is the longest in the continental United States.

Connect to
New York

Mountains in New York

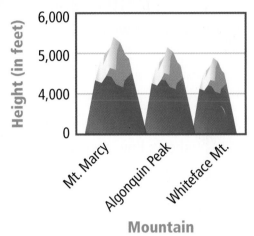

Height (in feet)

6,000
5,000
4,000
0

Mt. Marcy   Algonquin Peak   Whiteface Mt.

Mountain

Rivers in New York

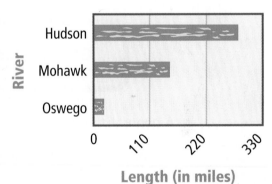

River

Hudson

Mohawk

Oswego

0   110   220   330

Length (in miles)

What is the difference in lengths between the Hudson and Oswego rivers?

Reading Social Studies

Generalize

Why It Matters Being able to generalize can help you better understand what you read.

Learn the Skill

A **generalization** is a broad statement that summarizes a group of facts and shows how they are related.

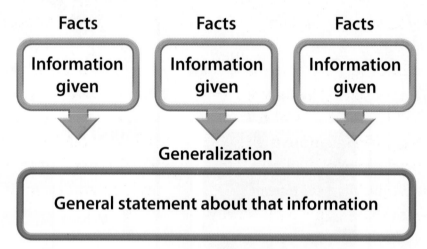

- A generalization is always based on facts.
- Signal words may include *most, many, some, generally,* and *usually.*

Practice the Skill

Read the paragraphs below. Make a generalization based on the information in the second paragraph.

Facts   Native Americans, such as the Lenape, used wood from trees to build their homes. They also used wood to make tools such as spoons and spears. **Generalization** Native Americans had many uses for wood.

European settlers used wood to build their homes. As more Europeans arrived, they needed more wood. To get this wood, people cut down more trees.

Apply the Skill

Read the paragraphs, and answer the questions.

New York City's Parks

The New York City park system includes more than 1,700 parks, playgrounds, and recreation areas. There are many different kinds of parks. Some parks are wooded areas. Others are made up of skating rinks or swimming pools.

New York City's parks come in many different sizes. The largest is Pelham Bay Park in the Bronx. It is 2,765 acres, which is more than three times the size of Central Park. The smallest park is Manhattan's Septuagesimo Uno. This park is only about 1,700 square feet—that's smaller than some big apartments!

Many people enjoy visiting New York City's parks for recreation. Depending on which park you visit, you might see people jogging, skating, or playing sports. On days with good weather, New Yorkers like to picnic in their favorite park. You can also see lots of pets at city parks. For pet owners, a day at the park can be a fun way for pets and their owners to enjoy fresh air and exercise.

Generalize

1. What generalization can you make about the kinds of parks found in New York City?

2. What generalization can you make about why people visit New York City's parks?

New York's Geography

Hudson River Valley

Study Skills

PREVIEW AND QUESTION

Previewing a lesson to identify main ideas, and asking yourself questions about those ideas, can help you read to find important information.

- To preview a lesson, read the lesson title and the section titles. Look at the pictures and read their captions. Try to get an idea of the main topic, and think of questions you have.

- Read the lesson to find the answers to your questions. Then recite, or say the answer aloud. Finally, review what you have read.

New York's Geography				
Preview	Questions	Read	Recite	Review
Lesson 1 You can describe New York's location in different ways	In which region of the United States is New York?	✓	✓	✓
Lesson 2				

Vocabulary Preview

continent

New York State is located on the **continent** of North America. North America is one of seven continents. **page 12**

landform

The state of New York has many **landforms,** such as mountains and islands. The Adirondack Mountains are in northern New York. **page 14**

Reading Strategy

Predict and Infer Use this strategy as you read this chapter. Look at the pictures in a lesson to predict what it will be about.

glacier

Large ice sheets once covered much of Earth. These **glaciers** helped shape many of the hills, plains, lakes, and rivers in New York. **page 14**

coastal plain

New York City is located near the ocean. Parts of the city are on the **coastal plain,** where the land is flat and level. **page 15**

Go Digital visit www.eduplace.com/nycssp/

New York's Location

WHAT TO KNOW
What are the different ways to describe the location of New York?

VOCABULARY
environment
region
continent
hemisphere

READING SKILL
Generalize As you read, find information that supports the general statement that there are many ways to describe New York's location.

New York's location

Before You Read How would you describe where you live? Are there mountains or plains? Do you go skiing in the winter or swimming in the summer? Landforms often affect what people do.

Understanding Geography

Main Idea Geography tells us about places and the people who live there.

There are many ways to describe New York State and New York City. You could describe the land, where people live, and what people do. You could compare New York's location to other states. When you study a place and its features, you are studying its geography. Geography is the study of the people and places of Earth.

Geographers study how people live in and use the environment. The **environment** includes the water, land, and air that surround us. Geographers ask many questions when they study a place: Where is it? What do people do there? How do they use the land?

Elk Lake This lake is located in the Adirondack Mountains of New York.

Albany Cities such as Albany grew up along the Hudson River because of the resources the river provided.

Looking at New York

Geographers use maps to study the location of a place. A map shows that New York is a state located in the northeastern region of the United States. A **region** is an area that has one or more features in common. New York shares its location in the northeast with several other states. Geographers often compare regions to learn how they are alike and different.

The geography of New York includes its features—mountains, plains, lakes, and rivers. It includes big cities, such as New York City, Buffalo, and Rochester, and small farming communities, such as Geneseo.

Geography is also about movement. It includes the ways people travel from place to place. It looks at how people exchange ideas with each other.

Shaping the Environment

Across New York, people interact with their environments. The environment influences what people eat, how they build homes, and the kind of work they do. Where people choose to live depends on the environment. People also change their environment. For example, they cut down trees and use the wood to build houses. People build roads, highways, and bridges to make traveling easier.

✓ READING CHECK GENERALIZE What generalizations can you make about New York's environment?

Describing Location

Main Idea There are many ways to describe the location of New York.

You can describe the location of your school in many ways. Your school has an address. It is located in a city. Your school is also located in a state, New York, and a country, the United States. Your school is located on a continent, too. A **continent** is a very large landmass. The United States is on the continent of North America.

Geographers also use another way to tell where people live. They divide Earth into hemispheres. A **hemisphere** is one half of Earth's surface. The equator is an imaginary line that divides Earth into Northern and Southern hemispheres. Another imaginary line, the prime meridian, divides Earth into Eastern and Western hemispheres. The United States is in the Northern and Western hemispheres.

You could say that New York State is in the northeastern part of the United States. You could point out that it is on the continent of North America. Then you could explain that it is in the Northern and Western hemispheres.

SKILL **Reading Maps** Which ocean borders New York?

Location of New York State

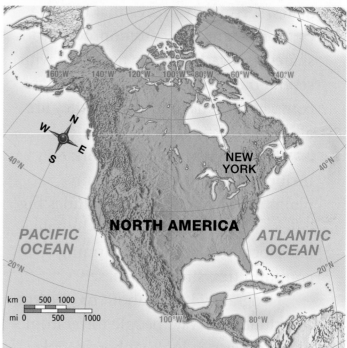

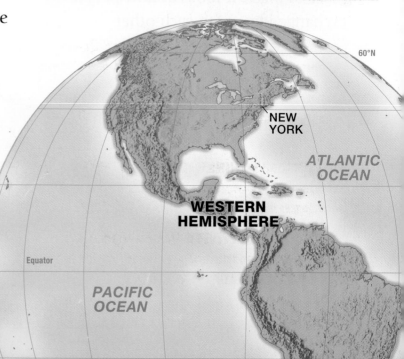

Using a Map

You can use a map to give more details about New York's location. You can say that New York's northern border separates Canada and the United States. Lake Ontario and Lake Erie lie to the west. The states of Pennsylvania and New Jersey are to the south. Connecticut, Massachusetts, and Vermont are on the eastern border.

Different maps can show different types of information about a place. Physical maps show where landforms such as mountains are located. Political maps show boundaries between states or nations. The kind of maps geographers use depends on the questions that they are asking.

✓ READING CHECK MAIN IDEA AND DETAILS
What states share a border with New York?

SUMMARY

Geography is the study of the people and places of Earth. There are many ways to describe the geographical location of New York. Maps give details about a place's location, and they can show different types of information about a place.

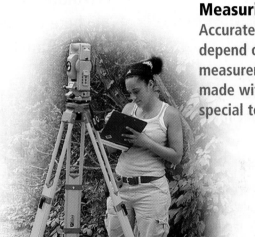

Measuring Tool
Accurate maps depend on exact measurements made with special tools.

Lesson Review

❶ **WHAT TO KNOW** What are the different ways to describe the location of New York?

❷ **VOCABULARY** Use **environment** and **region** in a sentence about where you live.

❸ **CRITICAL THINKING: Analyze** How have people in your community changed the environment?

❹ **WRITING ACTIVITY** Write a description of your community's location. Include at least five details.

❺ 🔄 **READING SKILL** Complete the graphic organizer to generalize about this lesson.

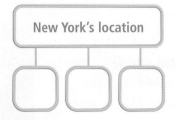

New York's location

N

20°N

0°

20°S

Geography of New York

WHAT TO KNOW
What are New York's major landforms and bodies of water?

VOCABULARY
landform
glacier
plateau
coastal plain

READING SKILL
Main Idea and Details
Write details about New York's landforms.

NEW YORK'S LANDFORMS

Before You Read When you look out of your window, what does the land look like? Depending on where you live, you might see a lake, a river, hills, mountains, or farmland.

New York's Land

Main Idea New York has many types of landforms.

If you drove across the state of New York, you would see many different landforms, including tall mountains, rolling hills, and flat plains. A **landform** is a natural feature of Earth's surface.

Long before the first people arrived, present-day New York was mostly low land with a range of mountains in the north. Then the climate became extremely cold for thousands of years. Giant glaciers moved across the land. A **glacier** is a huge, slow-moving sheet of ice. As they moved, the glaciers pushed rocks and soil. They flattened the land.

Then, about 10,000 years ago, the climate grew warmer. The glaciers melted. The land of New York had changed. The glaciers had created new landforms, such as valleys and islands.

Lake Placid Many of the lakes in the Adirondacks, including Lake Placid, were formed by glaciers.

New York Land Regions

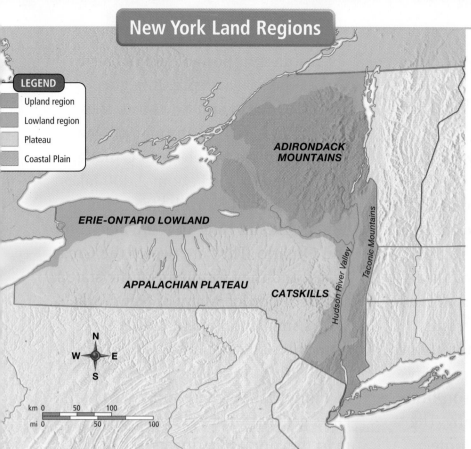

LEGEND
- Upland region
- Lowland region
- Plateau
- Coastal Plain

ADIRONDACK MOUNTAINS

ERIE-ONTARIO LOWLAND

APPALACHIAN PLATEAU

CATSKILLS

Taconic Mountains

Hudson River Valley

km 0 50 100
mi 0 50 100

Regions of New York
The state has several different regions. Dairy farms are found in the lowland regions.
SKILL **Reading Maps** Which region is in the southwestern part of New York?

Uplands and Lowlands

New York's uplands are in the northeastern part of the state. The Adirondack Upland includes Mount Marcy, the state's highest point. **Erin M. Crotty,** a New York State official who works to protect the environment, said that because of their history and natural beauty, the Adirondacks are

❝ one of the most important regions in the country. ❞

Some of the lowlands in New York follow the Hudson and Mohawk rivers. The Erie-Ontario Lowland is in the northwest along the Great Lakes. Fruit and vegetable farms, greenhouses, and dairy farms are found on the lowlands because of the rich soil and the mild weather near the lakes.

Plateaus and Plains

The Appalachian Plateau is in southern New York. A **plateau** is an area that rises above the nearby land. It may be flat or hilly. The Appalachian Plateau is New York's largest land region. Although the plateau has snowy winters, many small towns and dairy farms thrive there. Thousands of tourists visit the Catskill Mountains in this region.

The Atlantic Coastal Plain lies in southeastern New York. A **coastal plain** is flat, level land along a coast. The coastal plain includes Staten Island and Long Island. Long Island, with its popular sandy beaches, is the largest island on the East Coast.

✓**READING CHECK** MAIN IDEA AND DETAILS
Name some details of New York's lowlands.

New York's Waters

Main Idea New York State has many lakes and rivers.

New York's location between the Great Lakes and the Atlantic Ocean makes it a good place for trade and travel. So do the state's rivers and lakes. Beginning in the 1700s, settlers used waterways to travel the region. Many settlers built towns along the waterways.

The Hudson River flows south from the Adirondacks. It empties into the Atlantic Ocean at New York City. Ships can travel up the Hudson from New York City north to Albany. The Mohawk River begins near Rome, moves through central New York, and flows into the Hudson River.

Another important river in New York is the St. Lawrence. It begins in Lake Ontario and flows into the Atlantic Ocean. It forms part of New York's northern border with Canada.

Glaciers created about 2,000 lakes and ponds in New York State. The largest lakes in New York are lakes Erie and Ontario. They are two of the Great Lakes, and they form part of the state's northern border. Many of New York State's smaller lakes are in the Adirondack Mountains.

South of Lake Ontario are the 11 Finger Lakes. These long, skinny lakes get their name because on a map they look like fingers.

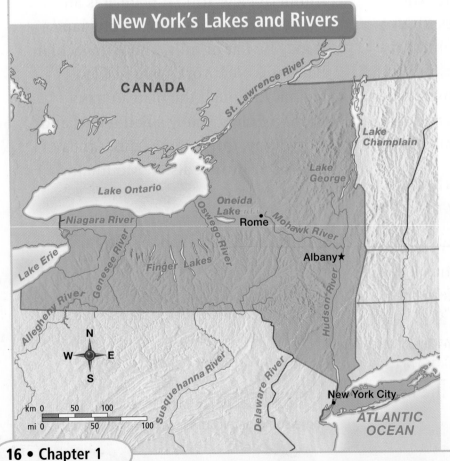

New York's Lakes and Rivers

CANADA

St. Lawrence River

Lake Champlain

Lake George

Lake Ontario

Oneida Lake

Niagara River

Oswego River

Rome

Mohawk River

Albany ★

Lake Erie

Genesee River

Finger Lakes

Allegheny River

Hudson River

Susquehanna River

Delaware River

New York City

ATLANTIC OCEAN

N W E S

km 0 50 100
mi 0 50 100

Water Resources The map shows some of the many lakes and rivers in New York.

SKILL **Reading Maps** What rivers flow into Lake Ontario?

Geography of New York City

New York City is made up of three major islands and part of the United States mainland. The three islands are Manhattan, Staten Island, and part of Long Island. Todt Hill on Staten Island is the city's highest area. The Hudson and East rivers connect to New York Harbor, one of the best large, natural harbors on the East Coast. The Harlem River separates Manhattan from the Bronx.

New York City's weather changes with each season. It has cold winters and hot, humid summers. Springs and autumns are milder, but can be stormy.

READING CHECK MAIN IDEA AND DETAILS
What are three important rivers in New York?

East River Flowing through New York City, this river separates Manhattan and the Bronx from Brooklyn and Queens.

SUMMARY

Glaciers shaped New York's land. Landforms include mountains, plateaus, and lowlands. New York also has many rivers and lakes.

Lesson Review

1 WHAT TO KNOW What are New York's major landforms and bodies of water?

2 VOCABULARY Complete the sentence below using one of these words.

coastal plain   plateau

A _____ is an area that rises above nearby land.

3 CRITICAL THINKING: Analyze How did rivers in New York help settlers?

4 ART ACTIVITY Create a postcard that shows a landform of New York. Include a drawing or photo and a short description of the area.

5 READING SKILL Complete the graphic organizer to show the main idea and details.

NEW YORK'S LANDFORMS

New York from Space

What does New York look like from high above? Satellite photographs can show you. A satellite is a machine that circles Earth miles above the surface. Satellites with cameras take photographs like the ones on these pages.

The geographic features of New York, such as lakes, rivers and mountains, can be seen from space. A satellite photo shows what those features look like.

New York City This satellite photo shows parts of New York City and New Jersey.

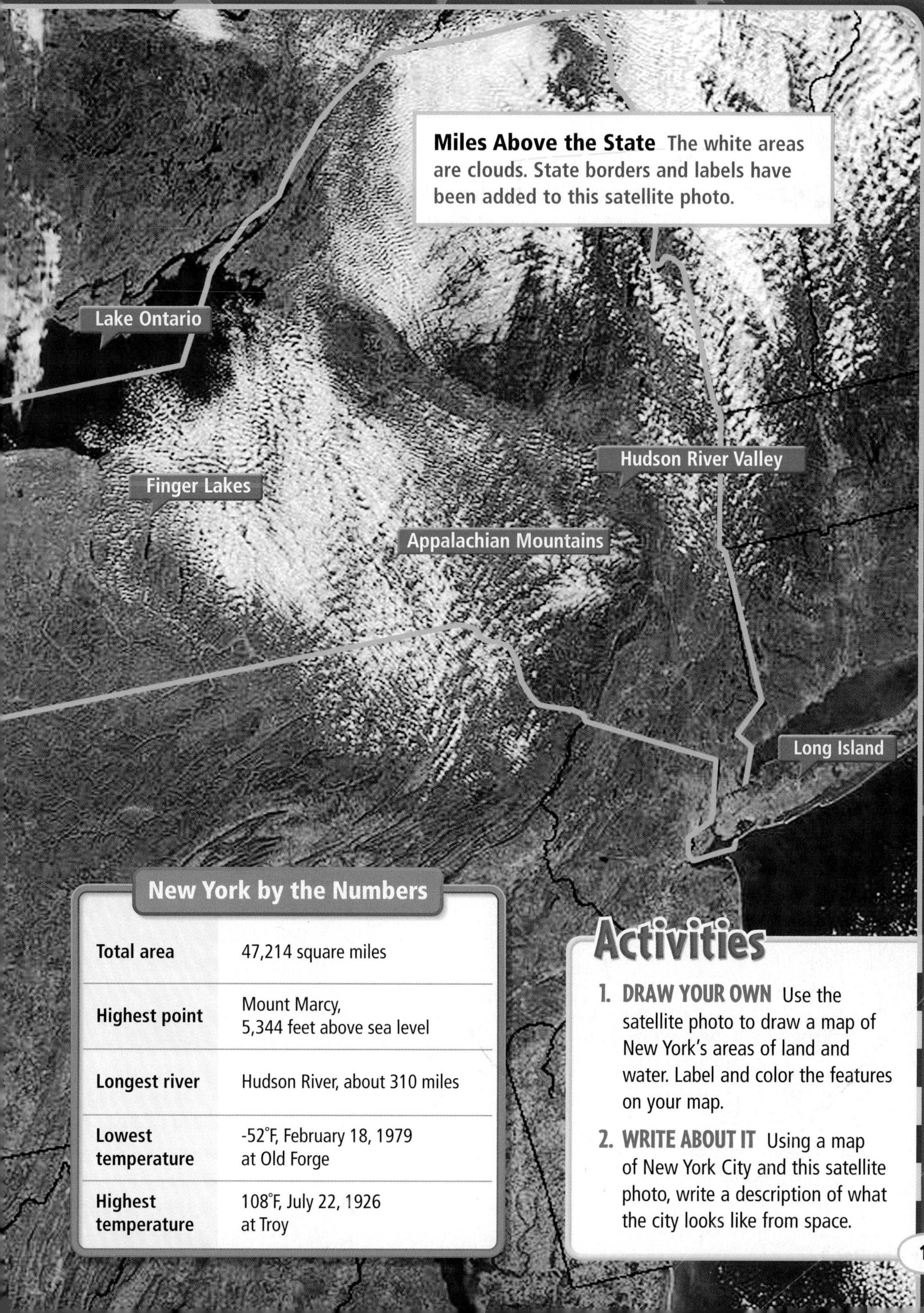

Miles Above the State The white areas are clouds. State borders and labels have been added to this satellite photo.

Lake Ontario

Finger Lakes

Hudson River Valley

Appalachian Mountains

Long Island

New York by the Numbers

Total area	47,214 square miles
Highest point	Mount Marcy, 5,344 feet above sea level
Longest river	Hudson River, about 310 miles
Lowest temperature	-52°F, February 18, 1979 at Old Forge
Highest temperature	108°F, July 22, 1926 at Troy

Activities

1. **DRAW YOUR OWN** Use the satellite photo to draw a map of New York's areas of land and water. Label and color the features on your map.

2. **WRITE ABOUT IT** Using a map of New York City and this satellite photo, write a description of what the city looks like from space.

Map and Globe Skills

Skillbuilder

Review Map Skills

Maps and globes show the surface of Earth. A map is a flat picture of all or part of Earth. A globe is a round model of Earth. People use maps and globes to locate places in the world.

New York State

CANADA

Plattsburgh

Lake Champlain

Adirondack Mountains

VERMONT

Lake George

NEW HAMPSHIRE

Lake Ontario

Rochester

Syracuse

Mohawk River

Buffalo

Lake Erie

Albany ★

Taconic Mountains

MASSACHUSETTS

Catskill Mountains

Hudson River

CONNECTICUT

LEGEND

★ State capital

• City

River

State boundary

PENNSYLVANIA

NEW JERSEY

Long Island

RHODE ISLAND

ATLANTIC OCEAN

km 0   50   100
mi 0   50   100

Learn the Skill

Step 1: Read the title of the map. It explains what the map is about.

Step 2: Study the map legend. The **legend** shows what the different symbols on the map mean.

LEGEND

★ State Capital

• City

∼ River

—— State Boundary

Step 3: Use the **compass rose** to find main directions such as north, south, east, and west. You can also use it to find directions such as northeast, northwest, southeast, and southwest.

Step 4: Use the **map scale** to find the distance between locations.

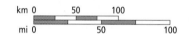

Practice the Skill

Use the map on page 20 to answer the questions.

1 What city is located near Lake Erie?

2 Are the Catskill Mountains north or south of the Adirondacks?

3 About how many miles apart are Albany and Plattsburgh?

Apply the Skill

Choose any starting point on the map on page 20. Write step-by-step instructions to tell someone how to get from that place to another place on the map.

Visual Summary

1–3.  For each item below, write details that describe New York's geography.

Landforms

New York's Geography

Bodies of Water

Regions

Facts and Main Ideas

Answer each question below.

4. **Geography** Explain where New York is located.

5. **Geography** In what ways did glaciers affect landforms in New York?

6. **Geography** What is the environment of New York's Appalachian Plateau like?

7. **Geography** What two lakes help form New York's northern border?

Vocabulary

Choose the correct word from the list below to complete each sentence.

hemisphere, p. 12
glacier, p. 14
plateau, p. 15

8. A _____ is a huge, slow-moving sheet of ice.

9. A flat or hilly area that rises above nearby land is a _____.

10. A _____ is one half of Earth's surface.

Apply Skills

Study the New York State map below. Then use your map skills to answer each question.

New York

11. If you traveled from Albany to Buffalo, in which direction would you travel?

   A. north

   B. south

   C. east

   D. west

12. Which part of the map would help you locate a river?

   A. legend

   B. title

   C. compass rose

   D. scale

Critical Thinking

Write a short paragraph to answer each question.

13. Classify If you made a map of the area around your school, what information would be good to include?

14. Compare and Contrast In what ways are a plateau and a mountain alike? In what ways are these landforms different?

15. Draw Conclusions How might the location of rivers affect where people choose to live in New York?

Activities

Map Activity Make a map of one of New York State's landforms, such as the Tug Hill Plateau, Allegheny Plateau, or St. Lawrence Lowlands. Label cities and bodies of water.

Writing Activity Write a paragraph describing the environment of New York City. Describe landforms and bodies of water.

Go Digital Get help with your writing at www.eduplace.com/nycssp/

New York's First People

Ganondagan State Historic Site, New York

Study Skills

ANTICIPATION GUIDE

An anticipation guide can help you anticipate, or predict, what you will learn as you read.

- Read the lesson titles and section titles for clues.
- Read the question at the end of each section.
- Predict what you will learn as you read.
- Check your prediction to see if you were correct.

Native Americans in New York

Lenape		
Question	Prediction	Correct?
How did the Lenape use the resources in their environment to meet their basic needs?	They used land for farming and they used trees to make shelters.	

Haudenosaunee		
Question	Prediction	Correct?

Vocabulary Preview

wigwam

Algonquian Indians of New York lived in **wigwams.** These homes were often made of hides and reeds. **page 28**

confederation

Some Native American nations formed a **confederation.** These nations still work together today on issues such as pollution and peace. **page 30**

Chapter Timeline

About 20,000 years ago
Land bridge connects Asia to North America

| 20,000 years ago | 16,000 years ago | 12,000 years ago | 8,000 years ago |

Reading Strategy

Monitor and Clarify As you read, use this strategy to check your understanding of the chapter. Reread, if you have to.

maize

Early Native Americans grew corn called **maize.** Maize was often dried, and the kernels were pounded into flour. **page 31**

agriculture

Native Americans used **agriculture** to raise crops. They grew plants for food, such as corn, beans, and squash. **page 38**

About 3,000 years ago
Algonquian-speaking people in New York

About 900 years ago
Haudenosaunee form confederation

4,000 years ago **Today**

Go Digital visit www.eduplace.com/nycssp/

Algonquians and Haudenosaunee

▶ **WHAT TO KNOW**
What was the
Haudenosaunee League?

VOCABULARY

wigwam
tradition
confederation
longhouse
maize

READING SKILL
Compare and Contrast
Use the Venn diagram to
show how the Algonquians
and the Haudenosaunee
were alike and different.

Algonquian Haudenosaunee

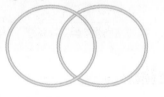

Before You Read If you have ever planted a seed
you know that you have to give it water and sun.
Native Americans who planted crops lived nearby
so they could take care of them.

How Algonquians Lived

Main Idea Hunting, gathering, and trading were important
to the Algonquian way of life.

No one knows exactly how the first people came
to North America because it happened thousands of
years ago. Many scientists think early people arrived
from Asia. About 20,000 years ago, Asia and Alaska
were probably connected by a land bridge, which
people could have crossed. Others believe people
may have come by boats.

By about 3,000 years ago, people who spoke
Algonquian (al GONG key uhn) languages lived
throughout New York State. Algonquian-speaking
people lived in wigwams. A **wigwam** is a house made
of a wood frame and covered
with hides or woven reeds.

Wigwams Families had
raised platforms for sleeping
and a stone fireplace.

Algonquian Craftwork
Algonquians made canoes from bark and bags from grass colored with natural dyes. This canoe is a model made around 1900.

Daily Life

Algonquians built canoes to travel long distances. As they traveled, they traded with other Native Americans. They traded food and furs for items such as copper from the Great Lakes area and seashells from the Gulf of Mexico. A hard black rock called obsidian came from the Rocky Mountains. A rock called mica came from present-day North and South Carolina. This rock separates easily into thin, shiny sheets. People used it to make decorations.

According to tradition, Algonquian men and women had different roles. A **tradition** is a way of life that has been followed for a long time. Algonquian men hunted, fished, and trapped. They also fought in wars. Women cared for the children, built wigwams, prepared food, and made clothing, mats, and most tools.

Using Resources

In the summer, the Algonquians camped near rivers or lakes to fish for trout, bass, and other fish. They hunted birds and gathered plants for food. They also got some of their food from farming. In the winter, the Algonquians moved from one place to another. They followed beaver, otter, moose, bear, and other animals that they hunted.

Animals and fish were used for more than food. Furs and animal hides were made into clothing. Bones were used as tools. For example, fish bones made good sewing needles. Deer antlers were used to make holes in animal skins so they could be sewn together. Algonquians also made tools and spear points from hard stones such as chert.

✔ **READING CHECK** COMPARE AND CONTRAST
In what ways were the roles of Algonquian men and women different?

The Five Nations

Main Idea The people of the five nations farmed and lived in settled villages.

Another group of Native Americans in New York State spoke Iroquoian (ihr uh KWOI uhn) languages. Five Iroquoian nations joined in a confederation that became known as the Haudenosaunee (ho deh no SAW nee) League. A **confederation** is a government in which separate groups of people join together, but local leaders still have power. The five nations were also called the Iroquois. They were the Mohawks, Oneidas (oh NY duhz), Onondagas (aw nuhn DAG uhz), Cayugas (ky YOO guhz), and Senecas (SEN uh kuhz).

The name Haudenosaunee means people of the longhouse. A **longhouse** is a long, narrow house that is home to many families.

Haudenosaunee Life

The Haudenosaunee spent more time farming than the Algonquians. They did not move from place to place to find food. Instead, they settled in villages. For protection from enemies and wild animals, some villages were surrounded by tall fences.

Like the Algonquians, the men and women each did different work. Men brought food to the village by hunting and fishing. They also chopped down trees used to build longhouses. They fought wars against enemies. Women planted and harvested crops in the fields near the village. They also made pottery and clothing, cooked food, and cared for children.

Native American Lands Over time, Native Americans in New York separated into two groups: the Algonquians and the Haudenosaunee.

SKILL **Reading Maps** Who lived in a larger area of land—the Algonquians or the Haudenosaunee?

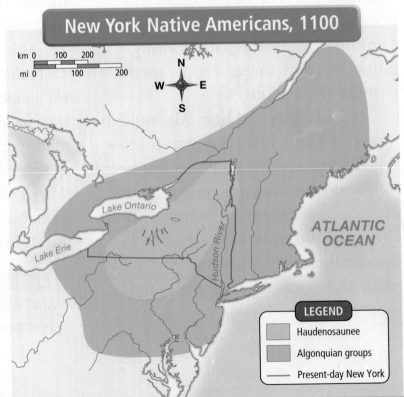

New York Native Americans, 1100

km 0   100   200
mi 0   100   200

Lake Ontario

Lake Erie

Hudson River

ATLANTIC OCEAN

LEGEND
Haudenosaunee
Algonquian groups
Present-day New York

Growing Food Crops

The Haudenosaunee hunted, gathered, and fished, but they depended on farming for much of their food. They grew several kinds of maize, beans, and squash. **Maize** is a form of corn. The Haudenosaunee called these important plants the "three sisters."

Maize was planted in small piles of soil about three feet apart. Later, beans were planted. Last came the squash, which was planted between the little hills of corn and beans. The crops could be stored for the winter, so people were able to stay in their villages all year.

1. Plant Maize   **2.** Plant Beans

✔ **READING CHECK** COMPARE AND CONTRAST
How were the Haudenosaunee different from the Algonquians?

SUMMARY

Native Americans in New York included the Algonquians and Haudenosaunee. Both groups hunted, gathered, fished, and traded. The Haudenosaunee also grew maize, beans, and squash.

"Three Sisters"
The maize supported the bean vines. The large leaves of the squash plants helped keep water in the soil.

3. Plant Squash

Lesson Review

❶ **WHAT TO KNOW** What was the Haudenosaunee League?

❷ **VOCABULARY** Write a paragraph comparing **wigwams** and **longhouses.**

❸ **CRITICAL THINKING: Cause and Effect** What effect do you think trading might have had on the Algonquians?

❹ **WRITING ACTIVITY** Write a paragraph explaining why planting three crops— maize, beans, and squash—in the same field was a good idea.

❺ 📷 **READING SKILL** Complete the graphic organizer to compare and contrast Native Americans in New York.

Algonquian   Haudenosaunee

Native American Artifacts

Digging into the past requires more than just a shovel. Scientists called archaeologists (ahr kee OL uh juhsts) use special tools to find prehistoric artifacts. They dig through layers of soil, looking for objects that tell about people long ago. Archaeologists keep almost everything they find, even bits of charcoal and bones.

Each summer, students from the State University of New York at Albany work in the Schoharie (sko HAHR ee) Valley, west of Albany. This region was home to Native Americans for thousands of years.

An Early Artifact In the Schoharie Valley, this student found a stone that Native Americans used for cracking nuts or grinding seeds. What features of the stone made it good for that type of work?

Digging The students remove dirt and objects from a square dig area.

Sifting A sifting box with a screen on the bottom may be used to separate solid objects from the dirt.

Floating The dirt may also be "floated" to recover objects that rise to the surface.

Discovering What clues suggest this was made by a person, not just found in nature?

Activities

1. **THINK ABOUT IT** Think about what you can learn from a primary source artifact. What clues might an artifact such as an arrowhead or a tool give you about Native American ways of life?

2. **WRITE IT** Choose three "artifacts" that belong to you. Write about what people in the future might learn from these things.

Go Digital Visit Education Place for more primary sources. www.eduplace.com/nycssp/

Skillbuilder

Make a Map

A map shows where cities, towns, rivers, mountains, and other features are located within a state, a region, a country, or the world. Making a map can help you to understand the features of your community.

Learn the Skill

Step 1: Decide what kind of map you want to make and how it will be used.

> Map of my town

Step 2: List the details to go on the map. Find other information that you want to include.

My house	Roads
My school	Chemung River
Shopping center	Town Hall

Step 3: Draw the outline shape of your map.

Step 4: Put your details on the map in the correct location. Use symbols, or label each point. Include a legend that explains your symbols.

Step 5: Think of a title for your map.

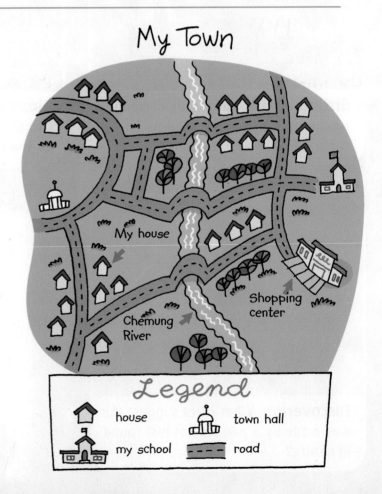

My Town

My house

Shopping center

Chemung River

Legend

house   town hall

my school   road

Follow the directions below to make a map of New York State.

1. List all the important cities and towns that you know in your state.

2. Name some rivers, mountains, or other natural features you might want to include on your map.

3. Write down any other information you want to show on your map.

4. Draw an outline of your state.

5. On your map, add the details you listed.

6. Include a legend that explains any symbols or colors you used.

7. Give your map a title.

Apply the Skill

Use what you learned to make a map of the world.
Label the seven continents and four oceans.

▶ **WHAT TO KNOW**
What natural resources did the Lenape use for food and shelter?

▶ **VOCABULARY**
clan
ancestor
natural resources
agriculture
culture

🎯 **READING SKILL**
Main Idea and Details As you read, list details about Lenape daily life.

Lenape daily life

The Lenape
An Algonquian People

Hundreds of years ago, the Lenape (luh NAH pay) Indians lived along the Delaware and Hudson rivers. They built villages in present-day New Jersey, Delaware, eastern Pennsylvania, and southeastern New York. Some Lenape settled the area that now includes New York City. The Lenape, also called the Delaware, were part of a larger group who spoke the Algonquian language.

Tools The Lenape used stone blades tied to pieces of bone to cut meat and plants.

Picture Stones The picture writing on the large stone tells the story of a Lenape boy and his dog. The small stone was a playing piece in a guessing game.

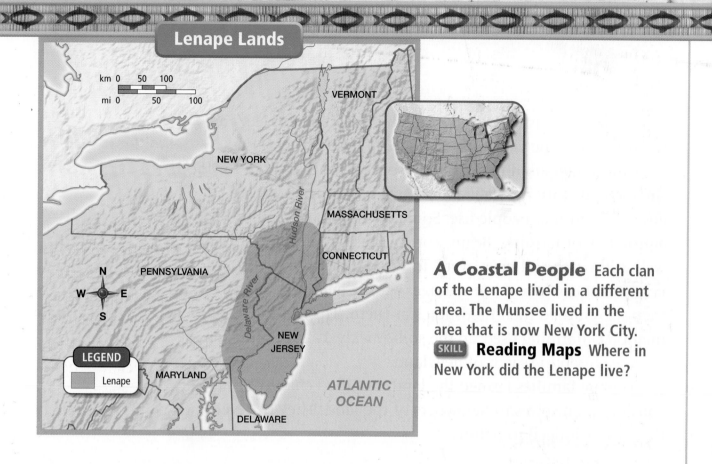

Lenape Lands

km 0 50 100

mi 0 50 100

VERMONT

NEW YORK

Hudson River

MASSACHUSETTS

CONNECTICUT

PENNSYLVANIA

N
W   E
S

Delaware River

NEW JERSEY

LEGEND

Lenape

MARYLAND

ATLANTIC OCEAN

DELAWARE

A Coastal People Each clan of the Lenape lived in a different area. The Munsee lived in the area that is now New York City. **SKILL** **Reading Maps** Where in New York did the Lenape live?

Lenape Government and History

The Lenape were divided into three clans: the Munsee, Unami, and Unalachtigo. A **clan** is a group of related families. Each clan had an animal name. They were known by names such as the wolf, the turtle, and the wild turkey.

The three clans spoke different versions of the Algonquian language and lived in different areas. Some people believe the clans' animal names are symbols for families who shared a common ancestor. An **ancestor** is a relative who was born long ago.

A sachem, or male leader, and a council of men led each Lenape village. The oldest woman in the village may have chosen the sachem.

Other Native American nations called the Lenape "grandfather" because they were thought to be the oldest Algonquian group. The Lenape recorded their history through a series of pictures carved into wood or bark, known as the Walum Olum. In later years, the Lenape wrote the events of the Walum Olum on paper.

✓ READING CHECK MAIN IDEA AND DETAILS
What were the names of the three Lenape clans?

Village Life

The Lenape usually lived on high ground near rivers and streams. A Lenape village could have up to 40 longhouses.

The Lenape used the natural resources around them for food, shelter, and clothing. **Natural resources** are things from the environment that people use. Some of their food came from **agriculture,** or farming. Beans, corn, squash, and pumpkins grew well in the rich soil near rivers. To open up land for crops, the Lenape cut down and burned trees. At the end of each harvest, they also burned their fields to clear them. This slash-and-burn method of farming used up the soil quickly. It forced the Lenape to move often in search of new land.

Lenape families farmed the land, but the Lenape did not consider themselves to be owners of the land. They believed the land belonged to nature.

Hunting Lenape men hunted animals using bows, arrows, and traps. They caught fish using harpoons as well as nets made from woven grasses.

Houses The Lenape lived in wigwams and longhouses made of poles cut from trees and covered with bark.

Sharing the Work

Lenape men and women had different responsibilities. Women farmed, gathered food, and cooked meals. They made clay pots and wove baskets from grasses and bark. Women also took care of children. According to tradition, children were born into their mother's clan. When a couple married, the husband moved into the longhouse of his wife's family.

Lenape men hunted, fished, and cleared fields. Using wood and stone, they made tools and weapons. Men also served as sachems and council members and defended their villages.

Older Lenape were honored and respected for their wisdom and experience. They also helped make pottery, fishnets, and wampum. Wampum was beads made of seashell. The Lenape used wampum in ceremonies, as gifts, and as money.

✓ READING CHECK MAIN IDEA AND DETAILS What kind of houses did Lenape families live in?

Work Lenape women roasted meats, made stews, and ground corn into flour to make corn cakes.

Legends and Ceremonies

Legends and ceremonies were important to Lenape culture. A **culture** is the way of life that people create for themselves and pass on to their children.

Different ceremonies took place during planting and harvesting seasons. For example, the Green Corn Ceremony celebrated the beginning of the harvest. Many of a village's ceremonies took place in a large central building known as the Big House.

Seasonal Ceremonies	
Month	**Ceremony**
March	Maple Sugar Dance
May	Planting Ceremony
June	Strawberry Dance
September	Green Corn Ceremony

Each ceremony celebrates a crop or event that was important to the Lenape at a certain time of year.

The Lenape also had many legends, or stories that have been handed down over time. One legend told the story of Earth's creation. According to the legend, Earth was made by a Creator who caused a giant turtle to rise from the sea. A large cedar tree grew on the turtle's shell and produced the first man and woman.

Today, many Lenape live in Oklahoma. They have modern jobs as teachers, bankers, and lawyers. The Lenape also continue to celebrate their nation's culture.

✓READING CHECK SUMMARIZE What were some important parts of Lenape culture?

SUMMARY

The Lenape lived in the area around New York City. They were divided into three clans and lived in villages. People hunted, farmed, and gathered crops.

Patience Harmon As a manager of the Nanticoke Museum, she helps preserve Native American history and traditions.

CASE STUDY REVIEW

❶ What to Know

What natural resources did the Lenape use for food and shelter?

❷ Reading Skill Main Idea and Details

Complete the graphic organizer to show the main idea and details.

> Lenape daily life

❸ Case Study Detective

The Lenape used wampum to trade for goods, much like we use money today. In what ways is wampum like money today? In what ways is it different?

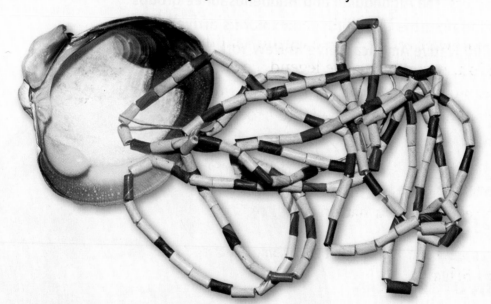

❹ Word Play

Use the following clues to figure out a mystery phrase about the Lenape.

[ ] [ ] [L] [ ] [ ] [ ] [ ] [U] [ ]

- This is what the Lenape called their history.
- It was originally carved into wood or bark.
- It was later written on paper.

Native Americans
~ Past and Present ~

New Yorkers build on traditions that go far into the past. The roots of New York's Native Americans run far deeper than those of other New Yorkers. The Algonquian and Haudenosaunee groups lived in New York before the first European explorers arrived. Today, more than 100,000 Native Americans live in New York State.

Ely S. Parker
(1828–1895)

Engineer, Government Official

Ely S. Parker was a Seneca Indian born on the Tonawanda Reservation in western New York. Parker became an engineer. He built canals in New York State before joining the army. During the Civil War, he served as General Ulysses S. Grant's close advisor. After the Civil War, Parker worked to bring the United States government and the nation's Native American groups closer together.

Joanne Shenandoah

Musician, Songwriter

Joanne Shenandoah's Indian name is "Tek-ya-wha-wha," which means "she sings" in the Oneida language. She is a world-famous singer, songwriter, and composer. Shenandoah's songs often reflect her Native American heritage. In 1993, she was given the "Native American of the Year" award.

The Mohawk Ironworkers

The Mohawks have a long history of building with iron and steel. You can see evidence of their labor all across New York City, from the Verrazano-Narrows Bridge to Kennedy International Airport. They have been building bridges, tall towers, and all kinds of other structures in New York City for decades. In the mid-1900s, many Mohawks lived in downtown Brooklyn, near Boerum Hill.

Activities

1. **TALK ABOUT IT** Discuss how the people in this feature have contributed to New York's past and present.

2. **SHOW IT** Make a fact card about one person from this feature. Include dates and accomplishments.

Visual Summary

1–3.  Write a description for each nation below.

Algonquian

Haudenosaunee

Lenape

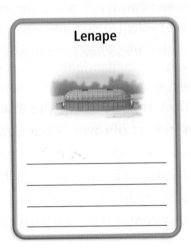

Facts and Main Ideas

Answer each question below.

4. **Culture** What were Algonquian houses like?

5. **Geography** Why did the Algonquians usually build camps near waterways?

6. **History** What plants did the Haudenosaunee call the "three sisters"?

7. **Government** What kind of people led each Lenape village?

8. **Culture** What was the Green Corn Ceremony?

Vocabulary

Choose the correct word from the list below to complete each sentence.

confederation, p. 30
longhouse, p. 30
culture, p. 40

9. The five nations of the Haudenosaunee joined into a _____.

10. _____ is the way of life people create for themselves.

11. The name Haudenosaunee means people of the _____.

Apply Skills

Map Skill Read the description of a town below. Then use your knowledge about maps to answer the multiple-choice questions.

A river runs south of the town. The southern part of town is flat and to the southwest lies the ocean. The northern part of town is hilly. The town hall is located in the center of town. A shopping center is to the northwest of it.

12. Where would you place hills on a map of the town?

   A. the entire southern border

   B. the southeastern section

   C. the northern part of town

   D. the center of town

13. What symbols should you have in the legend on your town map?

   A. a hill, a river, a shopping center, a town hall

   B. a river, a baseball field, a high school, a town hall

   C. a town hall, a post office, a fire station, a high school

   D. a post office, a football field, a road, a house

Critical Thinking

Write a short paragraph to answer each question below.

14. **Summarize** What was daily life like for the Lenape?

15. **Cause and Effect** What was one effect of the Lenape slash-and-burn method of farming?

Activities

Art Activity Make a list of the different resources that the Algonquians and Lenape used. Draw pictures to show how they were used.

Writing Activity Research to find out which groups of Native Americans lived near where your community is today. Write a report explaining what you learned.

Go Digital Get help with your writing at www.eduplace.com/nycssp/

Fun with Social Studies

This river flows from the Adirondack Mountains all the way to New York City.

Where in New York?

I live on the largest island on the East Coast.

Name the place in New York that each person is describing.

This large natural harbor is one of the best on the East Coast.

Museum Mix Up

Which two items do not belong in a Native Americans of New York exhibit?

Lenape pottery

Corn in Haudenosaunee garden

Lenape longhouse

Inuit igloo

Haudenosaunee arrow

Cheyenne tepee

What's Under There?

Write the letters that belong in the yellow squares and you'll know.

One half of Earth's surface.

An area that has one or more features in common.

A huge, slow-moving sheet of ice.

A very large landmass.

A relative who was born long ago.

A way of life that has been followed for a long time.

Go Digital → **Education Place®**
www.eduplace.com

Visit Eduplace!

Log on to Eduplace to explore Social Studies online. Solve puzzles to watch the skateboarding tricks in eWord Game. Join Chester in GeoNet to see if you can earn enough points to become a GeoChampion, or just play Wacky Web Tales to see how silly your stories can get. Play now at http://eduplace.com/nycssp/

New York History and Government

eGlossary

eWord Game

Biographies

Primary Sources

Write Site

Interactive Maps

Weekly Reader®: Current Events

GeoNet

Online Atlas

Review for Understanding

Reading Social Studies

A **generalization** is a broad statement that summarizes a group of facts and shows how they are related.

Generalize

1. Complete this graphic organizer to show that you understand generalizations about New York's geography.

New York's Geography

tall mountains	rolling hills	flat plains

 Write About the Big Idea

2. **Write a Short Story** Think about what it might have been like to be among the first people in New York. What difficulties might you have faced? Write a short story detailing the experiences.

Vocabulary and Main Idea

Write a sentence to answer each question.

3. In which **hemispheres** is New York located?

4. Into what three **clans** were the Lenape divided?

5. Where can you find a **plateau** in New York?

6. What **natural resources** did the Lenape use?

7. Why was **maize** important to the Haudenosaunee?

8. What are some features that **glaciers** formed in New York?

Critical Thinking

Write a short paragraph to answer each question.

9. **Main Idea and Details** List three details to support the idea that the environment influences people.

10. **Cause and Effect** Five nations of Native Americans made peace with each other and formed a confederation. How might forming a government have helped the five nations to work together?

Apply Skills

Study the Eastern United States Resources map below. Then use your map skills to answer each question.

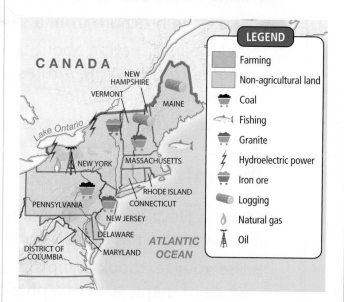

11. In which state on the map can natural gas be found?

    A. Maine

    B. New York

    C. New Jersey

    D. Pennsylvania

12. Which resource is found in large amounts in Maine?

    A. coal

    B. fossil fuels

    C. uranium

    D. forests

Unit 1 Activities

 Unit Writing Activity

Create a Brochure Create a brochure to interest people in visiting New York.

■ Make the brochure from a sheet of paper folded into thirds.

■ Include information about the land in New York to persuade people to visit. Write a fun slogan about New York that will catch people's attention.

■ Include pictures of places to see in New York.

 Unit Project

Make a New York Atlas Make at least two outline maps to include in an atlas of New York.

■ Use your textbook and other resources to make different kinds of maps, such as a physical map and a map that shows major cities.

■ Include labels and give your maps titles. Also use map keys to explain any symbols you use on your maps.

Read More

■ *Hudson River: An Adventure from the Mountains to the Sea* by Peter Lourie. Boyds Mills Press.

■ *The Rough-Face Girl* by Rafe Martin. Putnam Juvenile.

■ *Anna, Grandpa, and the Big Storm* by Carla Stevens. Puffin.

 visit www.eduplace.com/nycssp/

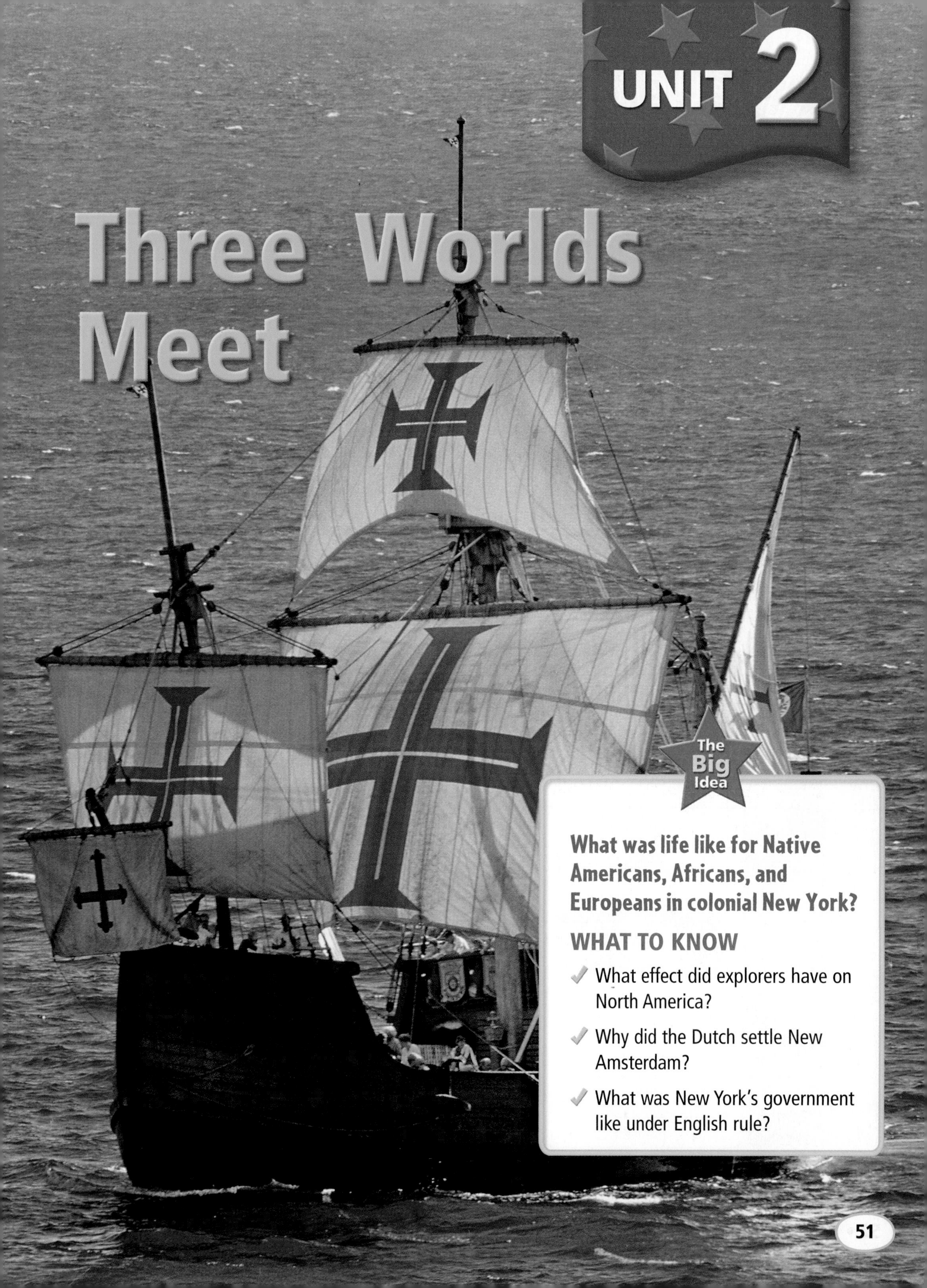

Three Worlds Meet

The Big Idea

What was life like for Native Americans, Africans, and Europeans in colonial New York?

WHAT TO KNOW

- ✓ What effect did explorers have on North America?

- ✓ Why did the Dutch settle New Amsterdam?

- ✓ What was New York's government like under English rule?

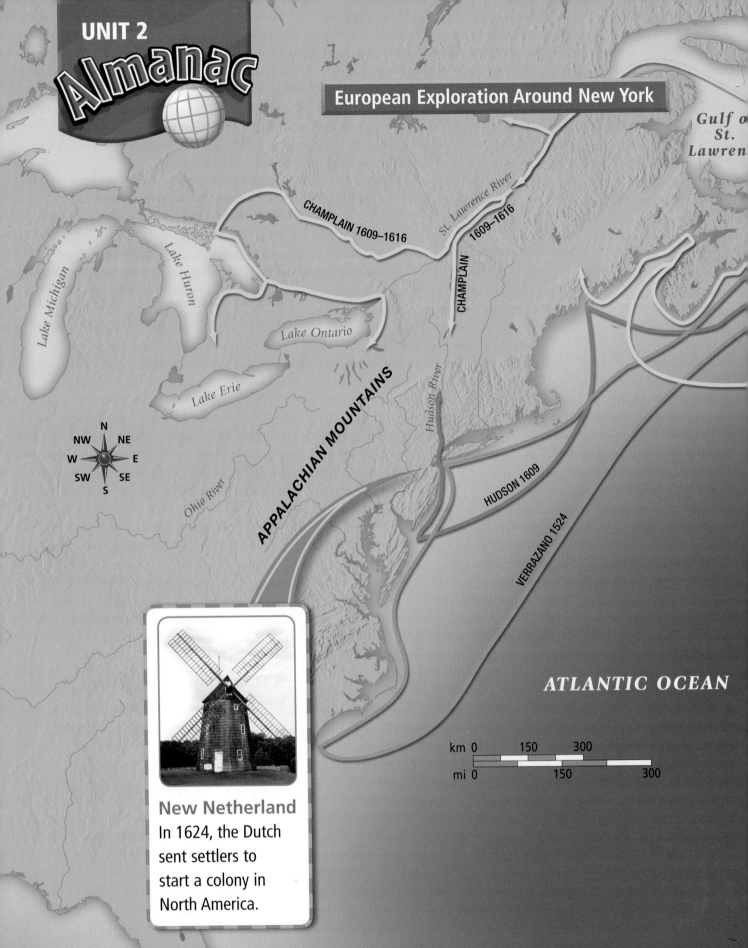

European Exploration Around New York

Gulf of
St.
Lawrence

CHAMPLAIN 1609–1616

St. Lawrence River

CHAMPLAIN 1609–1616

Lake Michigan

Lake Huron

Lake Ontario

Lake Erie

APPALACHIAN MOUNTAINS

Hudson River

Ohio River

HUDSON 1609

VERRAZANO 1524

N
NW   NE
W   E
SW   SE
S

ATLANTIC OCEAN

km 0   150   300
mi 0   150   300

New Netherland
In 1624, the Dutch
sent settlers to
start a colony in
North America.

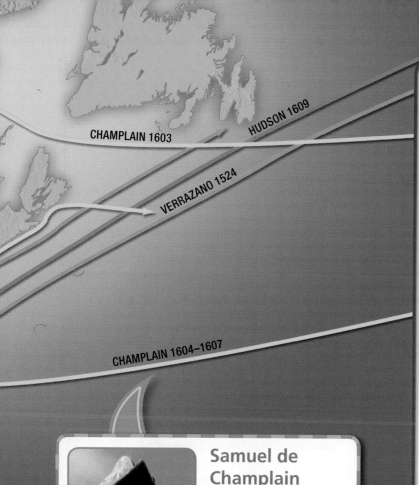

CHAMPLAIN 1603

HUDSON 1609

VERRAZANO 1524

CHAMPLAIN 1604–1607

Samuel de Champlain

During his 12 trips to North America, Champlain explored areas of New York.

LEGEND

→ Champlain's routes

→ Hudson's route

→ Verrazano's route

Crossing the Atlantic, 1492

Columbus and his three ships crossed the Atlantic in 70 days.

Crossing the Atlantic Through the Years

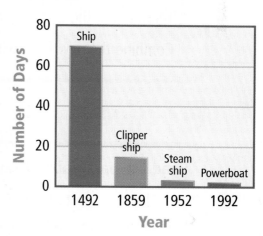

Five hundred years after Columbus, a powerboat crossed the Atlantic in 58 hours and 34 minutes.

Reading Social Studies

Draw Conclusions

Why It Matters Being able to draw conclusions can help you better understand what you read.

Learn the Skill

A **conclusion** is a general statement about an idea or an event. To draw a conclusion, you use evidence, or what you have learned. You also use knowledge, or what you already know.

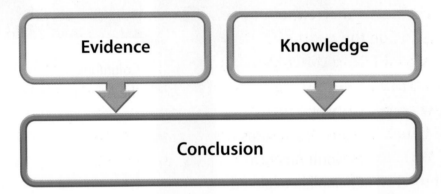

- Think about the new facts you read about a subject.

- Think about the facts you already know about that subject.

- Combine the new facts with those you already know to draw a conclusion.

Practice the Skill

Read the paragraphs. Draw a conclusion for the second paragraph.

> Evidence   Ships sailing to North America in the 1600s were often caught in storms.
> Knowledge   Bad weather can sink a ship. Sometimes ships sailing to North America would
> Conclusion meet bad weather and sink.
>
> In the 1600s, beaver furs were valuable in Europe. When Europeans arrived in North America, they met Native Americans who were skilled at hunting the many beavers there.

Apply the Skill

Read the paragraphs, and answer the questions.

Wind Power, Then and Now

For thousands of years, people have been using the wind to create power. Early European windmills looked like tall wooden buildings with a giant fan attached to the front. When the wind blew, it turned the fan, which was connected to wooden machines inside the windmill. These machines could serve different purposes. They could grind grain into flour, saw wood, or pump water.

The Dutch introduced windmills to New York, and later the English used them. The earliest Dutch windmills in New York were built on the southern tip of Manhattan, near what is now Battery Park. The Dutch used these windmills to grind grain for making bread. They also used them to saw the wood they needed to build homes.

Today, machines called wind turbines are used to power large batteries that store electricity. The turbines look like giant fans and can be up to 400 feet tall. They stand in groups called wind farms and can be seen from many miles away. The town of Fenner, near Syracuse, has one such wind farm. The wind farm produces enough electricity to power more than 7,000 homes.

Draw Conclusions

1. What conclusion can you draw about what would happen if a windmill did not receive wind?

2. What conclusion can you draw about the effect windmills had on early Dutch settlements in New York?

Early New York City

Old Hook Mill, East Hampton

Study Skills

POSE QUESTIONS

Learning to pose, or ask, questions as you read can help improve your understanding.

- Think of questions that might be answered by reading. For example, you might ask how events are related.

- Use the questions to guide your reading. Look for answers as you read.

Questions	Answers
What changes did English rule bring to colonial New York?	The English elected new leaders and passed new laws.
What helped New York's population grow in the late 1600s and early 1700s?	

Vocabulary Preview

colony

When a group of Dutch settlers came to North America to live, they started a **colony.** The colony belonged to the Netherlands. **page 62**

governor

The person in charge of a colony was a **governor.** Peter Stuyvesant was the governor of New Netherland in 1664. **page 62**

Chapter Timeline

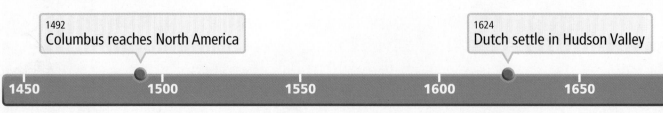

1492
Columbus reaches North America

1624
Dutch settle in Hudson Valley

| 1450 | 1500 | 1550 | 1600 | 1650 |

Reading Strategy

Summarize As you read, use the summarize strategy to focus on important ideas. What happens at the beginning, middle, and end of a lesson?

tolerance

The people who settled in New Netherland practiced **tolerance.** They welcomed people with different ideas and beliefs.
page 72

assembly

After the English took over, New York colonists wanted to elect an **assembly** to make laws.
page 77

1664
English control New Netherland

1700   1750   1800

Go Digital visit www.eduplace.com/nycssp/

First Explorers

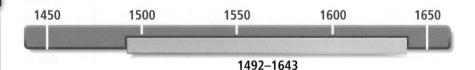

| 1450 | 1500 | 1550 | 1600 | 1650 |

1492–1643

WHAT TO KNOW
What effect did explorers have on North America?

VOCABULARY
route
claim
colony
governor

READING SKILL
Draw Conclusions
Write some facts about the exploration of North America. Draw a conclusion by putting those facts together.

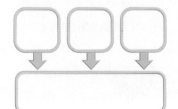

Before You Read Have you ever seen or found something you hadn't known existed? While trying to go to Asia, European explorers discovered a new and different land.

Searching for a New Route

Main Idea European explorers were looking for a new way to get to Asia, but instead arrived in North America.

People in Europe have traded with people in Asia for a long time. More than 500 years ago, places such as China had gold and valuable spices that many Europeans wanted. The trip from Europe to Asia by land was slow and dangerous, however. Explorers started looking for a faster, safer sea route. A **route** is a road or waterway that travelers follow.

In 1492, **Christopher Columbus** tried to reach Asia by sailing west from Spain. Instead, he landed in North America. Europeans had not known the Americas existed. They soon started competing for North American land.

Columbus's Ships
Columbus left Europe with the *Niña*, the *Pinta*, and the *Santa Maria*.

Lake Champlain In 1612, Samuel de Champlain (right) drew the map above. It shows the lake he named for himself.

Exploring North America

Europeans continued searching for a water route to Asia. In 1524, **Giovanni da Verrazano** (jee oh VAH nee duh vayr uh ZAH noh) sailed along the North American coast looking for that route. He did not find it, but he was the first European to reach New York Harbor. He wrote an account of the native people he met in North America.

French explorer **Jacques Cartier** (ZHAHK kahr TYAY) also explored North America. In 1535, he reached the St. Lawrence River. Another French explorer, **Samuel de Champlain** (shahm PLAYN) explored much of the land in northern New York. He set up a fur trade with the Huron (HYUR uhn) and Algonquian Indians.

Henry Hudson explored North America for the Netherlands. He looked for a way to sail across the continent. In 1609, Hudson sailed his ship into New York Harbor and up the Hudson River. He made it to present-day Albany. Hudson wrote,

> **“ The land is the finest . . . that I ever in my life set foot upon. . . . ”**

Hudson never found a way across North America. However, he did claim land that helped the Netherlands gain valuable resources such as furs. To **claim** is to declare that land belongs to a country.

✓ READING CHECK DRAW CONCLUSIONS Why did explorers begin to look for a different route to Asia?

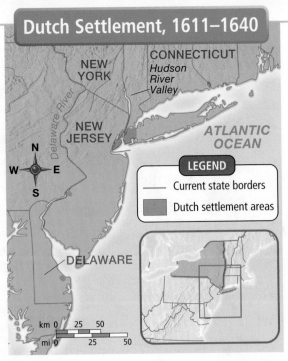

Dutch Settlement, 1611–1640

NEW YORK

CONNECTICUT
Hudson
River
Valley

Delaware River

NEW JERSEY

ATLANTIC OCEAN

N
W   E
S

DELAWARE

LEGEND
Current state borders
Dutch settlement areas

km 0   25   50
mi 0   25   50

Early Land Claims The Dutch settled along the Hudson River. They abandoned Fort Nassau (left) because of yearly flooding, but later returned to settle nearby areas.

Dutch Colonies

Main Idea The Dutch colony started peacefully, but soon conflicts began.

In 1614, the Dutch built Fort Nassau (NAS aw) near present-day Albany. They left the fort in 1618. Then in 1624, the Dutch sent settlers back to the Hudson River Valley to start a colony. A **colony** is land ruled by another country. The colony would keep other countries from claiming the land. Some Dutch settlers also claimed land along the Connecticut and Delaware rivers.

The Dutch settlers named their colony New Netherland. They traded furs peacefully with the Algonquian Indians there. The governor was **Cornelius May**. A **governor** was the official in charge of a colony.

The Algonquian War

As the Dutch colony of New Netherland grew, farmers wanted to move onto Algonquian hunting lands. This angered the Algonquians. Then in 1643, Governor **Willem Kieft** (keyft) asked the Algonquians to give the colonists food and furs. Kieft attacked those who refused. In response, Native Americans in the area joined together to fight the Dutch.

Many Native Americans in the Hudson River Valley moved away because of wars with each other and with the settlers. Some moved north to Canada, while others moved west. Others died of diseases, such as smallpox, that they caught from Europeans. Some were forced to leave by colonists who wanted their land.

Changes in New Netherland

When other Europeans first arrived in New Netherland, the Dutch were the only nation trading for furs there. By the mid-1600s, people from other nations also wanted to trade for furs in the region. Some of these nations started colonies near New Netherland.

The Dutch and the English claimed different areas around the Hudson River for themselves. Early settlements were far apart. Then the English began to build more colonies along the coast. The English population grew more quickly than the Dutch population. This English growth would soon lead to conflicts with the Dutch.

✓ READING CHECK GENERALIZE What did countries do to trade furs in North America?

Fur Fashion
The fur trade in North America grew because beaver hats were popular in Europe.

SUMMARY

Explorers came to North America looking for a shorter route to Asia. The Dutch formed the colony of New Netherland in the Hudson River Valley. Settlers forced some Native Americans off their lands.

Lesson Review

1524
Verrazano sails

1609
Hudson sails

1624
First Dutch colony

1475   1500   1525   1550   1575   1600   1625   1650   1675

1 WHAT TO KNOW What effect did explorers have on North America?

2 VOCABULARY Write a sentence about New Netherland using the word **colony.**

3 TIMELINE SKILL How many years passed between the time Verrazano sailed and the settlement of the first Dutch colony?

4 WRITING ACTIVITY Write a speech that an explorer might have given to get a European government to pay for his voyage. Explain the purpose of the trip.

5 📝 READING SKILL Complete the graphic organizer to draw conclusions.

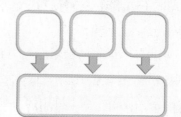

Explorers
of New York

What would you have seen if you had arrived in present-day New York 400 years ago? European explorers found an amazing world of soaring mountains, deep forests, rivers, and lakes. They also found the Native Americans who had lived on this land for thousands of years. When the explorers arrived, they brought many changes to the land and its people.

Giovanni da Verrazano
(1485–1528)

In 1524, this Italian explorer sailed along the east coast of North America. When Verrazano reached New York Bay, he anchored his ship at the place now called the Narrows. He explored the lower Hudson River in a small boat and traded with many Native Americans. Verrazano later wrote the earliest description of New York Bay and the different Native Americans who lived there. The Verrazano-Narrows Bridge across New York Bay was named in his honor.

Henry Hudson
(1575–1611)

When Hudson's ship, the *Half Moon*, sailed up what is now known as the Hudson River in 1609, about 10,000 Native Americans lived along the river's banks. To show Hudson they meant no harm, the Native Americans broke their arrows. Before returning to England, he lived on "Manna-hata"—a Lenape word for present-day Manhattan.

Samuel de Champlain
(1567–1635)

Beginning in 1603, this French explorer made 12 trips to present-day Canada. He founded the city of Quebec and a trading post at what is now Montreal. In 1609, Champlain discovered the lake that would be named for him: Lake Champlain.

Activities

1. **TALK ABOUT IT** In small groups, discuss questions you would like to ask one of New York's early explorers about the land or the Native Americans who lived there.

2. **WRITE ABOUT IT** Write a short diary entry from the point of view of an explorer or a Native American after the first meeting between the two.

Map and Globe Skills

Skillbuilder

Use Latitude and Longitude

▶ **VOCABULARY**

latitude

longitude

absolute location

To help find the exact location of a place on Earth, mapmakers created an imaginary grid of lines over the globe. These lines are called latitude and longitude. Lines of latitude go east and west. Lines of longitude go north and south.

Learn the Skill

Step 1: On the globe, find the lines of latitude. Lines of **latitude** measure how far something is north or south of the equator. The equator is at 0° (degrees) latitude. Lines of latitude north of the equator are labeled N. Those south of the equator are labeled S.

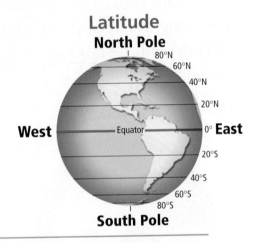

Latitude

Step 2: Find the labels for the lines of longitude. Lines of **longitude** measure how far something is east or west of the prime meridian. The prime meridian is an imaginary line that passes through Greenwich, England. The prime meridian is at 0° longitude. Lines of longitude east of the prime meridian are labeled E. Those west of the prime meridian are labeled W.

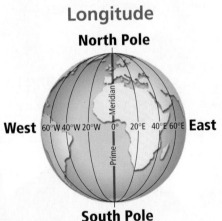

Longitude

Step 3: On a map, find where the lines of latitude and longitude cross. The exact latitude and longitude of a place on the globe is called its **absolute location.**

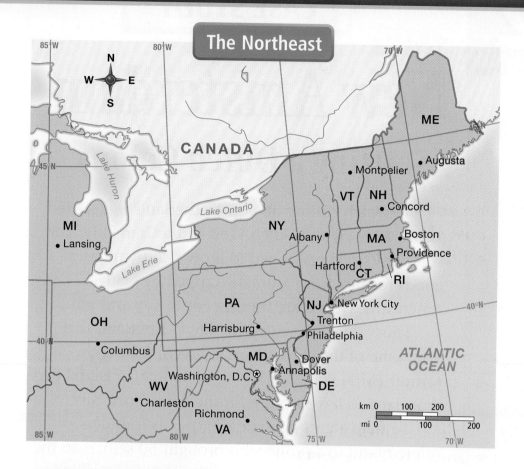

The Northeast

Practice the Skill

Use the map to answer these questions.

1 What city is located near 40°N, 83°W?

2 Which line of longitude is closest to New York's most western border?

3 What is the latitude and longitude of Philadelphia?

4 Which states have a northern boundary at about 45°N?

Apply the Skill

Locate New York City by using lines of latitude and longitude. You may have to estimate.

CASE STUDY

New Amsterdam
Settling a Dutch Colony

▶ **WHAT TO KNOW**
Why did the Dutch settle
New Amsterdam?

▶ **VOCABULARY**

founder
slavery
diversity
tolerance

READING SKILL
Main Idea and Details
Look for details of how
the Dutch treated people
with different ideas and
backgrounds.

The Dutch colony of New Netherland was started in 1624 by the Dutch West India Company. The company's owners hoped to grow rich by trading goods for furs from animals trapped by Native Americans. Goods are things people buy and sell.

Thirty families settled in New Netherland that year. One of the colony's early governors, **Peter Minuit** (MIN yoo IHT), bought Manhattan Island two years later to have a place for the colonists to live.

To help New Netherland grow, its founders offered land to anyone who brought 50 settlers to the colony. A **founder** is a person who starts something.

Manhattan Purchase Peter Minuit bought Manhattan Island from the Manhattan Indians in 1626.

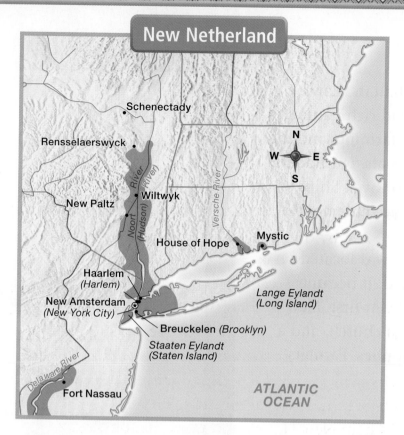

New Netherland

A Trading Colony Rivers were an easy way to travel inland.

SKILL **Reading Maps** Along which rivers did the Dutch settle?

New Netherland

People who accepted the founders' offer of land became wealthy. They were called patroons. Their lands were known as patroonships. One patroonship, Rensselaerswyck (REN suh LIHRZ vyk), became the center of the Dutch fur trade.

People from other European countries also settled in the area. Twelve French Huguenots (HYOO guh notz) started New Paltz in 1677 so they could have freedom of religion. Swedish colonists built log cabins along the Delaware River in the mid-1600s. English settlers also lived in and around New Netherland.

Slavery

The Dutch West India Company controlled trade between the Americas and Africa. The company captured Africans and forced them into slavery. **Slavery** is a cruel system in which one person owns another. Captive Africans and their children were enslaved for life.

Enslaved Africans were put onto ships that sailed to the Caribbean islands. During this trip, called the Middle Passage, many of them died. Some were brought from the Caribbean to New Netherland. There they had to work hard, doing such jobs as unloading ships and building.

✓ READING CHECK MAIN IDEA AND DETAILS
What group founded New Netherland?

Life in New Amsterdam

After the Dutch bought Manhattan Island, the settlement grew. The island had rich natural resources. The land was good for farming, and the forests were filled with many animals. Fur traders traveled along the nearby Hudson River. Ships could easily get into and out of the settlement's excellent harbor.

The town of New Amsterdam was located on the south end of Manhattan Island. It became a place where people met to trade. At first, New Amsterdam had mostly log huts, a church, and a building for storing food and supplies. Farmers lived outside the town.

A Dutch-Style City

New Amsterdam was similar to cities in the Netherlands. The main language was Dutch, and people followed Dutch laws. Until 1638, the Dutch Reformed Church gave children an education. After that date, the town had its own school founded by **Adam Roelantsen** (ROY lant sun).

The Dutch also brought their technology from the Netherlands. Technology is the use of scientific knowledge. The Dutch built windmills which used wind as power to grind grain, saw wood, and pump water.

As New Amsterdam grew, settlers moved to new areas of Manhattan. Nieuw (noo) Haarlem was one new settlement located at present-day Harlem. The original settlers included people from France, Sweden, Germany, and other countries.

✓ READING CHECK COMPARE AND CONTRAST How was New Amsterdam similar to cities in the Netherlands?

? Where did the Dutch build a fort with pointed corners?

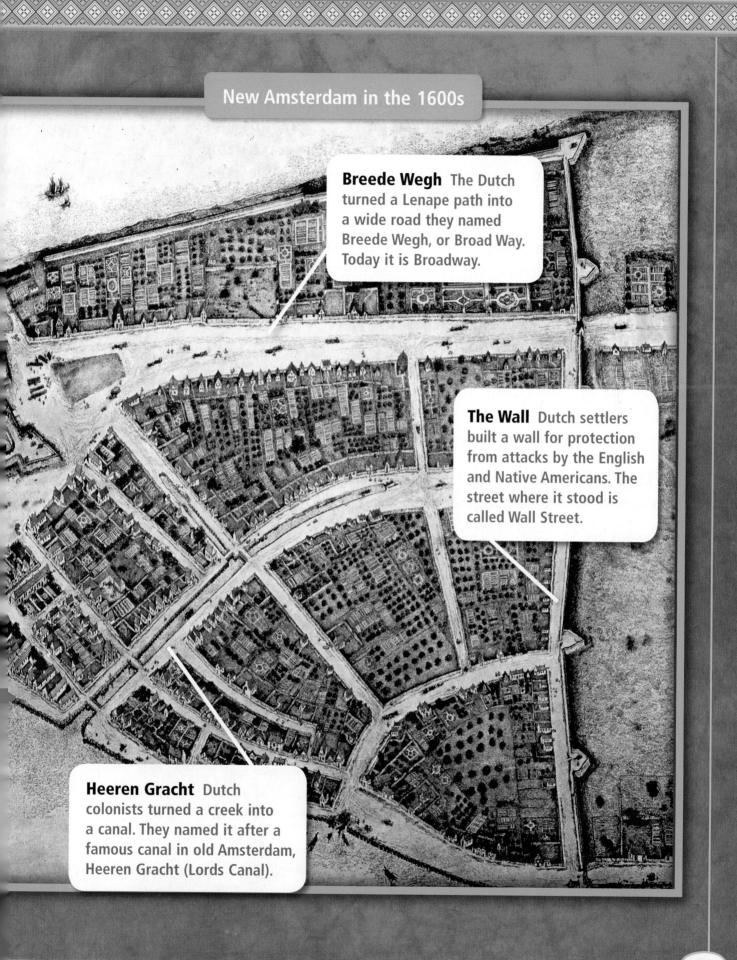

Breede Wegh The Dutch turned a Lenape path into a wide road they named Breede Wegh, or Broad Way. Today it is Broadway.

The Wall Dutch settlers built a wall for protection from attacks by the English and Native Americans. The street where it stood is called Wall Street.

Heeren Gracht Dutch colonists turned a creek into a canal. They named it after a famous canal in old Amsterdam, Heeren Gracht (Lords Canal).

Diversity and Tolerance

From its beginning, New Amsterdam had great diversity. **Diversity** means variety among the people in a group. In 1643, governor **Willem Kieft** told a visitor that the 500 people living in New Amsterdam spoke 18 different languages. People from the continents of Europe and Africa lived there. In 1654, the first Jewish settlers arrived in New Amsterdam.

New Amsterdam was a place where people from different countries were welcome. The Dutch had tolerance for many people who were not Dutch. **Tolerance** is respect for other people's differences.

The new colony, however, needed a bigger population to survive. Few people from the Netherlands wanted to travel across the Atlantic Ocean. To encourage people to move, Dutch leaders offered land and free supplies to people willing to live in New Amsterdam for more than a short time.

✓ READING CHECK CAUSE AND EFFECT Why did people from many countries feel welcome in New Amsterdam?

SUMMARY

New Amsterdam began in 1626 when Peter Minuit bought Manhattan Island. The city became a center of trade where people from many countries lived.

New Amsterdam In the mid-1600s, Pearl Street had a few Dutch buildings and a place for boats to dock in the harbor.

CASE STUDY REVIEW

❶ What to Know

Why did the Dutch settle New Amsterdam?

❷ Reading Skill Main Idea and Details

Complete the graphic organizer to show the main idea and details.

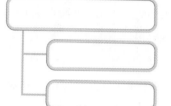

❸ Case Study Detective

Windmills in New Amsterdam had many important parts, and each part had to work for the windmill to grind grain. Look at the list of parts below. Match the parts to the numbers in the photograph.

gears to turn grinding stone

grinding stone

bucket to pour grain

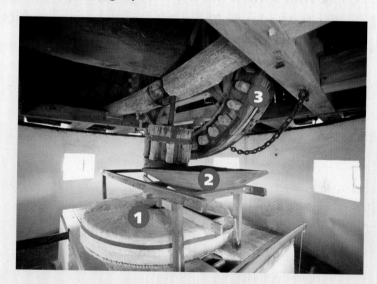

❹ Word Play

Use the following clues to figure out a mystery word about New Netherland.

_ _ T _ _ O _ S

- These people accepted land from the Dutch West India Company.
- They were wealthy landowners in New Netherland.
- The mystery word rhymes with "balloons."

Dutch Style in New Amsterdam

New Amsterdam was Dutch in more than just its name. People who settled the city brought Dutch style with them from the Netherlands. The design of the town and its houses reminded people of their home country.

① Waterways
In the Netherlands, the Dutch dug deep ditches to drain swampy land. They then used the ditches as waterways for transportation. They did the same in New Amsterdam.

①

A Changed City This picture shows lower Manhattan today. What are some ways it has changed since it was a Dutch colony?

② Bridges

Little bridges passed over the waterways—just as they still do over waterways in the Netherlands.

③ Stoops

At the front door of many homes was a small porch. It was called a stoop, a Dutch word we still use today for our front steps.

④ Dutch Doors

Dutch doors were split. The top could be opened to let in light. The bottom could stay closed to keep children safe inside and animals outside.

⑤ Steep Roofs

The steep, tiled roofs were faced on each end by walls. Today, some New York buildings still have this feature.

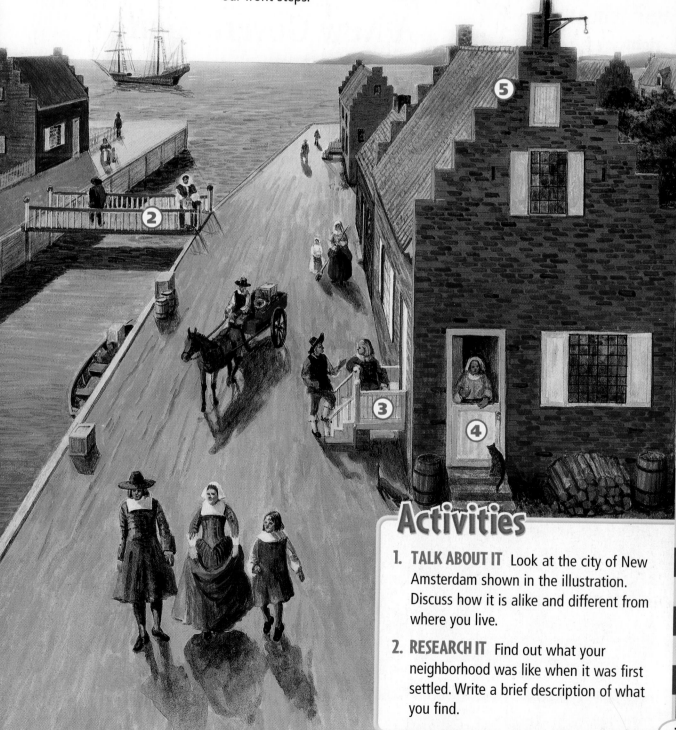

Activities

1. **TALK ABOUT IT** Look at the city of New Amsterdam shown in the illustration. Discuss how it is alike and different from where you live.

2. **RESEARCH IT** Find out what your neighborhood was like when it was first settled. Write a brief description of what you find.

English Rule in New York

A New Government

WHAT TO KNOW

What was New York's government like under English rule?

VOCABULARY

right
assembly
tax

READING SKILL

Categorize As you read, list ways that New York was influenced by the Dutch and the English.

DUTCH	ENGLISH

In 1664, the Netherlands and England were competing for control of North America. One day, the governor of New Netherland, **Peter Stuyvesant** (STY vih suhnt), saw English warships in New Amsterdam's harbor. The English were ready to go to war for control of New Netherland. English colonel **Richard Nicolls** told the Dutch to give up.

Most Dutch colonists did not want to fight. They were outnumbered. Also, they thought Stuyvesant's rule was unfair. The colonists convinced Stuyvesant to give up. New Amsterdam was now under English rule.

1664 Peter Stuyvesant gives up to the English

Under English Control

Nicolls renamed the colony New York, for **James, Duke of York,** who now owned the land. New Amsterdam became New York City. Nicolls was New York's first governor. He made laws that protected colonists' rights. A **right** is a freedom the government must protect.

One of the rights in New York was trial by jury. A group of colonists, called a jury, decided if someone had broken a law. Under Stuyvesant's rule, the government had controlled the courts.

By the late 1600s, New York's laws were similar to laws in England. New Yorkers did have some rights that other English colonists did not, however. The Dutch had allowed women and free Africans to own property. That right continued when the English took over.

The First Assembly

New Yorkers asked for more rights by calling for an assembly. An **assembly** is a group elected by the people to make laws. James refused their request. To force him to listen, colonists stopped paying taxes. A **tax** is a fee paid to the government for services.

James then agreed to an assembly. Members were elected in 1683. They wrote a "Charter of Liberties." It described how the government would work, and it listed people's rights.

In 1691, the Charter of Liberties became law. It protected freedom of religion. The charter said the governor did not control the assembly. It was New York's first plan of government.

✓ **READING CHECK** CATEGORIZE How did English control change New Amsterdam?

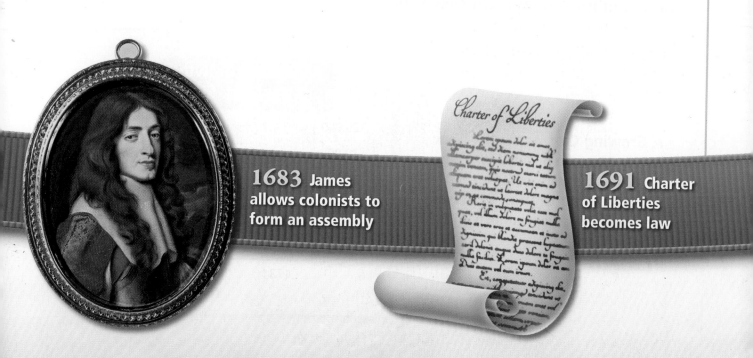

1683 James allows colonists to form an assembly

1691 Charter of Liberties becomes law

Charter of Liberties

A Growing Colony

When the English took over, about 9,000 people in New York lived on farms. Most people in the other colonies lived on farms as well. Few colonies had large cities. Only about 1,500 people lived in New York City. However, more people began coming to New York. By 1750, the colony's population had grown to about 27,000.

Ships carrying goods and people from many nations arrived in New York City's deep harbor. Settlers traveling to the rest of the colony often came through New York City, too. They included people from France, Scotland, Ireland, Germany, and England. Some came to New York from other North American colonies. For example, settlers from French colonies to the north built forts in northern New York.

Forced to Move

Not everyone who settled in New York chose to come there. Enslaved Africans could not choose where they lived. When the English took control of New York, about 150 Africans lived in New York City. By 1737, more than 1,700 lived there.

At the same time, the number of Native Americans in the city fell. Settlers forced many to sell their land. By 1684, Native Americans had given up all land in what is now Brooklyn.

✓ READING CHECK SUMMARIZE How did different groups of people come to New York?

SUMMARY

The English took control of New York and wrote a plan of government for the colony. New York City grew under English rule.

A Growing City As the New York colony grew, the population of New York City also increased.
SKILL **Reading Graphs** What was New York City's population in 1731?

Population Growth of New York City

CASE STUDY REVIEW

❶ What to Know

What was New York's government like under English rule?

❷ Reading Skill **Categorize**

Complete the graphic organizer to categorize information.

DUTCH	ENGLISH

❸ Case Study Detective

How is the photograph of New York City's harbor today different from the picture of the harbor long ago?

New York City's Harbor, 1700s

New York City's Harbor, Today

❹ Word Play

A *tax* is a fee paid to the government. *Tacks* are small nails.

Many words sound the same but have different spellings and meanings. Each of the following words has to do with trade, an important part of life in colonial New York City. What other words can you think of that sound the same as these?

buy

sale

cent

African Americans in New York City

The history of African Americans in New York City was buried under centuries of earth and stone. Clues dug up from historical sites are providing details about what their lives were like. We now know that, by the late 1730s, about one in every five people in New York City was of African descent. As you study this map of colonial New York City, look at the places that were important in the daily lives of African Americans.

Water Pumps
Getting water was a chore that many enslaved Africans did twice a day. They often met at pumps to talk and exchange news.

A man named David Grim drew this detailed map of New York City as it was in the 1740s.

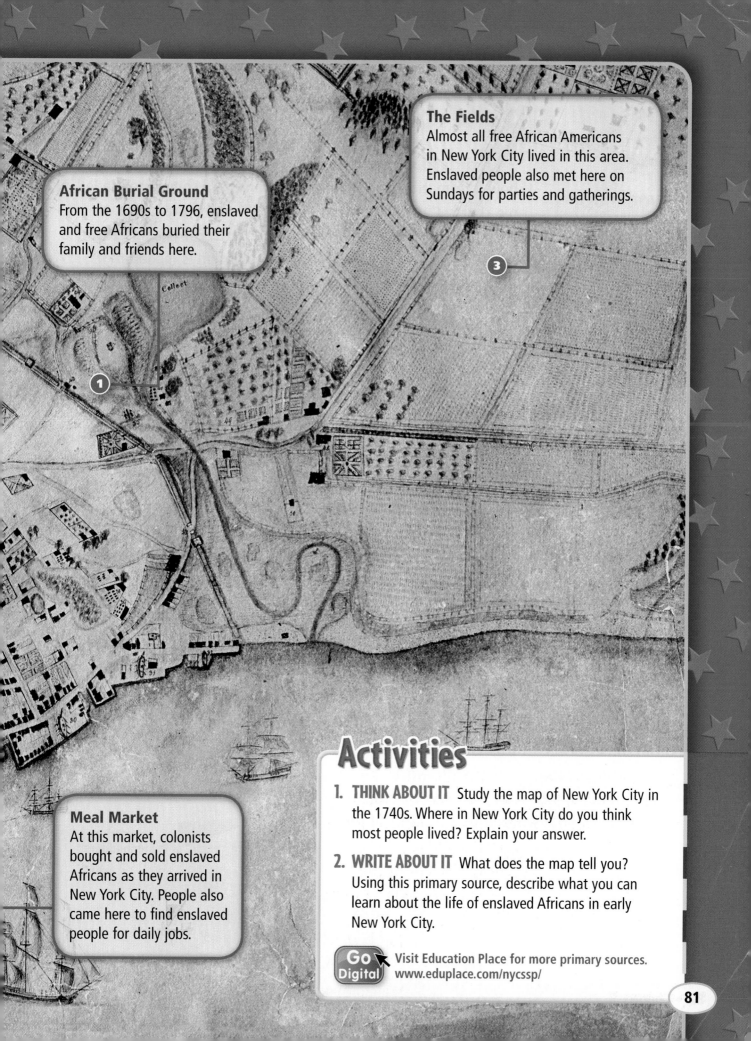

The Fields
Almost all free African Americans in New York City lived in this area. Enslaved people also met here on Sundays for parties and gatherings.

African Burial Ground
From the 1690s to 1796, enslaved and free Africans buried their family and friends here.

Meal Market
At this market, colonists bought and sold enslaved Africans as they arrived in New York City. People also came here to find enslaved people for daily jobs.

Activities

1. **THINK ABOUT IT** Study the map of New York City in the 1740s. Where in New York City do you think most people lived? Explain your answer.

2. **WRITE ABOUT IT** What does the map tell you? Using this primary source, describe what you can learn about the life of enslaved Africans in early New York City.

Go Digital Visit Education Place for more primary sources. www.eduplace.com/nycssp/

Skillbuilder

Read a Circle Graph

A **circle graph** is a circle that is divided into sections to show how information is related. Circle graphs are sometimes called pie charts. Circle graphs can help you see how the whole of something is broken up into different parts. For example, a circle graph can show you how a state's population is made up of different groups. It also lets you see how these groups compare to each other.

Learn the Skill

Step 1: Read the title to find out what information the graph presents. This graph gives information about jobs in New York in the 1700s. The whole circle represents the total number of jobs.

Workers in New York, 1700s

Step 2: Read the labels for each section of the circle. Each section of this graph represents people who worked in a certain kind of job.

Wood-workers

Step 3: Compare the sizes of the different sections. In this graph, a larger section means that more people worked in that kind of job. A smaller section means that fewer people worked in that kind of job.

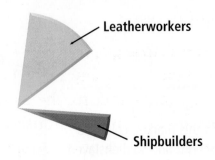

Leatherworkers

Shipbuilders

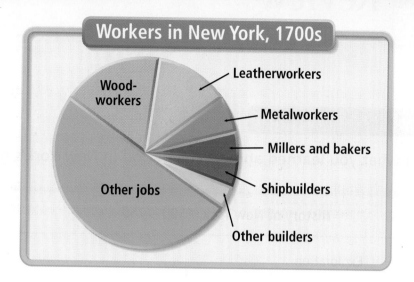

Workers in New York, 1700s

- Wood-workers
- Leatherworkers
- Metalworkers
- Millers and bakers
- Shipbuilders
- Other jobs
- Other builders

Practice the Skill

Use the circle graph to answer the questions.

1 List the jobs in colonial New York shown on the graph.

2 Which job category has the most workers?

3 Which job category has the fewest workers?

4 Did more colonial New Yorkers work with metal or wood?

Apply the Skill

Create a circle graph to show how you spend your time during a typical school day. First draw a circle that stands for the 24 hours in a whole day. Then divide it into sections to show all of your activities and the time you spend on them.

Visual Summary

1–3. ✏️ Write what you learned about each period in New York's history.

History of New York, 1500–1750	
 Exploration	
 Settlement	
 Government	

Facts and Main Ideas

Answer each question with information from the chapter.

4. **Geography** On what land in present-day New York did the Dutch first settle?

5. **Economics** With whom did the Dutch trade when they first arrived in New Netherland?

6. **Culture** In what ways did Dutch customs influence the English who took over colonial New York?

7. **History** What important right did James, the Duke of York, finally agree to give the colonists?

8. **History** Why was New York such a diverse place in the late 1600s?

Vocabulary

Choose the correct word from the list below to complete each sentence.

claim, p. 61
founder, p. 68
tax, p. 77

9. People have to pay a _____ to the government for services.

10. The person who started a colony was called its _____.

11. Explorers would _____ the land they found for their countries.

1609
Hudson explores

1664
English take over

1683
Charter of Liberties written

1600   1650   1700   1750   1800

Apply Skills

Use Latitude and Longitude Study the map below. Then use what you have learned about latitude and longitude to answer each question.

12. Which city is nearest to the 78°W line of longitude?

   A. Albany

   B. Rochester

   C. Syracuse

   D. West Point

13. Which of the following best describes the location of Syracuse?

   A. 76°N, 43°W

   B. 30°N, 42°W

   C. 43°N, 76°W

   D. 73°N, 35°W

Timeline

Use the timeline above to answer the question.

14. Did the English take over New York before or after the Charter of Liberties was written?

Critical Thinking

Write a short paragraph to answer each question.

15. **Generalize** Explain why New York grew so rapidly during the late 1600s.

16. **Cause and Effect** In what ways did the Dutch settlers affect the lives of Native Americans?

Activities

Drama Activity Write and perform a skit about life in New York under English control.

Writing Activity Write a description that could go on the back cover of a book called *Colonial New York*. Summarize what you think readers would want to know about this period in New York history.

Go Digital Get help with your writing at www.eduplace.com/nycssp/

Fun with Social Studies

Which Movies Don't Belong?

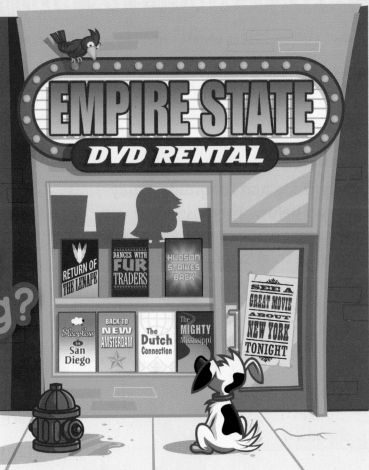

Some of these DVDs don't belong on the shelves. Which two titles are not related to New York?

Whose T-Shirt?

Who should wear each T-shirt?

LET'S GO Dutch

In 1492 I sailed the Ocean Blue

I've got a colony named after ME

Christopher Columbus

James, Duke of York

Peter Stuyvesant

Treasure Terms

abc VOCABULARY

Match the clues on the map to the correct vocabulary terms. The underlined letters in the correct terms will spell the name of a famous ship that sailed into New York long ago.

a_ssembly   founder
gover_nor   cla_im
co_lony   rig_ht

A freedom government must protect

A group elected by the people to make laws

A person who starts something

To declare that land belongs to a country

Land ruled by another country

The official in charge of a colony

Go Digital **Education Place®**
www.eduplace.com

New York History and Government
- eGlossary
- eWord Game
- Biographies
- Primary Sources
- Write Site
- Interactive Maps
- Weekly Reader®: Current Events
- GeoNet
- Online Atlas

Visit Eduplace!

Log on to Eduplace to explore Social Studies online. Solve puzzles to watch the skateboarding tricks in eWord Game. Join Chester in GeoNet to see if you can earn enough points to become a GeoChampion, or just play Wacky Web Tales to see how silly your stories can get. Play now at www.eduplace.com/nycssp/

Review for Understanding

Reading Social Studies

A **conclusion** is a general statement about an idea or an event. To draw a conclusion, you use evidence, or what you have learned. You also use knowledge, or what you already know.

 Draw Conclusions

1. Complete this graphic organizer to show that you understand how to draw conclusions about New York's colonial government.

New York Government

Colonists formed an assembly.	Colonists wrote the Charter of Liberties.

 Write About the Big Idea

2. **Write a Journal** Think about what life might have been like for a Native American, African, or European in colonial New York. Write a journal entry describing daily life.

Vocabulary and Main Ideas

Write a sentence to answer each question.

3. Why did European explorers **claim** land in North America?

4. Where did Dutch settlers start a **colony** in 1624?

5. What did the **founders** of New Netherland do to help the colony grow quickly?

6. In what ways did New Amsterdam have great **diversity?**

7. What is one **right** that colonists in New York had?

8. What did New York's first **assembly** accomplish in 1683?

Critical Thinking

Write a short paragraph to answer each question.

9. **Cause and Effect** What effect did Christopher Columbus's journey have on European countries?

10. **Compare and Contrast** How was New York's government the same as and different from those of other English colonies?

Apply Skills

Study the map below. Then use what you have learned about latitude and longitude to answer each question.

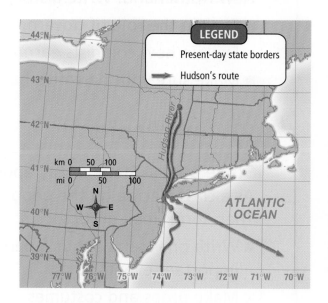

11. Which line of longitude does the Hudson River follow?

    A. 70°W

    B. 71°W

    C. 73°W

    D. 74°W

12. Hudson had to stop sailing north and turn around when the river got too shallow. Which line of latitude is closest to where Hudson turned around?

    A. 39°N

    B. 40°N

    C. 43°N

    D. 44°N

Unit 2 Activities

Show What You Know

Unit Writing Activity

Write a Narrative Imagine that you are a settler in New Netherland. Write a story about life in your colony.

- Explain the role of government in your society.
- Explain how colonists earn a living.
- Make sure your narrative has a story.

Unit Project

Stage a Play Stage a play about the early history of New York. As a class, decide on the people and events you want to show. Then form small groups.

- Write one scene about a person, a group of people, or an important event.
- Make props and costumes.
- Perform it for invited guests.

Read More

- *Peter Stuyvesant: Dutch Military Leader* by Joan Banks. Chelsea House.
- *Beyond the Sea of Ice: The Voyages of Henry Hudson* by Joan Elizabeth Goodman. Mikaya Press.
- *The Colony of New York* by Susan Whitehurst. Rosen.

 visit www.eduplace.com/nycssp/

The Revolution in New York

What was the effect of the American Revolution on people in New York?

WHAT TO KNOW

✓ Why did English colonists settle in North America?

✓ In what ways were the economies of the three colonial regions alike and different?

✓ Who were the people of the New York colony?

✓ Why did colonists fight back against British rule?

✓ What was New York's role in the American Revolution?

North America, 1740s

SKAGIT R.
BLACKFOOT
CHINOOK
Columbia
YAKIMA
TILLAMOOK
NEZ PERCE
YUROK
MODOC
PAIUTE
POMO
MIWOK
SHOSHONE
YOKUTS
CHUMASH
PUEBLO
NAVAJO
CAHUILLA
YUMA
APACHE

OJIBWA
CHIPPEWA
Lake Superior
WINNEBAGO
DAKOTA
Lake Michigan
SAUK
FOX
MIAMI

CROW
MANDAN
NAKOTA
LAKOTA
Missouri R.
SHOSHONE
CHEYENNE
BANNOCK
SHOSHONE
OMAHA
IOWA
PAWNEE
UTE R.
ARAPAHO
MISSOURI
ILLINOIS
Colorado
KAW
PUEBLO
KIOWA
OSAGE
Mississippi R.
CHICKASAW
PUEBLO
TUSKEGEE
Santa Fe
Albuquerque
CADDO
COMANCHE
CHOCTAW
El Paso
ATAKAPA
TONKAWA
New Orleans
Rio Grande
KARANKAWA

PACIFIC
OCEAN

Further Exploration
During the 1600s and 1700s, English sailors explored the Pacific coast searching for a water route to Asia.

LEGEND
English
New France
New Spain
Disputed territory
English port
Spanish mission
French trading post
PEQUOT Native Americans

Connect to

New York City

City Populations, 1740s

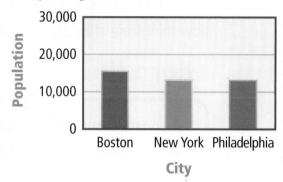

In the 1740s, Boston, New York, and Philadelphia were the three largest cities in the English colonies.

City Populations Today

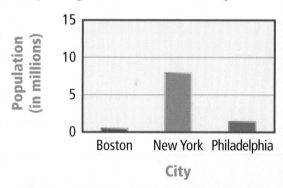

The population of New York City today is nearly 600 times larger than it was in 1740.

Quebec

Montreal

ABENAKI

TTAWA

HURON

Lake Ontario

MASSACHUSET

Boston

ERIE

HAUDENOSAUNEE PEQUOT

NATIONS

OTAWATOMI

Detroit

Lake Erie

SUSQUEHANNOCK

New York

Philadelphia

DELAWARE

Ohio R.

POWHATAN

Yorktown

HAWNEE

N
NW NE
W E
SW SE
S

TUSCARORA

ATLANTIC

OCEAN

CHEROKEE

CATAWBA

Charleston

CREEK

YAMASEE

St. Augustine

TIMUCUA

Victory at Yorktown
Colonists won the last major battle of the American Revolution at Yorktown, Virginia, in 1781.

CALUSA

Gulf of

Mexico

km 0 150 300
mi 0 150 300

Reading Social Studies

Compare and Contrast

Why It Matters Comparing and contrasting can help you understand how things are alike and how they are different.

Learn the Skill

When you **compare**, you think about how two or more items are alike. When you **contrast**, you think about how two or more items are different.

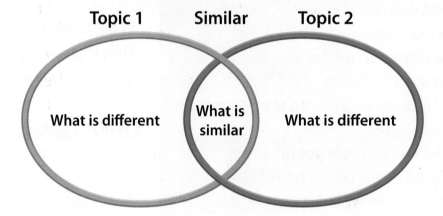

- *Like*, *alike*, *both*, *also*, *same*, and *similar* are words that compare.

- *Different*, *instead*, *however*, and *but* are words that contrast.

Practice the Skill

Read the paragraphs that follow. Compare and contrast the information in the second paragraph.

Similar
Different

In the early 1700s, New York and Virginia were both colonies ruled by England. Most people in both colonies worked as farmers. However, farms in Virginia were often much larger than farms in New York.

During the 1700s, all of England's colonies allowed slavery. Many enslaved people lived in both New York and Virginia. In Virginia, most enslaved people worked on large farms, but in New York most worked in homes and shops.

Apply the Skill

Read the paragraphs, and answer the questions.

Young Colonists

Have you wondered what life was like for children hundreds of years ago? How did they spend their days? The answer is that most children spent nearly all of their time working to help their families. However, unlike children today, most colonial children did not have the chance to attend school. There were few schools, and families needed children to work on their farms or in their shops.

Both boys and girls got up early, usually before sunrise. If a boy's father owned a shop, he would spend the day helping. Some boys were sent to live with other families to learn a trade.

For example, a boy might be sent to live with a carpenter so he could learn woodworking. Girls stayed home and helped their mothers clean, bake bread, and make soap, candles, and clothes. These were important skills that everyone valued.

Life was hard for colonial children, but they still found time to relax. They had few toys, but they liked playing games and sports. Most families had more than five children, so brothers and sisters always had others to play with when they finished their chores.

🎯 Compare and Contrast

1. What is the biggest difference between colonial children and children today?

2. What is one thing that is the same for colonial children and children today?

The Thirteen Colonies

Colonial Kitchen, 1700s

Study Skills

USE A K-W-L CHART

A K-W-L chart can help you focus on what you already know about a topic and what you want to learn about it.

- Before you read, use the K column to list things you know about a topic.

- Before you read, use the W column to list things you want to know about the topic.

- After you read, use the L column to list things you have learned about the topic.

The Thirteen Colonies		
What I **K**now	What I **W**ant to Know	What I **L**earned
The colonies were started by the English.	What was life like in the New York colony?	_____ _____

Vocabulary Preview

compact

The Pilgrims made a written agreement before they started their settlement. The **compact** was about the laws that would govern them. **page 103**

economy

The ocean shaped New England's **economy.** Many people used the region's resources to make a living by fishing or building ships. **page 104**

Chapter Timeline

1607
Jamestown founded

1620
Plymouth founded

1681
Pennsylvania founded

1600   1625   1650   1675   1700

Reading Strategy

Predict and Infer Use this strategy before you read. Look at the titles and pictures in a lesson to make predictions. What do you think you will read about?

cash crop

Indigo was an important **cash crop** in the Southern Colonies. Many farmers grew and sold indigo to earn money.
page 107

apprentice

A skilled worker such as a printer might need a helper. A young **apprentice** learned new skills by working at a trade.
page 113

1735
Zenger Trial

1725   1750

Go Digital visit www.eduplace.com/nycssp/

Starting the Colonies

1500   1550   1600   1650   1700   1750   1800

1600–1750

Before You Read Think about how you get around. What would travel be like in New York if there were not many roads? Hundreds of years ago, settlers in North America often used boats to travel.

Geography of the Colonies

Main Idea Geography influenced where people settled in the colonies.

During the 1600s and 1700s, thousands of settlers from England arrived in North America. Over time, they founded thirteen colonies along the Atlantic Ocean. The northernmost colonies were called New England. The Southern Colonies included the area that now stretches from Maryland to Georgia. In between were the Middle Colonies, including New York.

Hills and valleys covered much of the Middle Colonies. Farmers grew many crops in the rich soil. Ships traveled far inland on deep, wide rivers, such as the Hudson. Early settlers in the region relied on waterways to ship goods and to travel.

▶ **WHAT TO KNOW**
Why did English colonists settle in North America?

▶ **VOCABULARY**
fall line
self-government
compact

READING SKILL
Draw Conclusions Add facts to the chart that support the conclusion about the geography of the colonies.

The colonies were divided into three regions.

Middle Colonies
Gentle, rolling hills were a common feature of the Middle Colonies.

Geography and Settlement

Unlike the Middle Colonies, New England had few rivers large enough for ships to travel. Much of the land was either too rocky or sandy to farm. Farmers struggled to grow enough crops to feed their families. They had little left over to sell. New England had many other natural resources, however. Forests provided colonists with wood to build ships and houses. People caught fish and whales in the ocean for food and other uses.

Land in the Southern Colonies was low, with many rivers, bays, and wetlands. Settlers used boats to reach areas of rich farmland. Colonies developed across the flat coastal region and spread inland. Few people, however, settled on the rough, rocky land beyond the fall line. At the **fall line,** rivers from the higher land of the mountains flow to the lower lands near the coast and often form waterfalls.

✓**READING CHECK** DRAW CONCLUSIONS
Which colonial regions were good for farming?

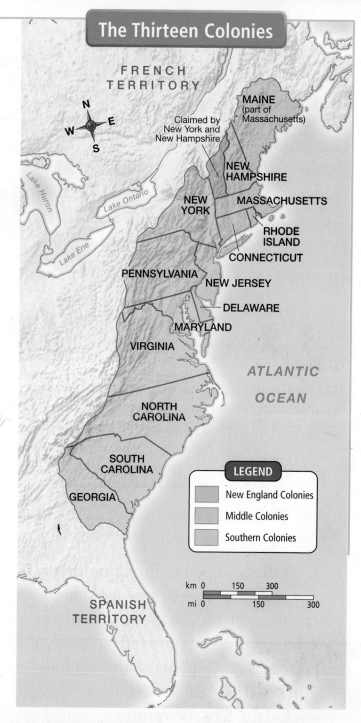

The Thirteen Colonies

FRENCH TERRITORY

MAINE (part of Massachusetts)

Claimed by New York and New Hampshire

NEW HAMPSHIRE

Lake Huron

Lake Ontario

NEW YORK

MASSACHUSETTS

RHODE ISLAND

Lake Erie

CONNECTICUT

PENNSYLVANIA

NEW JERSEY

DELAWARE

MARYLAND

VIRGINIA

ATLANTIC OCEAN

NORTH CAROLINA

SOUTH CAROLINA

GEORGIA

LEGEND

New England Colonies

Middle Colonies

Southern Colonies

km 0   150   300
mi 0   150   300

SPANISH TERRITORY

Three Regions This map divides the colonies into three regions. Each region has its own geography and climate.

SKILL **Reading Maps** Which were the Middle Colonies?

Jamestown, Virginia Today, visitors can tour a rebuilt Jamestown settlement and Native American village. This coin was used by people who lived in the Jamestown colony.

Reasons for Settlement

Main Idea Settlers came to the colonies for economic, religious, and political reasons.

Settlers moved to the colonies for many reasons. Some came looking for riches. In 1607, a group of settlers searching for gold founded Jamestown in present-day Virginia. Although they didn't find any gold, their town became the first successful English colony in North America.

Gold was not the only reason people moved to the colonies. James Oglethorpe created the colony of Georgia as a place for poor people to start new lives. He gave them land so they could start farms. He wanted Georgia to be a place where hard-working people could succeed.

Freedom of Religion

Some settlers came to North America in search of religious freedom. In England, people could be punished for not belonging to the Church of England. Thousands who refused to join the Church of England sailed to North America to escape punishment. The first group to arrive was known as Pilgrims. In 1620, they founded the colony of Plymouth, in what is now Massachusetts. Later, more colonists followed them to New England.

Other settlers made homes in the Middle Colonies. William Penn, a Quaker, founded Pennsylvania in 1681. Like the Pilgrims, Quakers in England could be punished for their beliefs. Penn wanted his colony to welcome people of all religions.

Political Freedom

The great distance between England and its colonies gave colonists new opportunities for self-government. **Self-government** is the power of people to make laws for themselves. For example, the Pilgrims created the Mayflower Compact. A **compact** is an agreement. In the Mayflower Compact, the Pilgrims agreed to be governed by laws that they made together. It was the first written plan of government in North America.

✔ **READING CHECK** CAUSE AND EFFECT Why did the Pilgrims and the Quakers move to the colonies?

SUMMARY

In North America, thirteen English colonies were founded along the coast of the Atlantic Ocean. The colonies had different types of geography. Colonists came to North America for many reasons, including the desire to find riches and to have religious freedom.

Mayflower Compact In this painting, Pilgrims write an agreement, or compact, aboard the *Mayflower.*

Lesson Review

1607
Jamestown founded

1620
Plymouth founded

| 1600 | 1610 | 1620 | 1630 |

❶ **WHAT TO KNOW** Why did English colonists settle in North America?

❷ **VOCABULARY** Write a sentence using **self-government** and **compact.**

❸ **TIMELINE SKILL** How many years after Jamestown's founding was Plymouth founded?

❹ **WRITING ACTIVITY** Write a description of an activity you do with friends in which you create your own rules.

❺ 🖉 **READING SKILL** Complete your graphic organizer to draw conclusions.

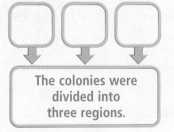

The colonies were divided into three regions.

Characteristics of the Colonies

WHAT TO KNOW

In what ways were the economies of the three colonial regions alike and different?

VOCABULARY

economy
proprietor
cash crop
plantation
mercantilism

READING SKILL

Compare and Contrast
List details that compare and contrast the governments of each colonial region.

New England	Middle Colonies	Southern Colonies

1500	1550	1600	1650	1700	1750	1800

1600–1750

Before You Read Think of a good friend or a relative. What makes the two of you alike? In what ways are you different? The thirteen colonies were alike in some ways, but different in others.

Life in the Colonies

Main Idea Each region of the colonies had different characteristics.

The thirteen English colonies had many things in common, but they differed in many ways too. New England, the Middle Colonies, and the Southern Colonies had different geographies, cultures, laws, and religions. The regions also built up different economies. An **economy** is the way in which the people of an area use the resources around them.

New England Coast Rocky coasts are common in New England.

New England Colonies

Government	**Town meeting:** a gathering where colonists held elections and voted on laws for their towns
Economy	**Farming:** rye, corn, wheat, barley, apples, cattle, sheep **Fishing:** cod, mackerel, whales **Trading:** fish, lumber
Culture and Daily Life	**Farms:** boys spent much of their time farming, but some also went to school; girls helped in the fields, prepared and preserved food
Science and Technology	**Improved shipbuilding:** better ship design – fishing ships could travel farther with smaller crews

SKILL **Reading Charts** **What details show that the ocean was important to colonists in New England?**

New England

A religious group known as the Puritans settled the Massachusetts Bay Colony in the early 1600s. Their religion shaped people's lives and the government. Everyone had to go to church, even if they weren't church members. Only men who were church members could vote or serve in town government.

The resources of the colonies affected the way colonists lived. Many New Englanders were farmers, but the ocean also shaped the region's economy. Fishing and shipbuilding brought many craftspeople and businesses to coastal towns and cities.

READING CHECK COMPARE AND CONTRAST Compare the daily lives of children in New England.

The Middle Colonies

In the Middle Colonies, most of the colonies were ruled by proprietors. A **proprietor** was a person who owned and controlled all the land in a colony. In 1664, **James, Duke of York,** became New York's proprietor.

The strong farming economy of the Middle Colonies helped some of the region's cities to grow larger. Farmers shipped their extra crops to be sold in New York City and Philadelphia, which were centers of shipping, trade, and culture.

Middle Colonies	
Government	**Proprietors:** people who owned colonies and chose governors to make important decisions for the colonies **Assembly:** landowning men elected to help make laws
Economy	**Farming:** wheat, oats, corn, barley, potatoes, hay, peaches, apples, farm animals **Trading:** crops, lumber
Culture and Daily Life	**Farms:** boys helped plant and harvest crops; girls cooked, sewed, and did housework **Cities:** people owned businesses or worked as shopkeepers, craftspeople, or laborers; children might learn a job or craft
Science and Technology	**Inventions:** bifocal glasses, a fireplace to better heat rooms, an early battery to store electricity – all invented by Benjamin Franklin

SKILL **Reading Charts** What did Benjamin Franklin contribute to the Middle Colonies?

Philadelphia By 1760, this fast-growing Pennsylvania city was the largest in the colonies.

Small Farms Virginia farmers harvest tobacco in the early 1600s.

The Southern Colonies

In the South, the good soil and warm climate were perfect for growing cash crops such as tobacco, rice, and indigo. A **cash crop** is a crop that people grow and sell to earn money.

Most Southern farms were small. Wealthy Southern farmers, however, grew large amounts of cash crops on plantations. A **plantation** is a very big farm.

Workers who lived on the farm raised the crops. Most plantation workers were servants or enslaved Africans. Though all the colonies had slavery, most enslaved Africans lived in the South.

READING CHECK MAIN IDEA AND DETAILS
Why did farmers in the Middle Colonies send extra crops to New York City?

Southern Colonies	
Government	**Proprietors:** people who owned and controlled many of the Southern Colonies **House of Burgesses:** a group of male, white landowners in Virginia elected to make and change laws for the colony
Economy	**Cash crops:** tobacco, rice, indigo **Trading:** cash crops
Culture and Daily Life	**Plantations:** children of owners lived fairly easy lives; enslaved African children had to work very hard and could be sold and separated from their families **Small farms:** children helped with farm work
Science and Technology	**Improved agriculture:** new type of indigo, a cash crop used to make a blue dye, was developed by Eliza Lucas Pinckney.

SKILL **Reading Charts** What cash crops did Southerners trade?

Valuable Resources

Main Idea The colonies provided England with valuable resources.

All along the coast of North America, colonists found valuable natural resources. The colonists shipped wood, fish, and crops to England, where people needed food and raw materials. To meet their own needs, colonists bought finished goods, such as furniture, cloth, and tools, from English traders.

Soon, a trade network developed among the colonies, Europe, and Africa. Each region provided things the others wanted. These shipping routes formed an imaginary triangle across the Atlantic Ocean. This became known as the triangular trade.

Controlling Trade

England was a powerful nation. Along with the thirteen colonies, it also controlled valuable land in the West Indies, or Caribbean. The English government believed it could use trade with the colonies to make itself even stronger. England was often at war with other European countries. It needed resources to keep its army and navy strong.

The English hoped to benefit from the colonies through mercantilism. **Mercantilism** was a system in which the government controlled the economy of its colonies in order to grow rich from trade. The English government believed that the thirteen colonies should provide for England's needs.

SKILL **Reading Maps** What types of goods were traded from the thirteen colonies to countries in Europe?

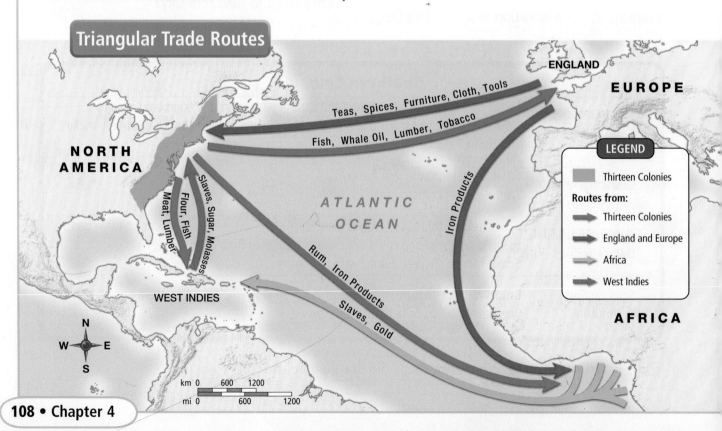

Triangular Trade Routes

ENGLAND

EUROPE

Teas, Spices, Furniture, Cloth, Tools

Fish, Whale Oil, Lumber, Tobacco

NORTH AMERICA

ATLANTIC OCEAN

Iron Products

Meat, Lumber

Flour, Fish

Slaves, Sugar, Molasses

Rum, Iron Products

WEST INDIES

Slaves, Gold

AFRICA

LEGEND

Thirteen Colonies

Routes from:

Thirteen Colonies

England and Europe

Africa

West Indies

N W E S

km 0 600 1200
mi 0 600 1200

Trade Laws

To gain more from trade with the colonies, the English government made new laws, called the Navigation Acts. The new laws controlled how the colonies could ship their goods, who they could trade with, and what products they could trade. The laws declared that colonists could sell products such as tobacco and cotton only to England. Over time, the list of goods that colonists could sell only to England grew larger. The laws became unpopular with many colonists.

READING CHECK CAUSE AND EFFECT
Why did the English government create the Navigation Acts?

SUMMARY

Although all the colonial regions had economies based on farming, each region developed in its own way. Over time, England found ways to gain more from trade with the colonies.

Shipping Goods
Many goods that traveled across the Atlantic Ocean were packed in barrels such as this one.

Lesson Review

1 **WHAT TO KNOW** In what ways were the economies of the three colonial regions alike and different?

2 **VOCABULARY** Write a short paragraph about the Southern Colonies using **economy** and **cash crop.**

3 **CRITICAL THINKING: Cause and Effect** What effect did the Navigation Acts have on the colonies?

4 **RESEARCH ACTIVITY** Use library or Internet resources to find out more about one of Benjamin Franklin's inventions. Present your research in a poster.

5 **READING SKILL** Complete the graphic organizer to compare and contrast the colonial regions.

New England	Middle Colonies	Southern Colonies

Trade with England

Sailors shout, shipbuilders pound nails, and wood creaks as big ships sail out to sea. These are some of the sounds New Yorkers heard 250 years ago at their busy port. Every year, more ships carried natural resources from North America to England and brought finished goods back the other way. New York City was on its way to being one of the world's greatest ports.

New York – England Trade

- ■ ships to England
- ■ ships to New York City

Number of Ships: 0, 100, 200, 300, 400, 500, 600

Year: 1734, 1754, 1768

Growing Trade As trade increased, more ships traveled beween England and the colonies.

Shipbuilding
New York Harbor, shown here, was a center of colonial shipbuilding. Raw materials for ships, such as the one above, came downriver from the surrounding countryside.

Traded Goods

From the colonies to England	ships and ship products, whale products, furs, tobacco, indigo, lumber
From England to the colonies	tea, spices, furniture, cloth, tools, glass, other finished goods

A Center of Trade

Ships from Europe, Africa, the Caribbean, and the other colonies carried goods in and out of New York's harbor. By 1760, New York City was the second-largest seaport in the colonies.

Activities

1. **EXPLORE IT** Put yourself in the scene of this painting. What do you see, hear, and smell?

2. **CHART IT** Use the information in the bar graph on page 110 to make a line graph showing the increasing number of ships that sailed to and from New York City.

The New York Colony

| 1500 | 1550 | 1600 | 1650 | 1700 | 1750 | 1800 |

1600–1750

Before You Read Have more people moved to your community over the years? As the colony of New York grew during the 1700s, people from different places, often with different cultures, moved there.

A Diverse Colony

Main Idea New York's population became more diverse as the colony grew.

As the thirteen English colonies grew and changed, so did New York. By 1750, New York City had more than 12,000 people. Twenty-five years later, its population had reached 20,000.

Dutch immigrants had been the first to come to New York. An **immigrant** is a person who leaves one country to live in another country. English settlers arrived in large numbers after their country took control of New York. Other settlers arrived from Sweden, Scotland, and Germany. Jewish immigrants came from Brazil and the Netherlands.

> **WHAT TO KNOW**
> Who were the people of the New York colony?

> **VOCABULARY**
> immigrant
> apprentice
> merchant

> **READING SKILL**
> **Main Idea and Details**
> Record details about the work people did in the New York colony.

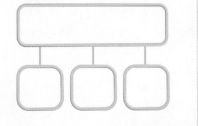

Brooklyn Ferry A ferry carried people between the growing towns of Manhattan and Brooklyn.

Daily Life

New York's colonists found different ways to earn a living. In New York City, immigrants started businesses using skills they had learned in Europe. Some immigrants made goods such as furniture, tools, and even ships. Others opened shops to sell these goods. People also worked as traders. They bought goods from England and sold them in the colonies.

Skilled workers, such as dentists and printers, provided valuable services to other colonists. In addition, they often took in young apprentices. An **apprentice** worked with a master to learn how to do a job. Apprentices did not get paid, but they received food, shelter, and clothes.

Many New Yorkers worked on farms. Men plowed and planted crops. Women made most of the clothing. Children fed farm animals and milked cows. Farm families often traded for things they could not make or grow.

Some colonists worked as indentured servants. These people did not have enough money to come to the colonies. They agreed to work for someone who would pay for their trip. After four to seven years, they were free to work for themselves.

Spinning Wool In colonial New York, women and girls made most of the cloth and clothing. This woman shows how they made wool into yarn.

Some workers were not paid at all. Enslaved Africans did much of the hard work in New York City, such as loading ships with goods. Others worked as house servants or in shops.

✓ **READING CHECK** MAIN IDEA AND DETAILS
What work did people do on farms?

Colonial Power In colonial government, gatherings of leaders such as the one shown here only included white, landowning men.

Colonial Rights

Main Idea Women, Native Americans, and Africans faced challenges in New York.

Most colonists in New York had little say in how the colony was run. A governor controlled the colony. The governor was chosen by the king of England. The colony also had an elected assembly. Only white men who owned property and went to church could vote, however. Women had fewer rights. They could own property, but were not allowed to vote or hold office.

Native Americans also had few rights. Colonists took so much land from the Munsee that many Munsee left the area. They traveled north and west, seeking new places to live.

As in the other colonies, people in New York treated enslaved Africans as property and denied them basic rights. Enslaved workers did not get paid and could not own property. Few were given an education.

Enslaved people struggled against harsh slave laws that made their lives harder. Parents and children could be bought or sold at any time, forcing families apart. Many enslaved Africans also lived separately from each other, because most slave owners in New York had only a few workers.

Even free blacks in New York had few rights. Those who owned property were not allowed to vote. By the early 1700s, newly-freed Africans could not own land.

Exercising Their Rights

Although the rights of some New Yorkers were limited, many found ways to exercise the rights they did have. **Mary Provoost Alexander** was a partner in her husband's trading business. She soon became one of the leading merchants in New York City. A **merchant** buys and sells goods.

Another New Yorker, **John Peter Zenger,** published a newspaper. In 1735, he printed complaints about the governor. Zenger was put on trial for this—and won. The court ruled that he could print bad things about the governor as long as they were true. Zenger's trial was one of the early victories for freedom of speech.

✓ READING CHECK COMPARE AND CONTRAST
In what ways were the rights of colonial men and women different?

SUMMARY

People from different places came to the colony of New York and worked at a variety of jobs. Many people, including women, Native Americans, and Africans, had little say in government and few rights.

Zenger's Paper Zenger accused the governor of cheating in elections and trying to limit rights.

Lesson Review

① **WHAT TO KNOW** Who were the people of the New York colony?

② **VOCABULARY** Use **immigrant** in a sentence about life in colonial New York.

③ **CRITICAL THINKING: Cause and Effect** What effect do you think New York's slave laws had on life for enslaved Africans? On free blacks?

④ **DRAMA ACTIVITY** Create a dialogue between a 12-year-old colonist and his or her parents about becoming an apprentice.

⑤ **READING SKILL** Complete the graphic organizer to show the main idea and details.

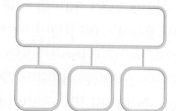

Skillbuilder

Write a Report

VOCABULARY
report

You have read that Jamestown was the first successful English colony in North America, but you want to learn more. What was life like? How did the colony become successful? You can answer these questions by writing a report. A **report** presents information that you have researched. Writing a report is a way to share what you have learned with others.

Learn the Skill

Step 1: Choose a topic. Then brainstorm key words and ideas about your topic.

Step 2: Use your key words and ideas to find information in reference materials.

Step 3: Take notes. Be sure to write down the name of the source. Then organize your notes according to main points and details. The details in these notes support the main point that life was difficult for early settlers in Jamestown.

> Source: Encyclopaedia Britannica
> What was life like in Jamestown?
>   difficult for early settlers
>   disagreements with Native Americans
>   colonists did not gather enough food
>   winter of 1609–10 known as
>   the Starving Time

Step 4: Write your report. Start with an opening paragraph that introduces your topic and main points. Then, write a separate body paragraph for each main point. Support the main points with details. Finally, write a closing paragraph that summarizes what you have written.

> Life was difficult for early settlers in Jamestown. The colonists had many disagreements with Native Americans. They also did not gather enough food to feed the colony. The winter of 1609–10 was known as the Starving Time. Many settlers did not survive.

Practice the Skill

Use the notes to write a sample body paragraph of a report on Jamestown.

How did Jamestown become successful?
  ships brought new settlers and supplies
  peace between the Native Americans
    and settlers
  settlers learned to plant tobacco
  tobacco became a cash crop for
    the colony

Apply the Skill

Use what you have learned to find information about colonial New York City. Write a report about the topic.

Visual Summary

1–3. ✏️ Write a description for each item below.

New England	Middle Colonies	Southern Colonies
		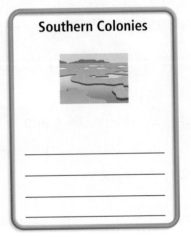
_____	_____	_____
_____	_____	_____
_____	_____	_____

Facts and Main Ideas

Answer each question with information from the chapter.

4. **Geography** What was the geography of New England like?

5. **History** What are two reasons that settlers came to the thirteen English colonies?

6. **Government** How were most of the Middle Colonies ruled?

7. **Economics** What goods did the colonists ship to England?

8. **Citizenship** What was one right women had in the New York colony?

Vocabulary

Choose the correct word from the list below to complete each sentence.

compact, p. 103
mercantilism, p. 108
immigrant, p. 112

9. Under the system of _____, England controlled the economy of the colonies.

10. The Pilgrims wrote a(n) _____ that was the first written plan of government in North America.

11. In New York City, a(n) _____ could use the skills he or she had learned in Europe to start a business.

Apply Skills

Write a Report Use what you have learned about writing a report to answer each question.

12. What is the main purpose of a report?

   A. to persuade

   B. to present information

   C. to describe a point of view

   D. to entertain

13. Colonists found many valuable natural resources in North America. Which detail supports this main point?

   A. Ships from Africa carried gold to the colonies.

   B. The colonies did not need to trade with England.

   C. Ships from Europe carried spices to the colonies.

   D. The colonies shipped wood, fish, and crops to England.

14. What is the main purpose of a closing paragraph?

   A. to introduce the topic and main idea

   B. to summarize what has been written

   C. to support main points with details

   D. to identify sources of information

Timeline

Use the timeline above to answer the question.

15. When was the first successful English colony in North America founded?

Critical Thinking

Write a short paragraph to answer each question. Use details from the chapter to support your responses.

16. **Compare and Contrast** How was government in New England different from that in New York?

17. **Generalize** Discuss the various ways that colonists in New York City earned a living.

Activities

HANDS ON **Citizenship Activity** The assembly in New York helped the governor make laws for the colony. Write a list of rules that you think your town should have. Explain the reasons behind each rule.

Writing Activity Write an editorial for John Peter Zenger's newspaper. Use it to speak out against something unfair in the New York colony, such as limited rights for women.

Go Digital Get help with your writing at www.eduplace.com/nycssp/

Chapter **5**

The American Revolution

Saratoga National Historical Park, New York

Study Skills

CONNECT IDEAS

Graphic organizers can help you connect ideas.

- On a bubble map, the main idea is written in the center bubble.
- Ideas that are related to the main idea are written in surrounding bubbles.

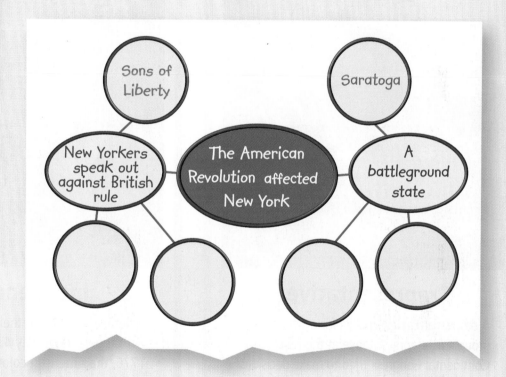

Vocabulary Preview

representative

A **representative** speaks for a whole group. Each representative at the First Continental Congress tried to make decisions to help the people in his colony. **page 124**

independence

Americans celebrate their **independence** with fireworks on July 4. On that day in 1776, the American colonies became a new nation. **page 126**

Chapter Timeline

1763
War between Britain and France ends

1767
Townshend Acts

1777
Battle of Saratoga

1750   1760   1770

Reading Strategy

Question As you read each lesson, ask yourself questions about important ideas. List the questions you have. Go back to them when you finish reading.

Patriot

Margaret Corbin was a famous New York **Patriot.** She fought for independence from Britain.
page 132

surrender

In 1777, the British **surrendered** to Patriot forces at Saratoga. More than 5,000 British soldiers became prisoners.
page 135

1783
Treaty of Paris

780   1790

 visit www.eduplace.com/nycssp/

Colonists Resist

| 1750 | 1755 | 1760 | 1765 | 1770 | 1775 | 1780 |

1754–1776

▶ **WHAT TO KNOW**
Why did colonists fight back against British rule?

▶ **VOCABULARY**
representative
protest
militia
revolution
independence

✓ **READING SKILL**
Cause and Effect List the laws Great Britain made for the colonies as causes. List the colonists' responses as effects.

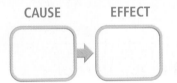

| CAUSE | EFFECT |

Before You Read Every day you make decisions, and that shows you are growing up. By the 1770s, the American colonists were tired of British control. They wanted to make their own decisions.

Disagreements with Britain

Main Idea The colonists disagreed with Britain over laws, taxes, and government.

In the 1700s, both Britain and France wanted to control land in western New York. Disagreements such as this led to war in 1754. The French and their Native American allies fought against the British and their Native American allies. After nine years of fighting, Britain won the war.

Britain expected the colonists to help pay for the war. To raise this money, the British government passed laws that taxed goods the colonists needed. The colonists had no representatives in the British government to stop these laws. A **representative** is someone who is chosen to speak for others.

Choosing Sides Colonists used this cartoon to show that working together was the only way to defeat the French.

Stamp Tax Colonists held meetings (left) to protest the tax that required stamps (above) on paper goods.

New Taxes

In 1764, Britain's government passed the Sugar Act. This act taxed sugar and many other imported goods. Some colonists tried to avoid paying the tax by secretly bringing goods into the colonies.

Britain created a new law called the Stamp Act in 1765. This law taxed anything printed on paper, including newspapers and calendars. Many colonists opposed the law and refused to pay for stamps.

The British government eventually canceled the Stamp Act, but it needed to find another way to make money. In 1767, Britain passed the Townshend Acts. One of the laws taxed tea, glass, lead, paints, and paper brought into the colonies. Colonists were just as angry about the Townshend Acts as they had been about earlier laws.

Conflict with Britain Grows

Colonists protested the new tax laws. To **protest** means to speak out against something. Groups called the Sons of Liberty spoke out against the tax laws. The Daughters of Liberty protested by making their own cloth instead of buying British cloth. Many colonists refused to buy goods that were taxed.

Because of the protests, all of the tax laws were canceled except the Tea Act, which taxed tea. In New York City and Boston, Massachusetts, protesters held "tea parties." They boarded ships that carried British tea and dumped it overboard.

In response, Britain passed more laws to show it had control of the colonies. Many of these laws limited colonists' rights.

✓ **READING CHECK** CAUSE AND EFFECT Why did Britain tax the colonies?

The Revolution Begins

Main Idea The colonists formed their own government and fought British rule.

In 1774, leaders from 12 colonies met to discuss the harsh new laws. This meeting was called the First Continental Congress. New York sent seven representatives, including **John Jay** and **William Floyd**. Representatives agreed to stop trade with Britain, and that each colony should form a militia. A **militia** is a group of citizens who fight in an emergency.

Then, in April 1775, British troops in Massachusetts marched from Boston to Lexington and Concord to look for weapons. The colonists were ready, and fighting broke out. The American Revolution had started. A **revolution** is a war fought to overthrow a government.

Fort Ticonderoga

In May 1775, colonial leaders held a meeting in Philadelphia, Pennsylvania, that became known as the Second Continental Congress. They formed a new army called the Continental Army and chose **George Washington** to lead it. These were big steps toward gaining independence. **Independence** is freedom from being ruled by another country.

That same month, American troops led by **Ethan Allen** and **Benedict Arnold** captured the British fort at Ticonderoga on Lake Champlain. Then in 1776, General **Philip Schuyler** (SKY lur) saw that Fort Ticonderoga would be hard to defend against the British. He tried to make the fort stronger by surrounding it with large dirt walls and high log fences.

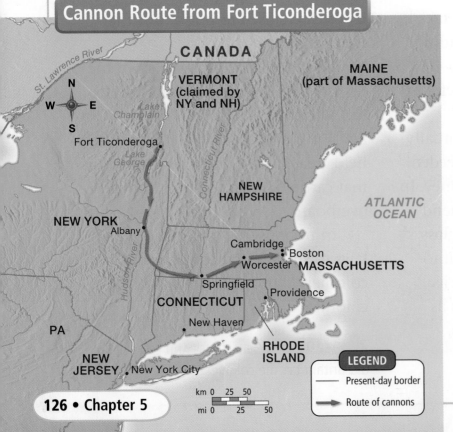

Cannon Route from Fort Ticonderoga

CANADA

St. Lawrence River

VERMONT (claimed by NY and NH)

MAINE (part of Massachusetts)

Lake Champlain

Fort Ticonderoga

Lake George

Connecticut River

NEW HAMPSHIRE

ATLANTIC OCEAN

NEW YORK

Albany

Hudson River

Cambridge

Boston

Worcester **MASSACHUSETTS**

Springfield

Providence

CONNECTICUT

New Haven

PA

RHODE ISLAND

NEW JERSEY • New York City

LEGEND
— Present-day border
→ Route of cannons

km 0   25   50
mi 0   25   50

Fort Ticonderoga to Boston
Continental soldiers moved 59 cannons from Fort Ticonderoga.

SKILL **Reading Maps** Which city in New York was on the route to Boston?

Signers of the Declaration
Four New Yorkers signed the Declaration of Independence.

The Declaration of Independence

In 1776, colonial leaders asked **Thomas Jefferson** to write a statement declaring independence. In the document, Jefferson explained that all people have rights to "life, liberty and the pursuit of happiness." He believed that Britain had not protected these rights, and wrote that the colonies were free from British rule. The Declaration of Independence was announced on July 4, 1776. This date, known as Independence Day, is when the United States of America became a nation.

✓ **READING CHECK** SUMMARIZE Why did the colonists declare their independence?

SUMMARY

Britain wanted the colonists to pay for its war with France. Colonists had no say in the laws that Britain passed to raise the money. Finally, the colonists declared independence.

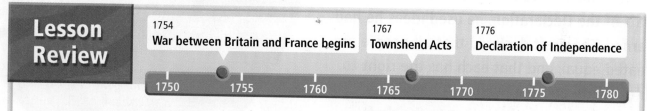

Lesson Review

1754 War between Britain and France begins	1767 Townshend Acts	1776 Declaration of Independence

1750 — 1755 — 1760 — 1765 — 1770 — 1775 — 1780

① **WHAT TO KNOW** Why did colonists fight back against British rule?

② **VOCABULARY** Write a paragraph about the American Revolution. Use the word **independence.**

③ **TIMELINE SKILL** How many years after the Townshend Acts was the Declaration of Independence written?

④ **SPEAKING ACTIVITY** List reasons colonists wanted independence. Then make a speech to persuade others to agree with your reasons.

⑤ **READING SKILL** Complete the graphic organizer to show cause-and-effect relationships.

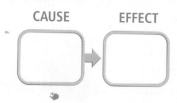

CAUSE   EFFECT

The Declaration of Independence

Thomas Jefferson is deep in thought. He must find the right words. Congress has chosen Jefferson to tell the king why the American colonies no longer belong to Britain. He is writing the Declaration of Independence.

Jefferson had read about government, history, and science as a young man. In his draft of the Declaration, he used ideas he had learned. The draft declared that all people are created equal, and that each has the right to "life, liberty and the pursuit of happiness." After making several changes to the draft, Congress approved the final version on July 4, 1776. The result was one of the most important documents in history.

Moving Toward Independence

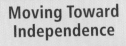

April 1775
American Revolution begins

May 1775
Second Continental Congress meets

June 1776
Writing begins on the Declaration of Independence

The handwritten draft of the Declaration of Independence:

> A Declaration by the Representatives of the UNITED STATES OF AMERICA, in General Congress assembled.
>
> When in the course of human events it becomes necessary for one people to dissolve the political bands which have connected them with another, and to assume among the powers of the earth the separate and equal station to which the laws of nature & of nature's god entitle them, a decent respect to the opinions of mankind requires that they should declare the causes which impel them to the separation.
>
> We hold these truths to be self-evident, that all men are created equal & independent, that from that equal creation they derive rights inherent & inalienable, among which are the preservation of life, & liberty, & the pursuit of happiness; that to secure these ends, governments are instituted among men, deriving their just powers from the consent of the...

> We hold these truths to be self-evident; ... created equal & independent that from that equal ... rights; that inherent & inalienable, among which are life, & liberty, & the pursuit of happiness; that to

Look Closely

In his draft, Jefferson put brackets around words he was not sure of.

Portable Desk

Jefferson wrote his draft on a portable desk, which he designed himself.

Activities

1. **TALK ABOUT IT** The Declaration of Independence is considered one of the most important documents in United States history. What ideas in the Declaration make it so important?

2. **WRITE ABOUT IT** What happens on June 28, 1776, when delegates in Congress hear the Declaration draft for the first time? Write a one-page story in the present tense.

Go Digital Visit Education Place for more primary sources. www.eduplace.com/nycssp/

July 1776
Declaration of Independence approved

129

Skillbuilder

Understand Point of View

▶ **VOCABULARY**

point of view

Citizens who live in the United States have a right to express a point of view. A **point of view** is the way someone thinks about a person, a situation, or an event. Citizens also have a responsibility to listen to the views of others.

Andrea's Point of View

"Our city has just opened a beautiful new park. I think that there aren't enough parking spaces for people who come to the park from other neighborhoods. In my opinion, a new parking lot would make it much easier for everyone to visit the park."

Michael's Point of View

"I live near the new park, and I believe there is already too much traffic on the streets. More parking spaces would make the problem worse. Visitors should walk or take a bus to the park. The noise and pollution of more cars would spoil the park."

Step 1: Read the statements carefully. Figure out what the subject is.

Step 2: Identify the point of view of the author or speaker. Look for phrases such as "I think," "in my opinion," or "I believe." These phrases help show a person's ideas about an issue.

Step 3: Think about the person who is speaking or writing. What experiences have helped shape the person's point of view? What facts does the person give? What basic ideas or beliefs does he or she have?

Step 4: Tell the person's point of view in your own words. Do you agree or disagree with this point of view? How is it similar to or different from the way you feel about this issue?

Practice the Skill

1 What is the subject of both statements on page 130?

2 Describe each person's point of view on the subject.

3 What facts does each person present? Do those facts support their points of view?

Apply the Skill

What is your point of view about providing more parking spaces? Write a paragraph that states your point of view. Be sure to provide good reasons for your opinion.

Role of New York in the War

1770   1775   1780   1785   1790

1776–1783

▶ **WHAT TO KNOW**
What was New York's role in the American Revolution?

▶ **VOCABULARY**

Patriot
Loyalist
retreat
surrender

 **READING SKILL**

Classify As you read, list Patriot and British victories.

PATRIOT	BRITISH

Before You Read Have you ever had to make a difficult decision? In 1776, colonists had to decide whether they were for or against independence from Britain.

Taking Sides

Main Idea The British retreated from Boston, and the fighting moved to New York State.

Not all New Yorkers agreed about the American Revolution. Some were Patriots. A **Patriot** was someone who wanted independence. Others were Loyalists. A **Loyalist** was a person who wanted British rule.

Native Americans also had to decide which side to support. This decision split the Haudenosaunee confederation. Some members fought for the Patriots and others fought for the British.

Declaring Independence
In New York City, Patriots tear down a statue of the British king.

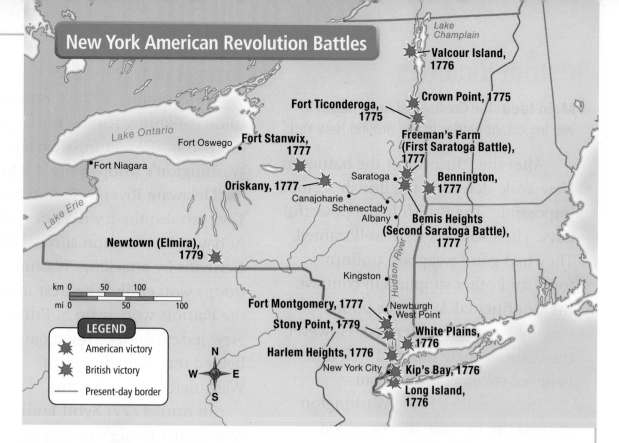

New York American Revolution Battles

- Valcour Island, 1776
- Crown Point, 1775
- Fort Ticonderoga, 1775
- Freeman's Farm (First Saratoga Battle), 1777
- Fort Stanwix, 1777
- Fort Oswego
- Fort Niagara
- Lake Ontario
- Lake Erie
- Oriskany, 1777
- Canajoharie
- Saratoga
- Bennington, 1777
- Schenectady
- Albany
- Bemis Heights (Second Saratoga Battle), 1777
- Newtown (Elmira), 1779
- Kingston
- Hudson River
- Fort Montgomery, 1777
- Newburgh
- West Point
- Stony Point, 1779
- White Plains, 1776
- Harlem Heights, 1776
- New York City
- Kip's Bay, 1776
- Long Island, 1776

km 0 50 100
mi 0 50 100

LEGEND
- ⭐ American victory
- ⭐ British victory
- — Present-day border

N W E S

Fighting in New York Many battles in New York were fought near major waterways. **SKILL** **Reading Maps** Who won the Battle of Crown Point?

Washington Marches to New York

Patriot and British leaders knew that to win the war, they would have to control New York. If British forces controlled New York, they could cut off communications and the flow of supplies between Patriots in the north and south. The British also wanted to control New York City because of its location. The city could serve as a base for the British army and navy.

In March 1776, the British left Boston. **George Washington** expected the British navy to sail toward New York City next. He marched the Continental Army to the city and arrived in April 1776. By late July, about 300 British warships had reached New York City's harbor.

Battle of Long Island

To defend New York City, Washington sent troops to Brooklyn. To defend means to protect from attack. In late August, the British general **William Howe** attacked. Protected by a thick fog, General Washington's army retreated across the river to Manhattan. To **retreat** means to turn back.

In Manhattan, the Patriots won a small battle against the British. However, the British took control of New York City, and won battles at several places along the Hudson River. It was becoming clear that the Continental Army had a long, hard fight ahead.

✓ **READING CHECK** CLASSIFY Why did the British classify New York City as important?

Patriot Victories

Main Idea The Continental Army began to win important battles in and around New York.

After the Patriots lost the battles in New York, defeating the British seemed impossible. The British had a powerful navy. Their soldiers were well trained. They had good weapons, uniforms, food, and other supplies. In contrast, the Continental Army was poorly supplied and poorly trained. However, the Patriots knew the land well and believed strongly in their cause.

In November 1776, Washington crossed the Hudson River and led his men south through New Jersey to Pennsylvania. Even though his men were hungry, cold, and ill, Washington knew he needed a victory soon.

Victories near New York

In December 1776, German soldiers fighting for the British were camped near Trenton, New Jersey. Washington's troops were across the Delaware River in Pennsylvania. They crossed the icy river overnight. At dawn, Washington surprised the Germans by attacking. Washington's troops won easily. The next month, the Patriots won again at Princeton, New Jersey. Both of these battles helped renew the hopes of Washington's tired troops.

In April 1777, **Sybil Ludington** warned her father's militia that the British were coming to Danbury, Connecticut. Because of Ludington's bravery, the militia arrived in time to protect the Patriot supplies there.

Sybil Ludington A 16-year-old New York girl saved Patriot supplies from being destroyed.

Control of the Hudson

In June 1777, the British general **John Burgoyne** (bur GOYN) came up with a plan. First, he would take over Albany, New York. Then he would move south along the Hudson River and gain control of the Hudson River Valley. Burgoyne thought this would divide the colonies and end the war.

Under this plan, the British general **Barry St. Leger** would move through the Mohawk River Valley and join Burgoyne near Albany. He sent Loyalists ahead, who attacked Patriots near Oriskany (aw RIHS kuh ney) Creek. The Loyalist Mohawk chief **Joseph Brant** and other Native Americans also took part. Many Patriots were wounded or died during the battles, but they finally stopped St. Leger.

Battle of Saratoga

About two months later, Patriot forces blocked the movement of Burgoyne's army. Under the command of generals **Horatio Gates** and **Benedict Arnold,** the Patriots fought the British at Saratoga. Many British soldiers were wounded in the battle, and their supplies were running low.

Finally, Burgoyne surrendered to Horatio Gates on October 17, 1777. To **surrender** means to give up. Saratoga was a turning point in the war. The Patriots proved that they were strong enough to defeat the British. Their success also helped convince France to send money, ships, and troops to help the American colonists.

READING CHECK SUMMARIZE Why was the Battle of Saratoga important for the Continental Army?

Victory at Saratoga This photo shows actors fighting the Battle of Saratoga. The painting shows Burgoyne surrendering.

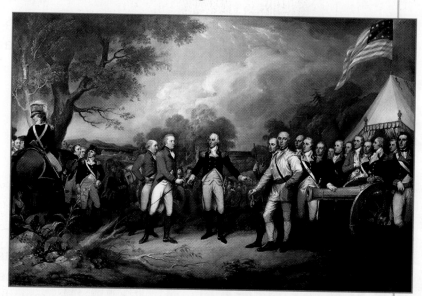

End of the War

Main Idea New Yorkers played important roles in the American Revolution.

The last major battle of the war happened in 1781. At Yorktown, Virginia, Washington's troops trapped a British army led by **Charles Cornwallis.** The French navy blocked the British from escaping in ships. Surrounded, Cornwallis surrendered on October 19.

The war ended in 1783 with the signing of the Treaty of Paris. The Patriots had won their independence. British troops and hundreds of Loyalists left New York City. Much of the city lay in ruins from a large fire in 1776. Roads, bridges, farms, and villages in New York had been destroyed during the war. New Yorkers now had to rebuild their lives and build a new nation.

New Yorkers in the War

Many New Yorkers served in the Continental Army. Two generals from New York were **George Clinton** and **Nicholas Herkimer.** Clinton became New York's first governor.

The American Revolution caused great changes for Native Americans in New York State, including the Haudenosaunee. Many had sided with the British because they wanted to keep settlers off their lands. After the war, however, many Native Americans were forced to move north to Canada.

African Americans from New York served in the Continental Army and took part in other ways, too. Historians think **Pompey Lamb** helped the Patriots capture a fort at Stony Point, New York. He knew the password that allowed Patriot soldiers to sneak into the fort. **Samuel Fraunces** owned a building in Manhattan where the Sons of Liberty met. At the end of the war, Washington and some of his troops had a farewell dinner in Fraunces's building.

Samuel Fraunces's Building
Members of the national government used this building between 1785 and 1788.

Women in the War

Women also played important roles during the war. Most stayed at home and did jobs that men had done before the war. One woman, **Margaret Corbin**, fought in New York. She was with her husband when he was killed in battle at Fort Washington. She fought in his place and was wounded in the battle.

✓**READING CHECK** CAUSE AND EFFECT What were the effects of the Treaty of Paris?

Margaret Corbin Corbin has a monument dedicated to her at the U.S. Military Academy in West Point.

SUMMARY

The Continental Army won important battles in and around New York, including the Battle of Saratoga. New Yorkers had many important roles in the war. The American Revolution ended in 1783 with the signing of the Treaty of Paris.

Lesson Review

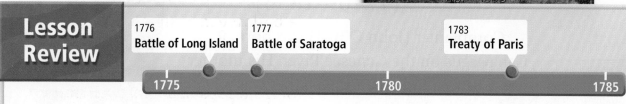

1776
Battle of Long Island

1777
Battle of Saratoga

1783
Treaty of Paris

1775   1780   1785

❶ **WHAT TO KNOW** What was New York's role in the American Revolution?

❷ **VOCABULARY** Write a paragraph explaining the difference between a **Patriot** and a **Loyalist**.

❸ **TIMELINE SKILL** What major battle took place in 1777?

❹ **ART ACTIVITY** Draw a scene from an event that happened in New York during the American Revolution. Write a caption to explain why the event was important.

❺ 🖋 **READING SKILL** Complete the graphic organizer to classify information.

PATRIOT	BRITISH

New York's Revolutionary Leaders

What qualities make a good leader? During the American Revolution, these three leaders showed courage and determination. Cornplanter supported the British, while George Clinton and John Jay were Patriots.

Cornplanter

(1740?–1836)

Cornplanter (John O'Bail) was born at Canawagus on the Genesee River. His mother was a Seneca Indian and his father was a Dutch trader. Cornplanter was chosen to be a leader of the Seneca during the American Revolution. Cornplanter believed that supporting the British was the best way to protect Haudenosaunee land and rights. He led attacks against American settlements in New York and helped to capture forts for the British. After the war, Cornplanter met with George Washington to make treaties between Native Americans and the United States government.

George Clinton

(1739–1812)

George Clinton had served as a soldier in Britain's war against France. George Washington made him a leader in the Continental Army. After the American Revolution, Clinton became New York's first governor, serving from 1777 to 1795 and again from 1801 to 1804. For this, he has become known as the "Father of New York."

John Jay

(1745–1829)

During his long career, John Jay used his experiences as a lawyer and his excellent writing skills to help the new nation. At the First Continental Congress, he wrote a document explaining the colonists' complaints against Great Britain. In 1777, he helped to write a plan of government for New York State. He also helped to draw up the Treaty of Paris of 1783. A college in New York City is named for Jay. Because Jay was a lawyer, students there study how people accused of crimes should be treated.

Activities

1. **TALK ABOUT IT** Why did people call George Clinton the "Father of New York"?

2. **PRESENT IT** Write and present a speech in favor of naming a college for John Jay.

Visual Summary

1–3. Write a description for each main event named below.

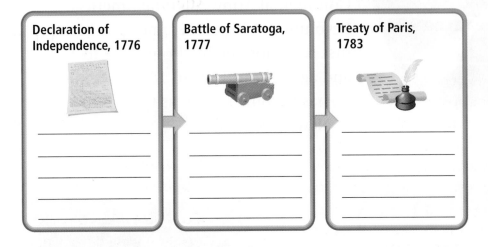

Declaration of Independence, 1776

Battle of Saratoga, 1777

Treaty of Paris, 1783

Facts and Main Ideas

Answer each question with information from the chapter.

4. **History** Why did the British pass laws that taxed the colonists?

5. **History** What did representatives at the First Continental Congress agree to do?

6. **Geography** Why did General Burgoyne want to control the Hudson River and the Hudson River Valley?

7. **History** What was the result of the Battle of Saratoga?

Vocabulary

Choose the correct word from the list below to complete each sentence.

representative, p. 124
militia, p. 126
surrender, p. 135

8. Each colony formed a _____ to fight in an emergency.

9. John Jay was a _____ for New York at the First Continental Congress.

10. The British general Cornwallis had to _____ at Yorktown.

1775	1777	1783
Ticonderoga captured	**Battle of Saratoga**	**Treaty of Paris**

1775	1780	1785	1790

Apply Skills

Point of View Use the passage and what you know about point of view to answer each question.

> The British government makes laws for the colonies, and we have no say about these laws. They have taxed many of the goods we need, including sugar, paper, and tea. These laws are terrible! Now there is a law against town meetings. How can the British government decide what's best for the colonies? Its laws have only hurt us. I say it's time to make our voices heard.

11. What is the subject of the passage?

- **A.** goods, such as sugar, paper, and tea
- **B.** protests against British laws
- **C.** unfair laws of the British government
- **D.** the Declaration of Independence

12. Which statement best describes the point of view of the passage?

- **A.** Britain does not need to raise money.
- **B.** Colonists should protest tax laws.
- **C.** Town meetings are a bad idea.
- **D.** Colonists don't like the British laws.

Timeline

Use the timeline above to answer the question.

13. In what year did the American Revolution end?

Critical Thinking

Write a short paragraph to answer each question.

14. **Compare and Contrast** In what ways were the British army and the Continental Army alike and different?

15. **Cause and Effect** What effects did the events of the American Revolution have on New York City?

Activities

Speaking Activity Find out more about one of the new tax laws mentioned in the chapter. Prepare a speech explaining why you agree or disagree with the law.

Writing Activity Write a story about two New York families, one a family of Loyalists and the other a family of Patriots.

 Go Digital Get help with your writing at www.eduplace.com/nycssp/

Fun with Social Studies

Help Wanted!

Who would apply for these jobs?

CLASSIFIEDS
HELP WANTED

Enjoy Learning New Skills?

If you enjoy learning new skills and would like to become a dentist or printer, an exciting career can be yours! There is no pay, but you will receive food, shelter, clothes, and expert training. Should have an open mind and be willing to learn.

Wanted: Citizens True to King George

We are looking for good citizens who are loyal to King George. Must support all British laws and must never have taken part in a protest against the King. Apply at General William Howe's headquarters.

Free Ride for Free Work

Are you tired of living in Europe? Would you like to see America, but you can't afford the trip? If so, there's a job waiting for you in the colonies. In exchange for free passage, you have to be willing to work without pay for four to seven years.

Believe in Liberty?

Do you believe New Yorkers have a right to govern themselves? Are you tired of leaders who live across the ocean making laws for us? If so, come to New York Harbor for a special tea party.

Match 'Em

Can you match the person to the correct item?

| Benjamin Franklin | Thomas Jefferson | Pompey Lamb | Eliza Lucas Pinckney | John Peter Zenger |

| indigo | bifocal glasses | Declaration of Independence | New-York Weekly Journal | secret password |

Crack the code...
and answer the riddle

Fill in the correct words and use the circled letters to answer the riddle.

A __ __ __ __ __ __ __ __(○)__ is a large farm.

An __ __ __ __ __(○)__ is the way people use an area's resources.

An __ __ __ __ __ __ __(○)__ works with a master craftsperson to learn a job.

To __ (○)__ __ __ __ __ something is to speak out against it.

A __ __ __ (○)__ __ is a group of citizens trained to fight in an emergency.

A __ __ __ __ __ (○)__ __ __ is a war fought to overthrow a government.

Where did the young Son of Liberty want to sleep?

On a __b__ __ __ __ __ __ __

Reading Social Studies

When you **compare**, you think about how two or more items are alike. When you **contrast**, you think about how two or more items are different.

Compare and Contrast

1. Complete this graphic organizer to show that you understand how to compare and contrast geographic characteristics of the colonies.

Middle Colonies **Southern Colonies**

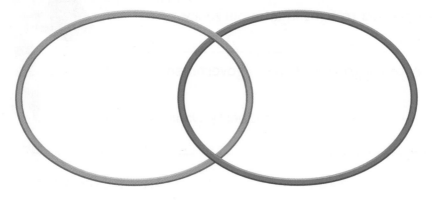

 ### Write About the Big Idea

2. **Write a Letter** Think about what life would have been like in New York during the American Revolution. Write a letter to a friend in another colony describing how the war affected your life.

Vocabulary and Main Ideas

Write a sentence to answer each question.

3. What effect did the **fall line** have on settlement in the Southern Colonies?

4. What kinds of work did people do in the **economy** of the Middle Colonies?

5. What did an **apprentice** receive for his or her work?

6. Why did people in each of the thirteen colonies form a **militia?**

7. Who wrote the Declaration of **Independence?**

8. Why did **Patriot** and British leaders want to control New York?

Critical Thinking

Write a short paragraph to answer each question.

9. **Generalize** What were the benefits of triangular trade for the colonies?

10. **Cause and Effect** What effect did the war between Britain and France have on taxes in the colonies?

Apply the Skills

Use the passage below and what you have learned about point of view to answer the questions that follow.

New York City's location makes it the most important city in the colonies. Britain needs to take control of the city if we are going to win this war. We need a base for our navy and soldiers. From New York City, we will be able to control the colony and cut off Patriot communications and supplies. I say it's time to show the colonists that Britain is in charge!

11. What is the subject of the passage?

   A. the British army and navy
   B. the Battle of Saratoga
   C. control of New York City
   D. New York City's colonists

12. Which statement best describes the speaker's point of view in the passage?

   A. Britain should control New York City.
   B. The Patriots should control New York City.
   C. Britain needs to create a navy to win the war.
   D. The Patriots need to create a navy to win the war.

Unit 3 Activities

 Unit Writing Activity

Write a Scene Write a scene in which the main characters discuss whether to declare independence from the British.

■ There should be at least one character who wants independence from the British and one who does not.

■ The characters should explain why they support or oppose independence.

 Unit Project

Honor a Hero Choose a New York hero from the American Revolution and prepare a presentation about him or her.

■ Write a speech about the hero, telling about the person's heroic deeds.

■ You may also reenact an event from the war where your hero was present.

■ Videotape your presentation and invite others to watch it, or perform the presentation live for them.

Read More

■ *Black Heroes of the American Revolution* by Burke Davis. Odyssey Classics.

■ *The Big Tree* by Bruce Hiscock. Boyds Mills Press.

■ *Charlotte* by Janet Lunn. Tundra Books.

Go Digital visit www.eduplace.com/nycssp/

The New Nation

The Big Idea

What is the importance of the United States Constitution?

WHAT TO KNOW

✓ How was the Constitution created?

✓ What does the Bill of Rights do?

Westward Expansion

PACIFIC
OCEAN

RED RIVER CESSION–1818

L. Superior

Columbia R.

Portland

OREGON TERRITORY–1846

Missouri R.

L. Michigan

Milwaukee

Chicago

Indianapolis

Salt
Lake
City

LOUISIANA
PURCHASE–1803

St. Louis

San Francisco

Colorado R.

Kansas City

MEXICAN CESSION–1848

Nashville

Memphis

Mississippi

GADSDEN PURCHASE–1853

TEXAS ANNEXATION–1845

Mobile

San Antonio

WEST FLORIDA
ANNEXATION–
1810, 1813

Gulf of Mexico

Louisiana Purchase
President Jefferson sent
an expedition to explore
this area.

Map Labels

WEBSTER ASHBURTON TREATY–1842

Portland

Boston

L. Ontario

Buffalo

L. Erie

Cleveland

New York

Philadelphia

Pittsburgh

Baltimore

Washington, D.C.

Ohio R.

UNITED STATES–1783

Norfolk

Lexington

Louisville

Wilmington

Atlanta

Charleston

Savannah

ATLANTIC OCEAN

Jacksonville

EAST FLORIDA –1819

N NE
NW E
W SE
SW S

km 0   150   300
mi 0   150   300

LEGEND

• Major city, 1850

New York City

George Washington was sworn in as President here in 1789.

Connect to
New York City

Population Growth, 1800s

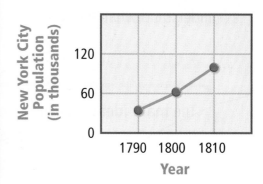

New York City attracted many new residents after the American Revolution. By 1790, it was the largest city in the country.

Population Growth Today

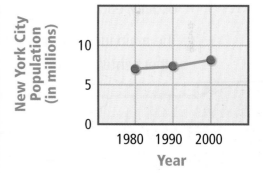

People continue to move to New York City from around the country and all over the world.

Reading Social Studies

Main Idea and Details

Why It Matters Finding the main idea and details can help you understand what you read.

Learn the Skill

The **main idea** is the most important idea of a passage. **Details** are facts, reasons, or examples that support the main idea.

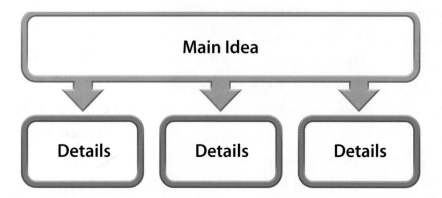

- Usually, each paragraph in a passage has a main idea and details.

- The main idea is often, but not always, stated in the first sentence. The other sentences often give the details.

Practice the Skill

Read the paragraphs below. Identify the main idea and details in the second paragraph.

Main Idea
Details

The United States Constitution is the basic law of our nation. The Constitution sets up our system of government. It also lists the rights of all Americans and the powers of each branch of the government.

During the American Revolution, the states created their own constitutions. In 1776, New Jersey and Pennsylvania both wrote constitutions. One year later, New York passed its first constitution.

Apply the Skill

Read the paragraphs, and answer the questions.

New York's Early Schools

During the early 1800s, most children in New York City did not attend school. Families needed children to work on their farms or in their stores. Children from wealthy families usually had private teachers who would teach them at home. Some children learned to read and write from a family member. However, many children grew up never knowing these skills.

New York's early schools were very different from schools today. To begin with, because so many children worked, there were far fewer schools.

Most schools had only one room and one teacher. A classroom was made up of students of all different ages. Boys and girls usually sat on opposite sides of the room. Most teachers were men, and many of them were very strict.

In the 1830s, people began to call for more schools. Leaders realized that offering education to all children would strengthen the country. During the 1900s, hundreds of schools were built all around the city. Today, more than 1 million students attend about 1400 schools run by the city.

◎ Main Idea and Details

1. What is the main idea of the first paragraph?

2. Which sentence tells the main idea of the second paragraph?

3. Which details explain how early schools were different from schools today?

The Challenge of Independence

Study Skills

USE VISUALS

Looking at visuals, such as photographs, charts, and maps, can help you better understand and remember what you read.

- Visuals often show the same information that is in the text but in a different way.

- Many visuals have titles, captions, or labels that help you understand what is shown.

✓	What kind of visual is shown?
✓	What does the visual show?
✓	How does the visual help you better understand the subject that you are reading?

George Washington being sworn in as President, Federal Hall, New York City, 1789

Vocabulary Preview

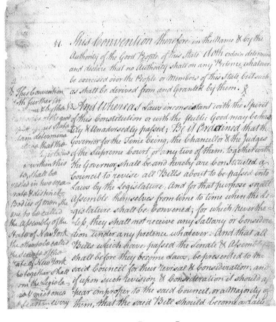

constitution

In 1777, New Yorkers planned their state government and wrote a **constitution.** The United States Constitution went into effect 11 years later. **page 156**

delegate

New York sent three **delegates** to the Constitutional Convention. They represented the state at the meeting.
page 157

Chapter Timeline

1777
New York's first
constitution ratified

1788
United States
Constitution ratified

1775   1780   1785

Reading Strategy

Summarize As you read, use the summarize strategy to focus on important ideas. Review the main ideas to get started. Then look for important details that support the main idea.

ratification

Alexander Hamilton wrote in support of **ratification** of the United States Constitution. New York approved it in 1788.
page 158

amendment

Many leaders wanted to make **amendments** to the Constitution. These changes became the Bill of Rights.
page 165

1791
Bill of Rights
ratified

1790   1795

Go Digital visit www.eduplace.com/nycssp/

155

The Constitution

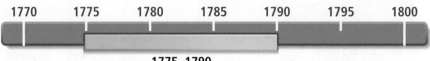

1770   1775   1780   1785   1790   1795   1800

1775–1790

WHAT TO KNOW
How was the Constitution created?

VOCABULARY
constitution
federal
delegate
democracy
ratification

READING SKILL
Main Idea As you read, list details about New York's role in the new nation's government.

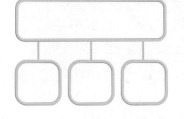

Before You Read You know that team members help each other reach a goal. After the American Revolution, New Yorkers had to work with other states to help their new country succeed.

Creating a State Government

Main Idea The state of New York and the United States each needed a plan for government.

When the United States declared independence in 1776, New Yorkers decided they needed a new government. In March 1777, some New Yorkers met in Kingston to write a new state constitution. A **constitution** is a plan for running a government. When describing the constitution, **Alexander Hamilton** said,

❝ I think your Government is . . . the best that we have yet seen. ❞

On April 20, 1777, the final draft was approved. Two days later, New York State had a government run by New Yorkers.

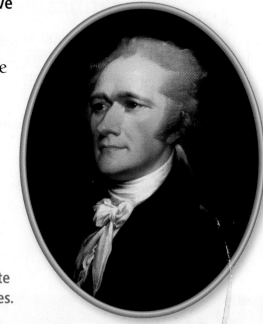

Alexander Hamilton This New York leader would later help create a constitution for the United States.

A New Capital Leaders had to decide which city should be named the national capital. After much consideration, New York City was chosen.

Capital City

After the American Revolution, the new nation also needed a government. The 13 states agreed to the Articles of Confederation. This document created a loosely united federal government. **Federal** describes a type of government in which states and the central government share power.

New York City was an important city in the new nation. Many people lived there. As a major port city, New York was also a center for trade and business. The national government chose it as the capital of the United States in 1785. It remained the capital until 1790, when the government moved to Philadelphia.

Constitutional Convention

Although the United States had a government, it was not working well. In 1787, delegates from 12 of the 13 states met in Philadelphia to fix it. A **delegate** is someone chosen to speak or act for others. The meeting became known as the Constitutional Convention. **Alexander Hamilton, John Lansing, Jr.,** and **Robert Yates** were New York's delegates.

During the Convention, the delegates decided that they needed a plan for a stronger national government. They argued about how much power large and small states should have. By working through their disagreements, they created a new plan: the Constitution.

READING CHECK MAIN IDEA AND DETAILS
Why was New York City important to the new nation?

A New Government

Main Idea The United States Constitution became the law of the land after the states approved it.

The United States Constitution created a national government. It is also the source of the United States' democracy. A **democracy** is a system in which the people hold the power of government. The Constitution protects the rights of citizens and gives them a say in their government. In addition, it declares that all government officials must obey the Constitution.

Under the Constitution, the national government is strong but still shares power with the states. The Constitution divides the government into three parts, or branches. Each branch has a different job and can limit the power of the other two. No one branch has too much power.

The Federalist Papers

After the Constitution was written, it still had to be approved by nine states. New Yorkers **John Jay** and Alexander Hamilton supported its **ratification,** or approval. Along with **James Madison** of Virginia, they wrote essays explaining the benefits of a strong national government. Their essays became known as the Federalist Papers.

Not all New Yorkers supported the new Constitution, however. Some believed that the state government should stay in control. They were concerned that a strong national government would take rights away from New Yorkers. The Federalist Papers helped convince people that the Constitution was necessary. New York State ratified the Constitution on July 26, 1788. It was the eleventh state to do so.

A Strong Argument
George Washington's copy of the Federalist Papers (below) shows his name in the top right corner.

Independence Hall The Constitution was written in this Philadelphia building.

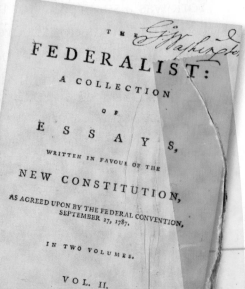

The First President

After the United States Constitution was ratified, George Washington was elected as the first President of the new nation. He took the oath of office at Federal Hall in New York City on April 30, 1789. A cheering crowd gathered on Wall Street to watch. The oath was a promise to perform his duties as President. One of his duties was to protect and defend the Constitution.

✓ **READING CHECK** MAIN IDEA AND DETAILS
How does the Constitution divide power in the national government?

SUMMARY

After the American Revolution, the states had to work together as one nation. They created and ratified the Constitution and then elected a leader for the new government.

Souvenirs These buttons celebrated the new Congress and President.

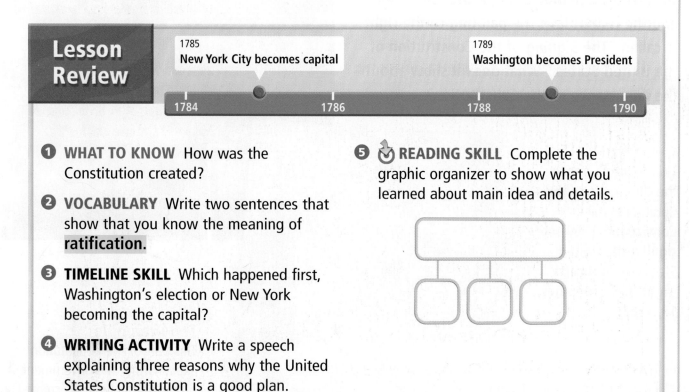

Lesson Review

1785
New York City becomes capital

1789
Washington becomes President

1784   1786   1788   1790

❶ **WHAT TO KNOW** How was the Constitution created?

❷ **VOCABULARY** Write two sentences that show that you know the meaning of **ratification.**

❸ **TIMELINE SKILL** Which happened first, Washington's election or New York becoming the capital?

❹ **WRITING ACTIVITY** Write a speech explaining three reasons why the United States Constitution is a good plan.

❺ **READING SKILL** Complete the graphic organizer to show what you learned about main idea and details.

Foundations
of our
Government

Where can you find the ideas that shaped our nation? Many of them are in documents such as the Mayflower Compact, the Declaration of Independence, New York's constitution, and the United States Constitution. These documents express ideas that continue to guide our democracy today, such as the common good, protecting rights, and the rule of law. The painting to the right is called "The Signing of the Constitution of the United States." What does it show about the importance of the Constitution?

This painting shows the delegates to the Constitutional Convention. They are signing the United States Constitution (right) on September 17, 1787.

The Preamble
This part of the Constitution explains that the government of the United States is created by and for the people.

George Washington
The artist shows us that Washington's leadership was very important to the new nation. How does he do this?

Delegates
The delegates are working while looking active and interested. Think about what this tells you about the Constitutional Convention.

Activities

1. **LIST IT** List details from the painting that show the event is an important one.

2. **WRITE ABOUT IT** If you were a reporter, what would you say about the signing of the Constitution? Write a news article based on the painting about the event.

Go Digital Visit Education Place for more primary sources. www.eduplace.com/nycssp/

Make a Timeline

VOCABULARY

decade

century

People often look at a timeline to find out when important events took place. A timeline shows events in the order in which they happened. Timelines are usually divided by years, decades, or centuries. A **decade** is a period of 10 years. A **century** is a period of 100 years. You can also use a timeline to find out the amount of time between events.

Learn the Skill

Step 1: Some timelines have titles. If there is a title, read it to find out the subject of the timeline.

Step 2: Look at the beginning date and the ending date to find out how much time the timeline covers.

Step 3: Look at the events described in the timeline. Read the dates on the timeline to find out when the events happened. Figure out how the events are related to each other.

History of the Constitution

1776
Colonies declare independence

1777
New York's first constitution ratified

1787
Constitutional Convention

1788
United States Constitution ratified

1775 1780 1785 1790

Use the timeline on page 162 to answer the questions.

1. What does the title tell you about the events in the timeline?

2. How many years does the timeline cover?

3. How long after the colonies declared independence was New York's constitution ratified?

4. How long after New York's constitution was ratified did the Constitutional Convention meet?

5. When was the United States Constitution ratified?

Apply the Skill

Read the paragraph below. List the events and their dates in the order in which they happened. Then use your list to create a timeline.

A meeting called the Constitutional Convention took place in 1787. During this meeting, the United States Constitution was written. Two years later, in 1789, George Washington was elected as the first President of the United States. At the time he was elected, New York City was the capital of the nation. It had been chosen as the capital in 1785. In 1790, Washington approved the selection of Philadelphia, Pennsylvania, as the new capital. The government remained in Philadelphia for 10 years. Washington, D.C. became the new capital in 1800 and is still the capital today.

1770	1775	1780	1785	1790	1795	1800	1805	1810

The Bill of Rights

WHAT TO KNOW
What does the Bill of Rights do?

VOCABULARY
amendment
bill

READING SKILL
Problem and Solution
How did people solve the problem of protecting individual liberties?

| People wanted the right to vote. | → | |

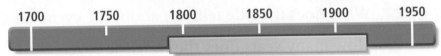

| 1700 | 1750 | 1800 | 1850 | 1900 | 1950 |

1791–1920

Before You Read Think about a time when you told someone your opinion. When citizens of the United States express opinions publicly, they are using one of the rights guaranteed in the Bill of Rights.

Changing the Constitution

Main Idea The Bill of Rights was added to the Constitution to protect freedoms.

When the states ratified the Constitution, many people thought it did not do enough to protect rights, which are also called liberties. Americans had been concerned with protecting their rights for a long time. In 1735, **John Peter Zenger** went on trial for criticizing New York's colonial government. A jury decided that it was legal to print criticisms of the government if they were true. Many citizens hoped to include freedom of the press in the Constitution.

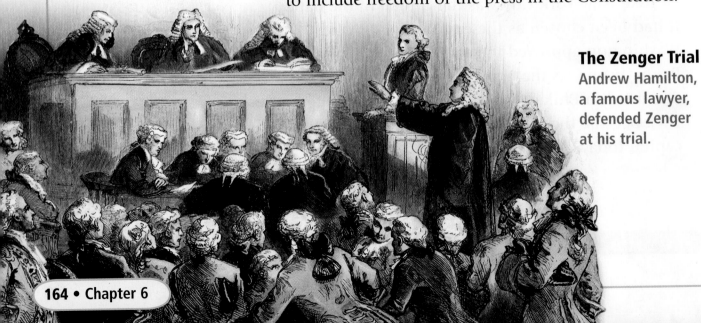

The Zenger Trial
Andrew Hamilton, a famous lawyer, defended Zenger at his trial.

Protecting Rights

Several states, such as New York and Virginia, wanted amendments added to the Constitution to protect rights. An **amendment** is a change to the Constitution. **Thomas Jefferson** wrote that such amendments were "what the people are entitled to against every government on earth." **James Madison** wrote 12 amendments. The states approved 10 of the amendments in 1791. They became known as the Bill of Rights. A **bill** can be a law that has been suggested, or a law that has been passed. The amendments in the Bill of Rights guarantee certain rights and freedoms to United States citizens.

The First Amendment guarantees many different rights. The freedoms of speech and press are two of these rights. They protect people who write or say things that others disagree with or who speak out against the government. Another First Amendment right is freedom of religion. The government cannot set a religion for the country or stop people from practicing their religion. The First Amendment also gives people the right to assemble, or come together peacefully, and to ask the government to change its laws.

✓ **READING CHECK** PROBLEM AND SOLUTION
What problem was the Bill of Rights written to solve?

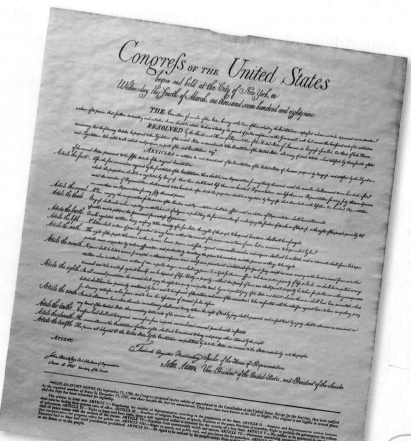

The Bill of Rights A copy of the original Bill of Rights is kept at the National Archives in Washington, D.C.

Unequal Rights

Main Idea The Constitution did not protect everyone's rights equally.

The Constitution and the Bill of Rights succeeded in protecting citizens' rights. However, not everyone living in the United States could enjoy those rights. At first, some states only allowed white men who owned land to vote. Therefore, people with little money often could not vote. Women also were not allowed to vote. Laws prevented African Americans from voting whether they were enslaved or free. The Constitution failed to protect African Americans in other ways as well. It allowed slavery to continue rather than ending it.

Some women were determined to win equal rights. In 1776, **Abigail Adams** wrote a letter to her husband, **John Adams.** At the time, he was in Philadelphia serving as a member of the Second Continental Congress. Abigail Adams asked her husband to "Remember the Ladies . . ." when the laws for the new country were written. However, the Constitution did not protect women's rights. Local laws did not allow them to own land or businesses. They also could not be elected to serve in government.

Abigail Adams She was the wife of one President and the mother of another, John Quincy Adams.

Olaudah Equiano A former slave, Equiano spoke out against slavery in writings and speeches.

The Expansion of Rights

In the more than 200 years since the Constitution and the Bill of Rights were written, much has changed. Many groups have fought for and won equal rights. For example, amendments have been added to the Constitution to guarantee the voting rights of men and women of all races. Others ensure that all people are treated equally by the government. Today, the United States Constitution protects more citizens than ever before.

READING CHECK MAIN IDEA AND DETAILS
Whose rights did the Constitution and the Bill of Rights originally protect?

SUMMARY

The Bill of Rights was added to the Constitution to protect the individual rights and freedoms of citizens. However, women and African Americans fought for years to gain equal rights under the law.

Voting Rights In the early 1900s, women held voting rights marches.

Lesson Review

❶ **WHAT TO KNOW** What does the Bill of Rights do?

❷ **VOCABULARY** Write a paragraph explaining why James Madison wrote a **bill** that added **amendments** to the Constitution.

❸ **CRITICAL THINKING: Analyze** Why do you think freedom of speech might be important in a democracy?

❹ **ART ACTIVITY** Review the First Amendment rights on page 165. On a separate sheet of paper or a poster board, illustrate a right that is important to you.

❺ **READING SKILL** Complete your graphic organizer to show what you learned about problem and solution.

| People wanted the right to vote. | → | |

Strengthening Democracy

When the United States was a young nation, no one was sure it would grow strong. Few countries at the time were based on democratic ideals. Many thinkers believed that democratic government in a large country would be impossible. New Yorkers helped prove them wrong. Alexander Hamilton, Samuel Eli Cornish, and many others helped democracy in the United States grow and become a model for other governments to follow.

Alexander Hamilton
(1757–1804)

Alexander Hamilton began fighting for liberty when he was a young man. He fought the British in the American Revolution. At the end of the war, he led New York soldiers at the Battle of Yorktown. Hamilton later supported the Constitution and a strong national government. He was also against slavery. As a government official, Hamilton gave strong support to the nation's businesses and trade. His portrait appears on the nation's ten-dollar bill to remind people of his contributions to the United States.

Samuel Eli Cornish
(1795–1858)

Samuel Cornish believed strongly in education and democratic values. As the pastor of New York City's first African American Presbyterian church, he encouraged African American parents to send their children to school. He also started the newspaper *Freedom's Journal* to "plead our own cause" for the end of slavery. The *Journal* was the first African American newspaper in the United States. Cornish helped start the American Anti-Slavery Society in 1833. Through church work, education, and writing, Samuel Cornish worked to include African Americans in the democratic future of the United States.

Freedom's Journal was the first African American newspaper in the United States.

Activities

1. **TALK ABOUT IT** How are Hamilton and Cornish alike and different? Talk about their similarities and differences.

2. **ACT IT OUT** Work with a partner to role-play a conversation between these famous New Yorkers.

Values and Traditions

The United States is home to a wide variety of people, but our values and traditions bring us together. The belief in freedom, equality, and the rule of law helped unite our nation long ago. We still practice these values and traditions in our daily lives. They make our national motto a reality:

E pluribus unum—out of many, one!

Values	Practices	Traditions
Freedom	By speaking out, practicing any religion or no religion, and calling for changes in the government, Americans exercise their freedoms.	**Independence Day** Each July 4th, we celebrate the day colonists declared independence from Britain to protect their freedoms. 
Equality	Americans show their belief in equality by respecting the rights of others.	**Martin Luther King, Jr. Day** On the third Monday in January, we honor the leader who worked peacefully for the freedom and equality of all citizens of the United States. 
Rule of Law	Everyone in the United States—citizens and elected leaders—must obey our nation's laws.	**Constitution Day** On September 17th, we celebrate the document that is the basis for the rule of law in our nation. Visitors to the National Archives can view the original Constitution. 

Activities

1. **TALK ABOUT IT** Compare the holidays on the chart. What similarities do you notice?

2. **WRITE ABOUT IT** Patriotic songs are an important part of the nation's traditions. In pairs, write a short song about one of the national holidays described in the chart above.

Skillbuilder

Interpret Historical Images

A photograph captures a moment in time. It can also provide valuable information about a subject or event. The photograph below was taken at a time when many people were demanding civil rights for all citizens. Civil rights are the rights guaranteed to citizens of a country. Study the photograph to learn more about people using the freedoms protected by the Bill of Rights.

Practicing Rights and Freedoms On August 28, 1963, about 250,000 people gathered in Washington, D.C. to protest the unfair treatment of African Americans in the South. They were practicing the rights protected by the First Amendment. Some carried signs calling for protection of the right to vote. Others demanded integrated schools, or schools where students of different races learn together.

Learn the Skill

Step 1: Look at the photograph carefully. Then read the title and caption to learn more about it. Add that information to what you already know about the subject.

Step 2: Ask yourself what you have learned from the photograph. How does the picture make you feel? What do you think is the photographer's point of view on the subject?

Practice the Skill

Use the photograph on page 172 to answer the questions.

1. What does the caption tell you about the event in the photograph?

2. The people in the photograph are using rights protected by the Bill of Rights. How many of these rights can you see being practiced?

3. Do you think the photographer supported the march or disapproved of it? Why?

Apply the Skill

Choose one photograph from the first five chapters of this textbook. Explain what information you can get from the photograph. Also explain how it helps you understand ideas in the text.

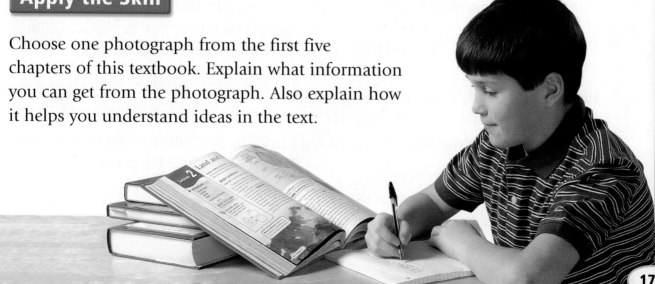

Visual Summary

1–3. ✏️ Write a description of each item named below.

Founding Documents

New York State Constitution	United States Constitution	Bill of Rights
_____	_____	_____
_____	_____	_____

Facts and Main Ideas

Answer each question with information from the chapter.

4. **History** Why was New York City chosen as the nation's capital in 1785?

5. **History** What was the purpose of the Constitutional Convention of 1787?

6. **Government** What is a federal government?

7. **History** What did John Jay and Alexander Hamilton do to support the approval of the Constitution?

8. **Citizenship** What groups of people were not protected by the Constitution and the Bill of Rights when they were written?

Vocabulary

Choose the correct word from the list below to complete each sentence.

delegate, p. 157
democracy, p. 158
amendment, p. 165

9. Alexander Hamilton was chosen to represent New York as a(n) _____ to the Constitutional Convention.

10. Freedom of speech is protected by a(n) _____ to the Constitution.

11. In the government of the United States the people hold the power, making our country a(n) _____.

1777
New York's constitution

1787
Constitutional Convention

1791
Bill of Rights ratified

1770   1775   1780   1785   1790   1795   1800

Apply Skills

Make a Timeline Use the information below and what you have learned about timelines to answer each question.

In 1777, New York approved a state constitution. Eight years later, New York City became the capital of the United States. After the new national Constitution was created, New York ratified it in 1788. George Washington was inaugurated in New York City the next year. In 1791, New York approved the Bill of Rights.

12. Where on a timeline would you place New York's ratification of the United States Constitution?

A. between 1775 and 1780

B. between 1780 and 1785

C. between 1785 and 1790

D. between 1790 and 1795

13. Which event took place first?

A. New York approves a state constitution

B. New York ratifies the United States Constitution

C. George Washington is inaugurated

D. New York City is chosen as the national capital

Timeline

Use the timeline above to answer the question.

14. How many years after the Constitutional Convention was the Bill of Rights added to the Constitution?

Critical Thinking

Write a short paragraph to answer each question below. Use details to support your response.

15. **Summarize** What was the result of the Constitutional Convention?

16. **Draw Conclusions** In 1791, not everyone had the same rights under the Constitution. What effect do you think this had on democracy?

Activities

HANDS ON **Art Activity** Make an illustrated timeline of events in the creation of constitutions for New York and the United States.

Writing Activity Write a letter to New York's delegates to the Constitutional Convention. Tell them what you think the Constitution needs to say.

Go Digital Get help with your writing at www.eduplace.com/nycssp/

Fun with Social Studies

What's Going On?

It's the late 1700s and New York's newspapers have big news. What has happened?

Changes Already!

Ten amendments added to document

Hamilton Signs

New York leader supports new plan of government

On the Move

Nation's leaders meet in New York City

Under Construction

abc VOCABULARY

Finish building the terms on the left by adding the word blocks on the right.

FE???AL

DE???ATE

???IFICATION

DE???RACY

AM???MENT

???STITUTION

MOC

END   LEG

CON   DER   RAT

Whose Views?

Match each person with the T-shirts they might own.

Abigail Adams

Samuel Eli Cornish

John Jay

I ♥ Freedom of the Press

Faithful Federalist

Remember the Ladies

Go Digital **Education Place®**
www.eduplace.com

New York History and Government
- eGlossary
- eWord Game
- Biographies
- Primary Sources
- Write Site
- Interactive Maps
- Weekly Reader®: Current Events
- GeoNet
- Online Atlas

Visit Eduplace!

Log on to Eduplace to explore Social Studies online. Solve puzzles to watch the skateboarding tricks in eWord Game. Join Chester in GeoNet to see if you can earn enough points to become a GeoChampion, or just play Wacky Web Tales to see how silly your stories can get. Play now at www.eduplace.com/nycssp/

Reading Social Studies

The **main idea** is the most important idea of a passage. **Details** are facts, reasons, or examples that support the main idea.

Main Idea and Details

1. Complete this graphic organizer to show that you understand important ideas and details about the Constitution.

The United States Constitution

The Constitution is a framework for the United States government.

 Write About the Big Idea

2. **Write a Story** People in the United States are guaranteed rights and freedoms in the Bill of Rights. Think about one right that is important to you. Write a story in which the characters learn why this right should be protected.

Vocabulary and Main Ideas

Write a sentence to answer each question.

3. Why did the states create a **federal** government after winning independence?

4. Why did **delegates** from 12 states meet in Philadelphia in 1787?

5. What makes the United States government a **democracy?**

6. Why did some people oppose the **ratification** of the United States Constitution?

7. What effect have **amendments** to the Constitution had on people's rights?

8. How many amendments are included in the **Bill** of Rights?

Critical Thinking

Write a short answer for each question. Use details to support your answer.

9. **Summarize** What events led to the writing of the Constitution and the Bill of Rights?

10. **Draw Conclusions** Why do you think the writers of the Constitution thought it was important to limit the power of government?

Apply Skills

Use the photo below and what you have learned about interpreting historical images to answer the following questions.

11. What are the people in the photograph asking for?

  A. higher wages

  B. men's right to vote

  C. freedom of religion

  D. women's right to vote

12. What does this photograph tell you about the protest?

  A. It was violent.

  B. It was peaceful.

  C. It took place last year.

  D. It took place in England.

Unit 4 Activities

Unit Writing Activity

Write an Oral Report Prepare an oral report about a person from the unit.

- Summarize the contributions of the person you chose.
- Describe that person's effect on others and on the government.
- Be sure to include important details and express main ideas in your oral report.

Unit Project

Build a Museum Display Create a museum display about early government in the United States.

- Choose people, places, and events to include in your display.
- Write brief reports about the people, places, and events.
- Create artifacts, drawings, timelines, maps, and journal entries to go with your reports.

Read More

- *We the Kids: The Preamble to the Constitution of the United States* by David Catrow. Dial Books.
- *The Constitution: The Story Behind America's Governing Document* by Kerry A. Graves. Chelsea House.
- *The Bill of Rights* by Karen Donnelly. Rosen Publishing Group.

 visit www.eduplace.com/nycssp/

Growth of New York

The Big Idea

What was the effect of industry and immigration on New York?

WHAT TO KNOW

- How did New York grow during the 1800s?
- For which rights did African Americans and women fight?
- What effects did the Civil War have on New York?
- What was daily life like for many immigrants?
- What do immigrants contribute to life in New York City?
- What effects did immigration have on New York City's growth?

181

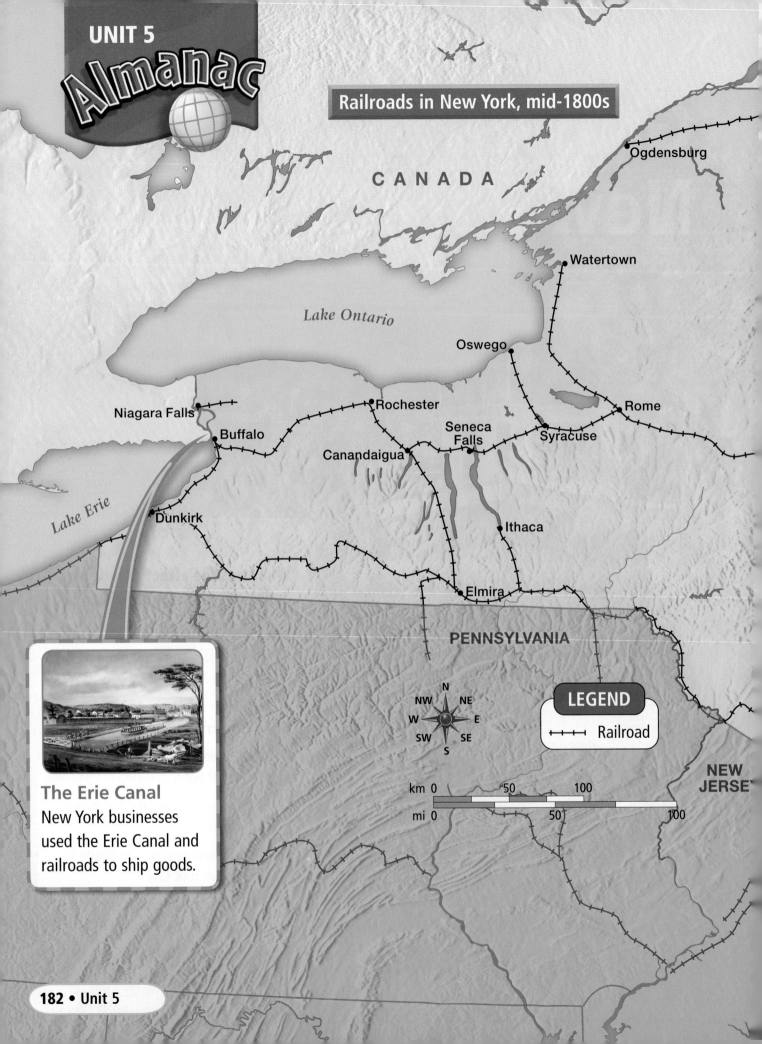

Railroads in New York, mid-1800s

CANADA

Ogdensburg

Watertown

Lake Ontario

Oswego

Rochester

Rome

Niagara Falls

Seneca Falls

Buffalo

Syracuse

Canandaigua

Lake Erie

Dunkirk

Ithaca

Elmira

PENNSYLVANIA

LEGEND

┼┼┼┼ Railroad

NEW JERSEY

N
NW   NE
W   E
SW   SE
S

km 0   50   100
mi 0   50   100

The Erie Canal
New York businesses used the Erie Canal and railroads to ship goods.

Immigration to New York State, 1860

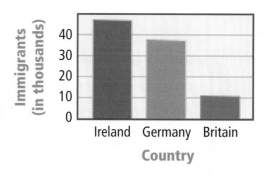

Immigrants (in thousands)

| | 40 | 30 | 20 | 10 | 0 |

Ireland   Germany   Britain

Country

In 1860, most immigrants came from northern Europe.

Immigration to New York State Today

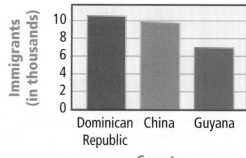

Immigrants (in thousands)

| 10 | 8 | 6 | 4 | 2 | 0 |

Dominican Republic   China   Guyana

Country

The greatest number of immigrants to New York now come from countries in the Americas and Asia.

VERMONT

NEW HAMPSHIRE

Schenectady

★Albany

MASSACHUSETTS

CONNECTICUT

RHODE ISLAND

Chester

New York City

Subways
Today, New York City's subway system is the largest in the world.

ATLANTIC OCEAN

Reading Social Studies

Cause and Effect

Why It Matters Understanding cause and effect can help you see why actions and events happen.

Learn the Skill

A **cause** is an action or event that makes something happen. An **effect** is what happens as a result of the cause.

Cause	→	Effect

- Words and phrases such as *because, since, so,* and *as a result* are clues that help identify cause and effect.

- A cause can have more than one effect. An effect may have many causes. Sometimes the effect may be stated before the cause.

Practice the Skill

Read the paragraphs below. Identify a cause and an effect in the second paragraph.

Cause
Effect

Starting in the 1800s, many people from other countries came to New York City. These new people brought new foods, customs, and traditions to the city. As a result, the city became more diverse.

In the mid-1800s, many people in Ireland did not have enough food. Because they were starving, thousands of people left Ireland and settled in New York. Today, New York continues to have a large Irish population.

Apply the Skill

Read the paragraphs, and answer the questions.

Taller Buildings

Have you ever wondered why New York City has so many tall buildings? One reason is right under your feet. Deep below the ground is a solid layer of bedrock that can support the city's many tall buildings. The biggest areas of bedrock are in midtown Manhattan and lower Manhattan. These areas have the tallest buildings.

For hundreds of years, most buildings in New York City were only a few stories tall. This started to change in the late 1800s as a result of new machines that allowed builders to make buildings taller than ever.

Manhattan's bedrock was important because these tall buildings had to stand on a strong base.

As more people moved to New York City, land became more valuable, so it made sense to build upwards. During the 1900s, hundreds of tall buildings went up all over the city. People called them skyscrapers because they seemed to scrape the sky. Many business offices and apartments fit in a single skyscraper. As a result, more people could live and work in New York City. Many of these buildings can still be seen today, and new ones are going up all the time.

Cause and Effect

1. What caused Manhattan to be a good place to build tall buildings?

2. Why were buildings made taller starting in the late 1800s?

3. What were some of the effects of skyscrapers on the growth of New York City?

Chapter 7

The United States in the Early 1800s

View from Brooklyn Heights, 1849

Study Skills

ORGANIZE INFORMATION

Graphic organizers can help you organize information.

- Graphic organizers help you categorize, or group, information.

- Putting people, places, and events into categories makes it easier to find facts and understand what you read.

The United States in the Early 1800s

Settling western New York
- Haudenosaunee sell their land

Transportation and Communication
- _____
- _____

Industrial Revolution
- _____
- _____

Vocabulary Preview

canal

Boats may travel through a **canal** as they move goods from place to place. The Erie Canal connects the Hudson River to Lake Erie. **page 191**

turnpike

A pike, or log, blocked a private road called a **turnpike.** Travelers paid a fee, and the pike was turned out of the way. The logs were later replaced with gates. **page 194**

Chapter Timeline

1825
Erie Canal opens

1800　1805　1810　1815　1820　1825　1830　1835　1840

Reading Strategy

Monitor and Clarify Check your understanding of the text using this strategy. Reread if you need to.

suffrage

In the 1800s and early 1900s, Susan B. Anthony and other women fought for **suffrage.** They worked to help women gain the right to vote. **page 198**

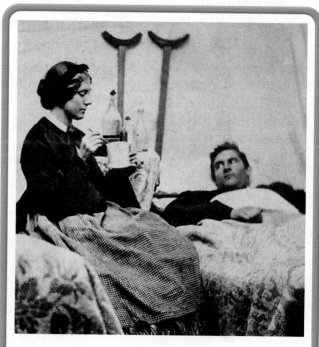

volunteer

During the Civil War, some women served as **volunteers** to help wounded soldiers. A volunteer helped without being paid. **page 203**

1848
Seneca Falls Convention

1861
Civil War begins

1865
Civil War ends

1850   1855   1860   1865   1870

Go Digital visit www.eduplace.com/nycssp/

The Industrial Revolution

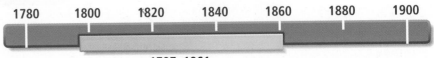

| 1780 | 1800 | 1820 | 1840 | 1860 | 1880 | 1900 |

1797–1861

Before You Read Think about how machines help you do work. During the 1800s, new inventions and ways of working helped Americans produce more goods in less time.

WHAT TO KNOW
How did New York grow during the 1800s?

VOCABULARY

assembly line
canal
turnpike
steamboat

READING SKILL
Cause and Effect
Look for effects that the Industrial Revolution had on New York.

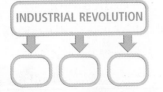

INDUSTRIAL REVOLUTION

The Growth of Business

Main Idea In the late 1700s and early 1800s, land treaties and the Industrial Revolution led to the growth of New York cities.

After the American Revolution, New Yorkers started moving to lands in western New York State. The Haudenosaunee lived on most of that land.

In 1797, the Haudenosaunee signed the Big Tree Treaty, giving up land to the Holland Land Company. The company wanted to build towns and factories in western New York. After selling their land, many Haudenosaunee were forced to move to reservations. These are lands set aside for Native Americans by the government.

The Big Tree Treaty
Red Jacket, a Seneca leader, signed the treaty.

Mills Before the 1820s, western New York had many small mills, like this one in Rochester.

Work in Factories

In the early 1800s, the Industrial Revolution started in the United States. The Industrial Revolution was a time of great advances, especially in New York. Before the 1800s, most products had been made by hand in workshops. During the Industrial Revolution, large groups of people began working together in factories. Machines made products faster than people could make them by hand.

The Industrial Revolution helped New York's economy grow. Factories opened throughout New York State. People worked on assembly lines. An **assembly line** is a series of work stations where workers put together products one step at a time. Assembly lines allowed workers to make products faster. Companies then made more products and more money.

Western New York

At first, factories did not grow as quickly in western New York State because travel by land was slow and expensive. This made it difficult for people to reach distant towns. Businesses needed better and faster ways to deliver goods. Traveling by rivers was cheaper and quicker, but not always reliable. Heavy rains could flood rivers, making travel impossible. During dry weather, rivers might be too shallow. When travelers came to a waterfall, they had to leave the river and carry their goods and boats along the shore.

New Yorkers began to think about ways to solve their transportation problem. Some of them wanted to build a canal. A **canal** is a waterway made by people.

✓ READING CHECK CAUSE AND EFFECT What effect did the Industrial Revolution have on the way many people worked?

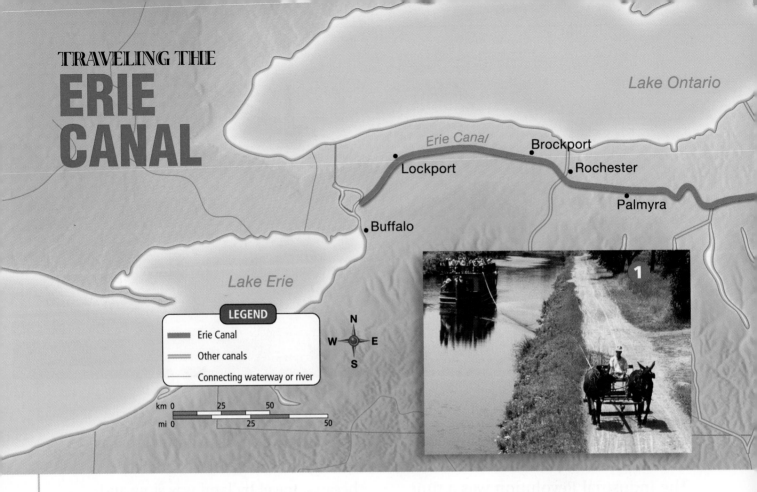

TRAVELING THE ERIE CANAL

Lake Ontario

Erie Canal

Brockport

Lockport

Rochester

Palmyra

Buffalo

Lake Erie

LEGEND

Erie Canal

Other canals

Connecting waterway or river

N
W E
S

km 0   25   50

mi 0   25   50

The Erie Canal

Main Idea The Erie Canal made travel and shipping quicker, cheaper, and easier.

DeWitt Clinton and **John Stevens** believed that building a canal would improve transportation. This canal would connect the Great Lakes to the Hudson River and New York City. Moving goods by canal would lower the cost of shipping.

Many people did not believe it was possible to build a canal that long. Others thought it would cost too much. However, in 1817, Clinton became governor of New York. He convinced enough people that building a canal was the right thing to do.

Building and Opening the Canal

On July 4, 1817, work began on the Erie Canal near Rome, New York. Local workers and Irish immigrants built the canal. They dug the canal forty feet wide and four feet deep. A ten-foot-wide towpath was built along the bank.

In 1825, Governor Clinton opened the Erie Canal. He traveled on it from Buffalo to New York City. In New York City, he poured a barrel of Lake Erie water into the Atlantic Ocean to celebrate the canal's completion. The canal stretched more than 360 miles across New York. By traveling along the Erie Canal and the Hudson River, boats could finally move from Lake Erie all the way to New York City's harbor.

To New York City

CANAL TRAVEL

1

Barges were loaded with goods. Mules then towed, or pulled, the barges along a towpath.

2

Along the canal, boats and barges were weighed. Drivers had to pay a toll, or fee. Those with heavier barges paid higher tolls.

3

Boats traveling the length of the canal passed through 83 locks. A lock is a part of a canal where boats are raised or lowered.

Impact of the Erie Canal

Almost immediately, the Erie Canal became the major route for goods and people moving in and out of New York City. Goods could be shipped directly to the city from the Great Lakes region. The Erie Canal made it possible to ship goods more quickly and less expensively. This made New York City the most important city for shipping on the East Coast.

As a result, more business owners were willing to build factories in the towns along the canal. The populations of those towns grew at an amazing rate. Across the state, people left their farms and crowded into the new towns looking for work and better wages.

During the first 10 days that the canal was open, 40,000 barrels of flour were shipped from Rochester to eastern cities by way of the canal. Thanks to the canal, Rochester grew from a town of 2,500 people in 1823 to a city of 9,207 by 1830.

Other western New York towns grew into cities as well. In Utica, three large wool and cotton mills were built in the late 1840s. The city's population rose from 2,861 in 1817 to 17,556 in 1849. By the mid-1800s, the Erie Canal had helped western New York become a center for industry.

READING CHECK DRAW CONCLUSIONS
How did the Erie Canal help the economy of New York?

Steam Power

Main Idea The steam engine led to more improvements in transportation.

The Erie Canal was not the only improvement in transportation during the Industrial Revolution. New Yorkers continued to look for better and faster transportation. Some people concentrated on improving ways to travel by water. Others worked to improve land travel by constructing a railroad system and building better roads. States asked turnpike companies to build and take care of roads. A **turnpike** is a road that travelers pay to use.

Steamboats

Pulling barges on a river such as the Hudson could be difficult because of the river's strong current. In 1807, **Robert Fulton** used a steam engine to solve the problem. He built the first useful steamboat. A **steamboat** is a boat powered by a steam engine.

The invention of steamboats made river transportation easier, but Fulton's first steamboat could travel only at 5 miles per hour. However, **John Stevens** and his son, **Robert Stevens,** worked to make the steam engine better. By the mid-1820s, Robert Stevens used a different technology for steam engines. With this technology, boats could travel at speeds of up to 18 miles per hour. These improved steamboats were soon used all across the United States.

Robert Fulton
Fulton (above) traveled on his first steamboat, the *Clermont.* He went from New York City to Albany on the Hudson River.

Railroads, Roads, and Telegraphs

Trains powered by steam engines could reach over 25 miles per hour—faster than a steamboat. By 1831, New York's first railroad opened. Railroads soon connected New York City to the rest of the state and country. Steam engines also improved roads. Steam-powered stone crushers and steamrollers built roads with hard surfaces that did not wear out easily. Travel by road became quicker.

Communication also improved. **Samuel Morse** invented the telegraph, a way to send signals by electricity over wire. A message using Morse's code of dots and dashes was first sent in 1844. By 1861, a telegraph line crossed the country. People could now communicate long distances almost instantly.

✓ READING CHECK MAIN IDEA AND DETAILS

What new methods of travel did New Yorkers have by the mid-1800s?

SUMMARY

The Industrial Revolution and the Erie Canal caused towns throughout New York to develop into cities that still exist today. Canals, railroads, steamboats, and better roads improved transportation. Telegraphs improved communication.

Railroads In the 1800s, railroad companies advertised this new form of travel.

Lesson Review

1807
Fulton's steamboat

1825
Erie Canal opens

1831
New York's first railroad

1800 1810 1820 1830 1840 1850 1860

❶ **WHAT TO KNOW** How did New York grow during the 1800s?

❷ **VOCABULARY** Write a short paragraph explaining how **assembly lines** changed the way people worked. Use the phrase in your paragraph.

❸ **TIMELINE SKILL** What event happened 24 years before New York's first railroad opened?

❹ **RESEARCH ACTIVITY** Locate the branches of the Erie Canal. Make a list of present-day towns and cities that grew along these branches.

❺ 🔄 **READING SKILL** Complete the graphic organizer to show cause-and-effect relationships.

INDUSTRIAL REVOLUTION

The Struggle for Rights

1780   1820   1860   1900   1940   1980

1799–1920

▶ **WHAT TO KNOW**
For which rights did African Americans and women fight?

▶ **VOCABULARY**
emancipation
abolitionist
suffrage

 READING SKILL
Sequence As you read, list events that affected African Americans and women during the early 1800s.

1	
2	
3	
4	

Before You Read Have you ever wanted to change something that you thought was unfair? In the early 1800s, African Americans and women fought to be treated more fairly.

Slavery in New York

Main Idea In the early 1800s, abolitionists in New York fought to end slavery.

Slavery had a long history in New York, beginning when the Dutch brought enslaved Africans in the 1600s. New York had one of the highest populations of enslaved people among the northern colonies. After the American Revolution, however, some states in the north chose to end slavery. People in New York began to join the call for emancipation. **Emancipation** is the freeing of enslaved people.

Call to Action Posters were used to bring together opponents of slavery.

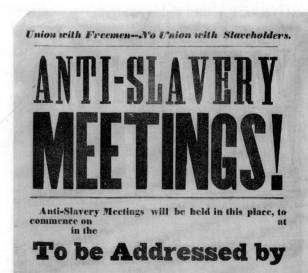

Union with Freemen--No Union with Slaveholders.

ANTI-SLAVERY MEETINGS!

Anti-Slavery Meetings will be held in this place, to commence on   at
in the

To be Addressed by

Agents of the Western ANTI-SLAVERY SOCIETY.

Three millions of your fellow beings are in chains--the Church and Government sustains the horrible

Fighting to End Slavery

Many years passed before New York abolitionists were successful. An **abolitionist** is someone who joined the movement to end slavery. In 1799, New York passed a law to end slavery in the state over time. Abolitionists were not satisfied, and they continued their fight. Slavery finally ended in New York in 1827.

Slavery was still legal in other states, though. New York abolitionists wanted to end slavery throughout the country. Weeksville, New York, became a center for abolitionists. The Brooklyn community was part of the Underground Railroad. This was not a real railroad. It was a secret network of people who helped enslaved people escape.

Frederick Douglass He started *The North Star* to "hasten the day of FREEDOM to the Three Millions of our enslaved fellow countrymen."

New York Abolitionists

In New York City, on March 16, 1827, **Samuel Cornish** and **John Russwurm** published the first African American newspaper in the country. It was called *Freedom's Journal*. Cornish and Russwurm wrote articles against slavery. Two other New Yorkers, **Arthur** and **Lewis Tappan,** helped found the American Anti-Slavery Society in 1833.

Sojourner Truth, another abolitionist, escaped slavery in New York before it was outlawed. By the 1840s, Truth had become famous for her powerful antislavery speeches. Another escaped slave, **Frederick Douglass,** also spoke against slavery. In 1847, Douglass began publishing an abolitionist newspaper in Rochester called *The North Star*.

READING CHECK SEQUENCE What happened in 1833 to help the cause of emancipation?

Women's Rights

Main Idea Women struggled for their rights in the 1800s.

During the 1800s, many people worked for women's rights, too. At that time, women could not own property, attend most schools or colleges, or vote.

Two New Yorkers, **Elizabeth Cady Stanton** and **Lucretia Mott**, became well known in the fight for women's suffrage. **Suffrage** is the right to vote.

Susan B. Anthony, who lived in Rochester, also called for suffrage and other rights for women. She said,

> " There never will be complete equality until women themselves help to make laws and elect lawmakers. "

Seneca Falls

Stanton and Mott organized a convention, or meeting, to discuss women's rights. In 1848, about 250 women and 40 men gathered at Seneca Falls, New York. The meeting is known as the Seneca Falls Convention. They heard speeches and discussed ways to fight for women's rights.

Stanton presented *The Declaration of Sentiments* at the convention. This document was modeled after the Declaration of Independence. It said,

> " We hold these truths to be self-evident; that all men and women are created equal . . . "

The document demanded that women be allowed to vote.

Seneca Falls These statues show the moment when Susan B. Anthony met Elizabeth Cady Stanton in Seneca Falls in 1851.

A Long Struggle

The Seneca Falls Convention inspired others to join the struggle for women's rights. Stanton and Anthony began working together for women's suffrage. The two met to plan and write speeches. Anthony would then travel the country to deliver the speeches.

Over many years, states began to recognize women's rights, including the right to vote. In 1917, New York State allowed women to vote. In 1920, the Nineteenth Amendment to the Constitution was ratified to guarantee the right of women to vote in all states. The goal of Anthony, Mott, Stanton, and many others was reached as last.

READING CHECK CAUSE AND EFFECT What effect did the Seneca Falls Convention have on women's rights?

SUMMARY

New York abolitionists fought to end slavery in New York and throughout the United States. Women from New York State also led the fight for women's suffrage during the 1800s.

Susan B. Anthony These one-dollar coins honor Susan B. Anthony's fight for women's rights.

Lesson Review

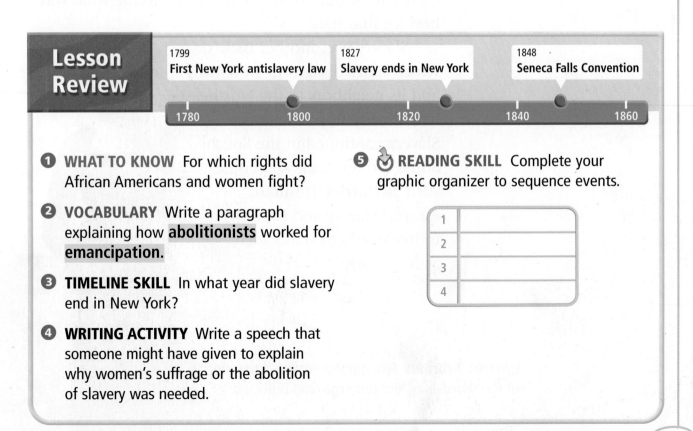

1799	1827	1848
First New York antislavery law	Slavery ends in New York	Seneca Falls Convention

1780 — 1800 — 1820 — 1840 — 1860

❶ **WHAT TO KNOW** For which rights did African Americans and women fight?

❷ **VOCABULARY** Write a paragraph explaining how **abolitionists** worked for **emancipation.**

❸ **TIMELINE SKILL** In what year did slavery end in New York?

❹ **WRITING ACTIVITY** Write a speech that someone might have given to explain why women's suffrage or the abolition of slavery was needed.

❺ **READING SKILL** Complete your graphic organizer to sequence events.

1	
2	
3	
4	

The Civil War

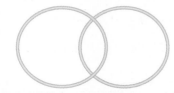
Before You Read Sometimes people have very different ideas about things. In the early 1800s, the northern and southern United States had different ideas about how to make the economy strong.

The Country Divides

Main Idea Disagreements over slavery and states' rights split the United States and led to the Civil War.

The United States had 34 states in 1860, and people in the northern and southern states did not always agree. People in New York and other northern states wanted a strong national government. Most southerners supported states' rights. They thought each state should have the power to decide what was best for that state.

Slavery was another issue on which states disagreed. New York and its neighbors in the Northeast had already stopped slavery. Slavery continued in the South. Some former enslaved people, such as **Harriet Tubman,** escaped slavery and moved to free northern states such as New York.

Harriet Tubman She guided enslaved people to freedom along the Underground Railroad.

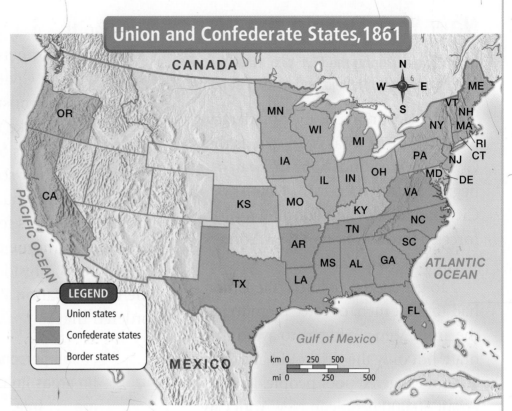

Union and Confederate States, 1861

CANADA

Legend
- Union states
- Confederate states
- Border states

A Nation Divided
The United States split into the Union and the Confederacy in 1861. Border states were slave states that stayed in the Union.

SKILL Reading Maps
How many states were border states?

Different Economies

Many southerners thought that ending slavery would harm their farming economy. The plantations of the South had grown to depend on the work of enslaved people. A plantation is a large farm. Most plantation owners believed that without enslaved workers the cost of producing cotton and other raw materials would increase.

Northern states had many farmers as well, but the economy was changing. Cities in the North were growing quickly, and factories were being built. By 1860, fewer than half of northerners farmed. The North and South were becoming more and more different.

Moving Toward War

In 1860, Americans elected **Abraham Lincoln** to be President. Many southerners disagreed with Lincoln because he had spoken out against slavery. As news of Lincoln's election spread, they argued that their states should leave the Union.

Eleven southern states decided to secede. To **secede** means to leave the nation to which a state belongs. These states formed the Confederate States of America, or the Confederacy. The remaining states, including New York, formed the Union.

READING CHECK COMPARE AND CONTRAST
What issues divided the North and South?

New York During the War

Main Idea During the Civil War, New Yorkers fought on the battlefield and helped at home.

The Union and the Confederacy went to war in what is known as the Civil War. A month after the war began, 30,000 men from New York City had already joined the Union forces. However, not all New Yorkers wanted to go to war.

To get enough soldiers, the Union had to draft men, or force them to join the army. Men could pay to avoid the draft, but only the rich could afford this. The rule angered poor people. In 1863, about 50,000 people in New York City protested. This event became known as the Draft Riots. Rioters robbed stores and destroyed buildings. Lincoln had to send soldiers to stop them.

Fighting the War

At first, northerners thought they would win the Civil War easily. Union factories made most of the weapons for the war. Unlike much of the South, they had railroads to move supplies and food to their soldiers. However, the Confederacy had better generals, and their soldiers fought hard to defend their home ground.

In 1863, President Lincoln signed the Emancipation Proclamation. He ordered that

> **❝ . . . all persons held as slaves [in areas fighting the Union] . . . are . . . free. ❞**

After the proclamation was signed, many newly freed African Americans joined the Union forces.

New York Soldiers
In support of President Abraham Lincoln (above), New York sent about 100,000 soldiers into battle—more than any other Union state.

Helping During the War

New York City women helped the Union, too. Some ran farms or businesses while men were away at war. Others served as volunteers. A **volunteer** is someone who chooses to do work without pay. Many were nurses who treated injured soldiers.

Finally, in 1865, the Civil War ended when the Confederacy gave up. The Union had won. The United States became one nation again. The Constitution was changed to outlaw slavery. New Yorkers celebrated and prepared to rebuild a divided nation. Newly freed African Americans began moving to New York and other northern states.

✓ **READING CHECK** MAIN IDEA AND DETAILS
In what ways did New Yorkers help the Union army during the Civil War?

SUMMARY

Conflicts between northern and southern states led to the Civil War. Some New Yorkers fought, while others protested against the war. Because the North won the Civil War, the United States remained one country and slavery was ended throughout the nation.

Civil War Hat This hat was worn by a soldier in the Union army.

Lesson Review

1861 Civil War begins	1863 Emancipation Proclamation	1865 Civil War ends

1860   1861   1862   1863   1864   1865

❶ **WHAT TO KNOW** What effects did the Civil War have on New York?

❷ **VOCABULARY** Choose the word that best completes the sentence.

secede   volunteer

To _____, a state has to leave the nation to which it belongs.

❸ **TIMELINE SKILL** How long did the Civil War last?

❹ **WRITING ACTIVITY** Write a letter that a young volunteer from New York might have written during the Civil War. Describe what the person did to help others.

❺ 🔄 **READING SKILL** Complete the graphic organizer to compare and contrast the Union and the Confederacy.

UNION   CONFEDERACY

CIVIL WAR PHOTOGRAPHS

Images of war can change the way people feel about war. During the Civil War, photographers such as Mathew Brady took pictures of soldiers, battles, and ruined buildings. Before the war, photography was still new. Most newspaper and magazine pictures were illustrations. During the war, newspapers began printing war photographs. For the first time, people in homes far from the battlefield could see what actually happened in war.

Working at Camp Photographs showed that some women and their children followed their husbands from camp to camp.

Mathew Brady Brady is in this photograph with New York soldiers in Virginia. He left his New York City studio to take photographs of the Civil War.

Activities

1. **TALK ABOUT IT** How might photography have changed people's feelings about war?

2. **WRITE ABOUT IT** Choose one of the photographs of the Civil War on this page. Write a description of what you see.

Go Digital Visit Education Place for more primary sources. www.eduplace.com/nycssp/

Skillbuilder

Resolve Conflicts

▶ **VOCABULARY**

compromise

Sometimes, differences in opinions and beliefs can lead to a conflict. A conflict is a disagreement between groups of people or individuals. By working together, both sides in a conflict can overcome their disagreements and find a solution.

Learn the Skill

Step 1: Identify the conflict.

Step 2: Understand the reasons for the conflict. Have the people involved in the conflict state their goals.

Step 3: Think of all the possible ways to solve the conflict.

Step 4: Choose the plan that is most acceptable to everyone involved. Each side may need to make a compromise. A **compromise** is when a person or group gives up something it wants in order to move closer to an agreement.

Conflict: The softball team and the school band both want to use the auditorium after school on Tuesdays.

Goal: The softball team wants to hold meetings on Tuesdays.

Goal: The school band wants to rehearse on Tuesdays.

Possible Solution: The softball team offers to hold meetings every other Tuesday.

Possible Solution: The school band offers to practice at a later time.

Solution: The softball team will hold meetings every other Tuesday. The band will practice in the evening on the days that the softball team has meetings.

Both the Union and the Confederacy began ordering men to join their armies. On both sides, wealthy people could pay to avoid military service. They could either pay a fee to the government or pay others to take their places. Some people thought paying to get out of military service was fine because the army would still have enough men. Others believed it was unfair because only poor people would end up in the army. They thought that rich people should fight as well.

Practice the Skill

Read the paragraph above. Then answer the questions.

1. Identify the conflict. What differences in opinion did people have about allowing men to pay to get out of serving in the army?

2. What were the goals of the people involved in the conflict?

3. Brainstorm ways that both groups can work together to solve this conflict.

Apply the Skill

Find out about a conflict that exists in your community. Learn about ways that people have tried to compromise in order to find a solution.

Visual Summary

1–3. ✏️ Write a description of each item or event shown below.

Industrial Revolution, 1800s

Struggle for Rights, mid-1800s

Rights for Women

Civil War, 1861–1865

Facts and Main Ideas

Answer each question below.

4. **History** What effect did the Erie Canal have on New York City?

5. **Technology** How did the steam engine affect transportation in the 1800s?

6. **History** What did Frederick Douglass do to support emancipation?

7. **Citizenship** In what ways did some New Yorkers and other Americans work for women's rights?

8. **History** Describe events that led to the Civil War.

Vocabulary

Choose the correct word from the list below to complete each sentence.

canal, p. 191
turnpike, p. 194
volunteer, p. 203

9. A person could choose to serve as a _____ by doing jobs for free.

10. A _____ is a waterway made by people.

11. A road that travelers pay to use is called a _____.

Apply Skills

Resolve Conflicts Read the paragraph. Then use what you have learned about resolving conflicts to answer each question.

> Mrs. Lee's fifth-grade class wants to volunteer in the community. They all agree about the importance of volunteering, but they disagree about what to do. Some students want to visit elderly neighbors who cannot leave their homes. Others think it is more important to collect food for the food bank. Still others want to help the recycling center in town.

12. What is the first step the students should take to resolve the conflict?

   A. Forget about volunteering.

   B. Ask Mrs. Lee to decide what to do.

   C. Identify the conflict.

   D. Come up with more suggestions.

13. How can the students best resolve the conflict?

   A. Compromise on a project that most students would like to do.

   B. Let someone outside the class decide for them.

   C. Argue until some people give up.

   D. Decide not to compromise.

Timeline

Use the timeline above to answer the question.

14. How many years passed between the opening of the Erie Canal and the beginning of the Civil War?

Critical Thinking

Write a short paragraph to answer each question below.

15. **Cause and Effect** How did the Erie Canal help New York grow?

16. **Infer** Why do you think it took so long for women to win the right to vote?

Activities

Science Activity The steam engine helped power the Industrial Revolution. Read about steam engines in a book or on a website. Then draw your own version and explain how steam can provide power.

Writing Activity Write a story about New Yorkers' reactions to the end of the Civil War. Use dialogue to make your characters seem real.

Go Digital Get help with your writing at www.eduplace.com/nycssp/

Immigration and Migration

Statue of Liberty,
Liberty Island

Study Skills

VOCABULARY

Using a dictionary can help you learn new words.

- A dictionary shows the meanings of a word and tells its origin, or where it came from.

- You can use a chart to organize unfamiliar words.

immigration (ĭm´ mĭ grā´ shən) *noun* [from the Latin *immigrāre,* to remove or go into] 1. Movement from one country to another to live.

Word	Syllables	Origin	Definition
immigration	im•mi•gra•tion	Latin	Movement from one country to another to live

Vocabulary Preview

immigration

During the late 1800s, many people moved from Europe to live in New York. This **immigration** made the population of the United States grow. **page 215**

heritage

New immigrants to New York City bring with them their **heritage,** including traditions such as music and dance. **page 224**

Chapter Timeline

| 1870 New York City Fire Department created | 1892 Ellis Island opens | 1900 Garment workers organize union |

1840   1870   1900

Reading Strategy

Predict and Infer Use this strategy as you read the lessons in this chapter. Look at the pictures in a lesson to make predictions. What do you think you will read about?

skyscraper

Inventions such as the **skyscraper** helped change New York City. In these tall buildings, more people could live and work in a small area. **page 231**

labor union

Many workers in New York joined groups called **labor unions.** Each union tried to gain higher wages and better working conditions. **page 234**

1954
Ellis Island closes

1930   1960   Today

Go Digital visit www.eduplace.com/nycssp/

The Melting Pot
Immigrants in New York

▶ **WHAT TO KNOW**
What was daily life like for many immigrants?

▶ **VOCABULARY**

melting pot
immigration
tenement
discrimination

READING SKILL
Draw Conclusions Add facts to the chart below that lead to the conclusion.

Many people moved to New York City.

At the beginning of the 1800s, the area that is now New York City had a population of under 90,000 people. One hundred years later, that population had grown to nearly 3.5 million.

During the 1800s, many people from other parts of the country and from around the world were moving into New York City. The city's population became more varied than ever before, making it one of the great melting pots in the United States. **Melting pot** is a term used to describe a place where people from many different cultures come together to form a new, diverse society.

New Arrivals People from around the world arrived in New York City in search of a better life.

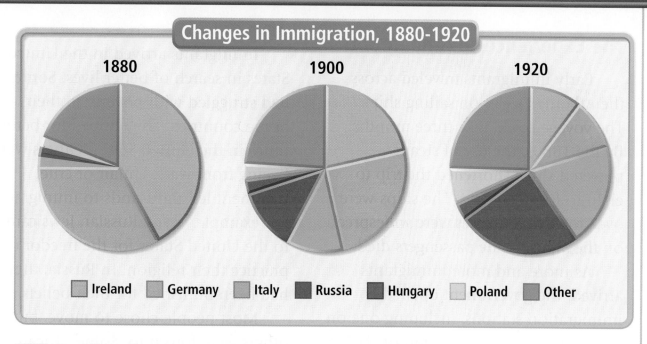

Changes in Immigration, 1880-1920

1880   1900   1920

Ireland   Germany   Italy   Russia   Hungary   Poland   Other

SKILL **Reading Charts** From which country did more immigrants come in 1880, Russia or Ireland? In 1920?

Immigration Patterns

Many immigrants to New York City in the 1800s came from Ireland. Between 1846 and 1850, a disease destroyed the Irish potato crops. Most poor people depended on potatoes for their food. A famine, or lack of food, spread across the country. Hundreds of thousands of Irish people moved to New York to escape the famine.

Large numbers of Germans also came to New York City during the mid-1800s, as well as Swedes and Czechs. Some stayed, but many bought farm land in other parts of the country.

In the late 1800s, immigration to New York City reached one of its highest points ever. **Immigration** is the movement of people to a new country. The newer immigrants came from countries in southern or eastern Europe, such as Russia, Italy, and Poland.

Many of the new immigrants chose to stay in New York City, where they first landed. New York had industries and a busy harbor. Immigrants needed work, and the growing city provided hundreds of thousands of jobs.

✓READING CHECK DRAW CONCLUSIONS What effect did immigration have on New York City's population?

The Experiences of Immigrants

Early immigrants traveled across the Atlantic Ocean on sailing ships. The voyage could take three months. By the 1880s, the use of steam-powered ships shortened the trip to eight to fourteen days. The ships were overcrowded. Diseases were widespread on the ships. Some passengers died.

As more and more immigrants arrived, the government opened immigration stations, including one on Ellis Island in New York Harbor. At Ellis Island, government workers examined newcomers. Inspections often took three to five hours.

Immigrants arrived in the United States in search of better lives. Some had struggled with poverty in their home countries. They hoped for better times in the United States. Others were fleeing from wars. Unfair or cruel treatment led thousands to immigrate. For example, many Russian Jews came to the United States for the freedom to practice their religion. In Russia, they had been punished for their beliefs.

Most people chose to move, but others were forced to. Some African Americans migrated north after slavery ended. In the South, they had faced unfair treatment.

JOURNEY TO NEW YORK

New Beginnings
① Immigrants arrived hoping to be allowed into the United States. They carried the few things they had brought from their home country.

Daily Life of Immigrants

Once in New York City, immigrants had to learn a new way of life in an unfamiliar place. Most of them arrived with little money and few items from their old homes.

The jobs immigrants found in New York City paid better than in their homelands. Some eastern Europeans earned more than double the wages they made in their home country.

Many immigrants lived in tenements. A **tenement** is a poorly built apartment building. Tenement apartments were crowded, and some did not have running water.

Immigrants sometimes faced discrimination. **Discrimination** is when people treat others unfairly based upon their differences. Immigrants often had to take unsafe jobs because it was the only work they could find.

Over time, immigrant families moved out of tenements. Some bought their own homes. The children of immigrants attended high school and college in greater numbers than their parents. Better education led to better jobs and new opportunities.

✓ READING CHECK GENERALIZE What was the journey to the United States like for many immigrants?

(2) Inspection Immigrants were asked about where they planned to live and work. Doctors checked them for diseases that could spread to others.

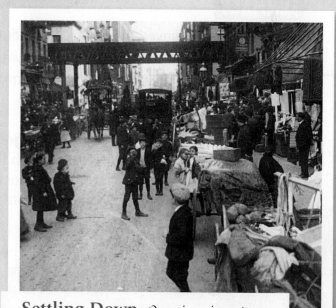

(3) Settling Down Once immigrants passed inspection, they often moved to crowded areas. New York City neighborhoods had some of the highest populations per square mile in the world.

A World City

People have continued to move to New York City since the 1920s. From 1940 to 1950, New York City's population grew by more than 400,000 people. Many of them were Puerto Ricans. Recent newcomers also include many people from Asia, Africa, Latin America, and from rural areas of the United States.

New York City also became a world business capital during the 1940s. Banks and other large businesses moved offices there. The city had one of the world's biggest ports, handling 150 million tons of cargo a year.

Today, New York City still has a very large economy that is interdependent with New York State and with the rest of the world. **Interdependent** means depending on each other. Goods such as milk, meat, and fruit come into New York City from other parts of the state. Goods made in New York City or brought in through its port are sent throughout the state and nation.

✔**READING CHECK** DRAW CONCLUSIONS Why could New York City be called a world business capital?

SUMMARY

Many immigrants moved to New York City during the late 1800s and early 1900s. They came for new jobs and a new way of life, but they also faced new challenges. New York City grew into one of the world's leading cities.

Continued Immigration Immigrants continue to come to New York City. Some make their home in the Queens neighborhood of Little India (right).

❶ What to Know

What was daily life like for many immigrants?

❷ Reading Skill Draw Conclusions

Complete the graphic organizer to draw a conclusion.

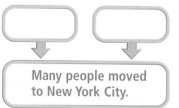

Many people moved to New York City.

❸ Case Study Detective

Look closely at the picture below. Where is the family? What are they doing? Can you locate items that people still use today?

❹ Word Play

Use the following clue to unscramble the letters below and form a word from the lesson.

N E E T N E M T

Clue: If you were an immigrant in the late 1800s, you might have lived in one of these.

Study Skills

Skillbuilder

Identify Primary and Secondary Sources

▶ **VOCABULARY**

primary source

secondary source

A **primary source** is a firsthand account of an event. It has been recorded by a person who was there. Autobiographies, speeches, photos, and letters are examples of primary sources.

A **secondary source** is recorded by someone who was not present at an event. History books, encyclopedias, and biographies are secondary sources.

The sources below give information about Ellis Island.

Immigration authorities [officials] came on board at Ellis Island. They were not very nice. . . . They checked visas [passports], calling people in alphabetical order. Then people were turned over to a health inspector. But my father didn't hear our name, so they said, "Wait till the end," . . . We were afraid we were going to be stuck on the boat.

—David Froelich, arrived at Ellis Island in 1939 at age 11

The government began using Ellis Island as an immigration station in 1892. About 35 buildings were constructed on the island. Newcomers were taken to the main building. . . . The immigrants were questioned by government officials and examined by doctors. Certain people were prohibited [forbidden] by the federal law from immigrating to the United States.

—from an encyclopedia entry on Ellis Island

Step 1: Identify the subject of both passages.

Step 2: Read both passages. Look for clue words such as *I, my, me,* and *we.* These words are often used in primary sources. Also look for personal details.

Step 3: Identify each passage as either a primary or a secondary source. To help you figure this out, ask yourself these questions: *Who wrote the passage? What event does the writer talk about? Was the writer at the event?*

Practice the Skill

Answer these questions about the primary and secondary sources on page 220.

1. Which passage is a primary source? How do you know?
2. Which passage is a secondary source? How do you know?
3. What kinds of information does the primary source give you that the secondary source cannot?

Apply the Skill

Use the Internet or library resources to find one primary source and one secondary source about tenement life. Write a paragraph to tell how each source helps you understand tenement life.

Living in New York

A Changing City

VOCABULARY

ethnic group
migrate
heritage

READING SKILL
Cause and Effect As you read, note the effects that immigrants have on New York City.

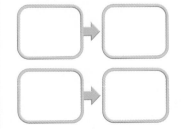

As more people came to New York City, they often settled near friends and family. They formed neighborhoods mostly made up of a single ethnic group. An **ethnic group** is a group of people who share a race, nationality, religion, or culture. In an ethnic neighborhood, immigrants could speak their own language and practice their own customs.

Immigrants have settled in ethnic neighborhoods throughout New York City. In Queens, Forest Hills has long been a Jewish neighborhood. Richmond Hill is known as "Little Guyana" because of its large Guyanese population.

A Growing City By 1900, over 3,400,000 people lived in New York City. Many came from other countries and settled in ethnic neighborhoods such as Little Italy.

New York City, 1900

Foreign-born population

Population born in the U.S.

Lafayette Theater By 1930, more than 200,000 African Americans lived in the area known as Harlem. Places such as the Lafayette Theater became important centers of culture.

New York City Neighborhoods

Chinatown is one of New York City's most famous ethnic neighborhoods. The Chinese faced discrimination in many places, but in Chinatown they could speak Chinese, read Chinese-language newspapers, and practice their customs.

People from within the United States have also settled in ethnic neighborhoods. Between 1916 and 1930, 1.5 million African Americans migrated from the South to the North in search of better jobs and lives. To **migrate** is to move from one region and settle in another. Many African Americans settled in the Manhattan neighborhood called Harlem. Like other neighborhoods, however, Harlem has changed. Today, it is home to people from the Caribbean, Mexico, Senegal, and other countries.

READING CHECK CAUSE AND EFFECT What caused many Chinese people to settle in Chinatown?

Cultural Contributions

When new immigrants arrived, they brought their heritage. **Heritage** is something that is passed down from one generation to the next, such as language, traditions, food, or skills.

Many immigrant languages have contributed words that are now common in American English. From the German language, we have the word "kindergarten." African Americans from the South brought such words as "banjo" and "gumbo" with them. The Spanish introduced such words as "alligator" and "guitar."

The music and festivals of immigrant groups are part of life in New York City. Today, festivals such as the West Indian Carnival in Crown Heights, Brooklyn, and the Puerto Rican Day Parade in Manhattan celebrate the traditions of diverse cultures.

The heritages of different groups have also combined to form new American arts. Tap dancing is a blend of Irish and African dances. It was first performed on Manhattan's Lower East Side.

✓ READING CHECK CLASSIFY What are two words the Spanish introduced to American English?

Savion Glover This famous tap dancer draws from a blend of cultural traditions in a performance at the Joyce Theater in New York City.

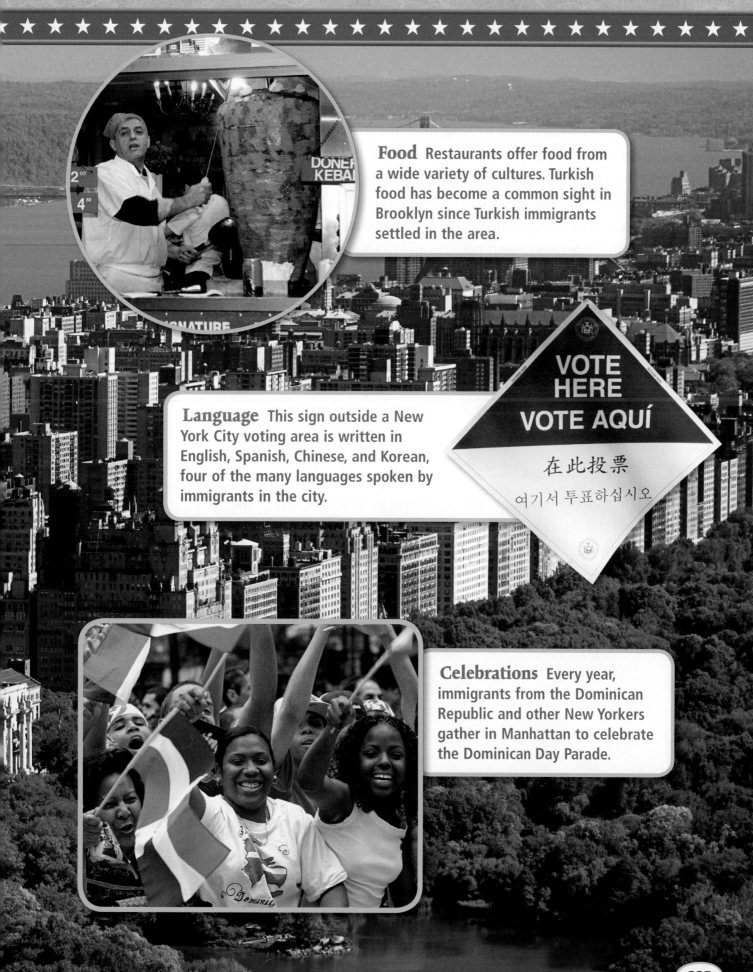

Food Restaurants offer food from a wide variety of cultures. Turkish food has become a common sight in Brooklyn since Turkish immigrants settled in the area.

VOTE HERE
VOTE AQUÍ
在此投票
여기서 투표하십시오

Language This sign outside a New York City voting area is written in English, Spanish, Chinese, and Korean, four of the many languages spoken by immigrants in the city.

Celebrations Every year, immigrants from the Dominican Republic and other New Yorkers gather in Manhattan to celebrate the Dominican Day Parade.

Building a Diverse City

The contributions of immigrants skilled in arts, crafts, engineering, and the sciences can be seen all over the city today. German immigrant **John A. Roebling** and his son, **Washington Roebling,** were engineers who designed the Brooklyn Bridge. The bridge has become a major New York landmark.

Hispanic artists began painting murals on buildings in New York City in the 1960s. Local artists, teenagers, and people from the neighborhood would gather to paint the murals.

As more people arrive, they will add their own contributions. Today, immigrants continue to bring their languages, food, and customs to New York City.

READING CHECK SUMMARIZE What contributions of immigrants can be seen around New York City today?

SUMMARY

Large numbers of immigrants began coming to New York City in the 1800s and still do so today. They have created ethnic neighborhoods and enriched city life with their languages, skills, and traditions.

Brooklyn Bridge When the bridge opened in 1883, the distance between its towers was the longest of any bridge in the world.

CASE STUDY REVIEW

❶ What to Know

What do immigrants contribute to life in New York City?

❷ Reading Skill Cause and Effect

Complete the graphic organizer to show cause-and-effect relationships.

❸ Case Study Detective

Every year, people in Chinatown celebrate the Chinese New Year. Find three examples of Chinese heritage in this photograph.

❹ Word Play

The letters from *neighborhood* can be used to spell other words. Here are three:

| rein | big | horn |

- How many other words can you spell using letters from *neighborhood*?

New York City Neighborhoods

Walking through New York City, you might hear dozens of languages spoken. The smells of many kinds of food fill the air outside restaurants. By 1920, immigrants from all over the world had settled in ethnic neighborhoods across the city. These communities were a home away from home, where people shared their heritage with friends and neighbors from the same culture. In time, these neighborhoods became a part of the culture of all New Yorkers.

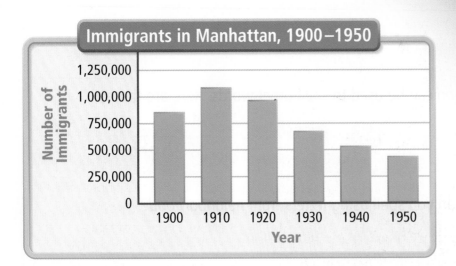

Broadway

Canal St.

Immigrants in Manhattan, 1900–1950

Number of Immigrants

- 1,250,000
- 1,000,000
- 750,000
- 500,000
- 250,000
- 0

Year: 1900 1910 1920 1930 1940 1950

Peak of Growth By 1910, the immigrant population of Manhattan was more than 1 million. New laws later limited the number of immigrants allowed into the country.

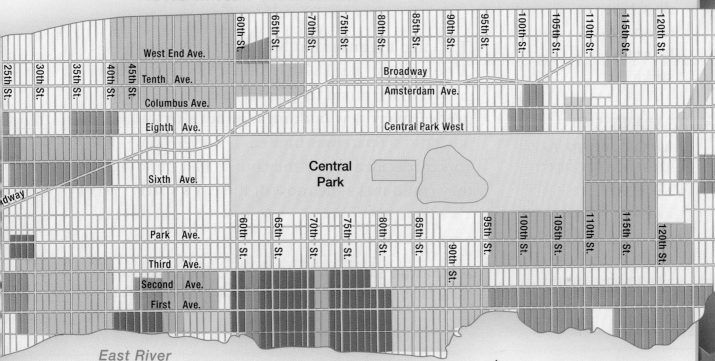

LEGEND

Ethnic Neighborhoods of New York, 1920

- African American
- Chinese
- Czech, Hungarian
- French
- German
- Irish
- Italian
- Russian, Polish, Jewish
- Scandinavian
- Turkish, Greek, Syrian

A Patchwork Quilt Different groups settled in their own neighborhoods of Manhattan. Some neighborhoods today still have the special characteristics of those groups.

Hudson River

West End Ave.
Tenth Ave.
Columbus Ave.
Eighth Ave.
Sixth Ave.
Park Ave.
Third Ave.
Second Ave.
First Ave.

Broadway
Amsterdam Ave.
Central Park West

Central Park

East River

25th St. 30th St. 35th St. 40th St. 45th St. 60th St. 65th St. 70th St. 75th St. 80th St. 85th St. 90th St. 95th St. 100th St. 105th St. 110th St. 115th St. 120th St.

Activities

1. **TALK ABOUT IT** Why do you think immigrants settled near other people from the same culture? Explain your answer.

2. **WRITE ABOUT IT** Choose an immigrant group shown on the map. Write a paragraph explaining where they settled in Manhattan and what groups settled near them.

▶ **WHAT TO KNOW**
What effects did immigration have on New York City's growth?

▶ **VOCABULARY**
skyscraper
reservoir
labor union
strike

◎ **READING SKILL**
Draw Conclusions As you read, list facts that support this conclusion.

Immigration changed New York City.

New York City Expands
Building Upward

Immigrants arrived in New York City in large numbers in the 1800s. As the city's population grew rapidly, it had to adapt. For example, people needed many new buildings for housing and businesses. Space was limited, however. New Yorkers decided that if they built taller buildings, they could make the most of the city's space.

Manhattan Skyline New York City is famous for its many tall buildings, including the Empire State Building.

Carnegie Hall Tower

One Worldwide Plaza

New Technology

Before people could build tall buildings, they had to solve several problems. One problem was how to get to the top. Not many people wanted to climb long staircases to reach the upper floors. Early elevators were unsafe for passengers. In the 1850s, though, new technology made them safe. Workers soon put elevators in stores, hotels, and other tall buildings.

People could now reach upper floors more easily, but there were still limits as to how high buildings could be. In the 1800s, buildings were made mainly of wood and bricks. The walls needed to be very thick to support the weight of the upper floors. Thicker walls made taller buildings much more expensive.

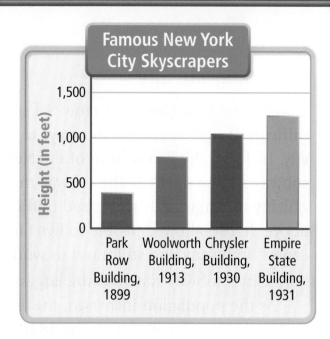

Famous New York City Skyscrapers

Height (in feet)

| 1,500 |
| 1,000 |
| 500 |
| 0 |

Park Row Building, 1899 — Woolworth Building, 1913 — Chrysler Building, 1930 — Empire State Building, 1931

Standing Tall At 391 feet, the Park Row Building was once the tallest in the world.

In the 1880s, workers began to construct buildings with steel frames. Steel frames made it possible to build taller, stronger buildings with thinner walls. They were called skyscrapers. A **skyscraper** is a very tall building.

✓**READING CHECK** DRAW CONCLUSIONS Why were skyscrapers made of steel?

Condé Nast Building

Empire State Building

Improving the City

As New York City grew, crowded streets made travel difficult. People needed better ways to move around the city. In 1904, the first section of the New York City subway system opened. The subway moved people quickly underground. This eased traffic on the streets above. It also allowed people to live farther from the center of the city and still travel to work. Today, New York City's subway system is the largest in the world.

As the population increased, the city's wells, springs and streets became dirtier. In the 1830s and 1840s, workers built a system of pipes, tunnels, and reservoirs to supply clean water. A **reservoir** is a place where water is collected and stored for use. The clean water kept people healthier and was used to fight fires.

The city also needed to get rid of dirty water. In 1850, New York City began building sewers, or underground pipes, to carry away waste. By 1902, the sewer system had grown to more than 1,400 miles.

Living conditions within New York City also improved. Many of the city's immigrants had been living in crowded, unsafe tenements. In 1867, New York State passed laws to make tenements safer, such as by requiring them to have fire escapes.

Even in safer buildings, crowding was a problem. Diseases spread easily. The city's government passed laws to fight disease. Officials made sure trash was picked up, the water supply was clean, and that food in the city was safe to eat. Individuals made the city healthier, too. For example, **Dr. S. Josephine Baker** created a school health program.

✓READING CHECK CAUSE AND EFFECT Why did New York City build a subway system?

ABOVE THE GROUND Fire Safety

The New York City Fire Department was set up in 1870. Members used the city's water system to fight fires.

Modern firefighters use advanced equipment and trucks, but they still need city water to fight fires.

BELOW THE GROUND Subway Systems

When New York City's first subway opened in 1904, more than 100,000 people took a ride.

Today, more than 7 million people a day ride the New York City subway.

Working in New York

The people who arrived in New York City needed work. Many men, women, and children in the growing city found jobs in factories. There, they often worked long hours with dangerous machines for low pay. Some people fought to protect young workers and end child labor. New laws reduced the hours children could work and kept them from doing dangerous jobs.

Workers formed labor unions as a way to win better working conditions. A **labor union** is a group organized to protect workers' rights. To fight for rights, labor unions organized strikes. A **strike** is when workers refuse to work as a way to force business owners to improve their conditions.

In 1909, thousands of garment workers, or people who made clothing, went on strike for better pay. Without workers, business owners had no clothing to sell. They agreed to increase workers' pay. The garment workers also won shorter workdays.

✓**READING CHECK** MAIN IDEA AND DETAILS What actions did workers take to improve their working conditions?

SUMMARY

New York City expanded with the building of skyscrapers and the subway. New laws on health, water, and firefighting, as well as better working conditions, improved daily life.

Clothing Factory In the mid-1800s, women sewed by hand or used a hand-cranked sewing machine.

CASE STUDY REVIEW

❶ What to Know

What effects did immigration have on New York City's growth?

❷ Reading Skill Draw Conclusions

Complete your graphic organizer to draw conclusions.

Immigration changed New York City.

❸ Case Study Detective

What's the evidence that life in New York City changed? Find three ways in which the photographs show differences between the past and today.

❹ Word Play

Like *skyscraper,* many words are compounds made up of more than one word. Combine words from the left and right boxes to create compound words about travel.

cross	way
rail	plane
street	walk
air	car

235

Labor Union
LEADERS

In the late 1800s and early 1900s, many New Yorkers faced serious problems at work. The workday was long, the workplace was often dangerous, and the pay was low. Labor unions and their leaders worked to solve these problems.

Rose Schneiderman
(1882–1972)

When Rose Schneiderman was about 16, she got a job in a New York City hat factory to help earn money for her family. By the time she was 21, she had organized a union there. In 1905, Schneiderman led a 13-week strike for better hours and fair pay. Her success as a leader led to her election as president of a national women's union. She also advised President Franklin D. Roosevelt about workers and unions.

Kate Mullany
(1845–1906)

At age 19, Irish immigrant Kate Mullany took a job in Troy. She worked in a laundry fourteen hours a day for six days a week, earning only $2 a week. To improve the pay and poor conditions, Mullany started the Collar Laundry Union in 1864. It was the first major women's labor union in the United States. She led 200 workers in a strike and won a pay increase.

Asa Philip Randolph
(1889–1979)

In 1917, Asa Philip Randolph started *The Messenger*, a magazine that reported on African American labor unions. He helped African American railroad workers organize a union in 1925. During his time as union president, workers received better pay and worked shorter hours. Randolph also worked for equal job opportunities for all Americans.

Activities

1. **THINK ABOUT IT** In what ways did Schneiderman, Mullany, and Randolph affect the lives of workers?

2. **PRESENT IT** Write a list of reasons a business should provide workers with a safe workplace. Use these reasons to write a letter to a business owner.

Visual Summary

1–3. ✏️→ Write a description of each item shown below.

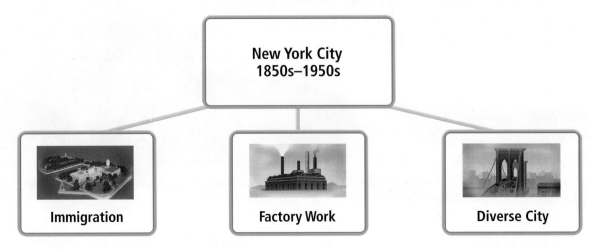

New York City
1850s–1950s

Immigration

Factory Work

Diverse City

Facts and Main Ideas

Answer each question below.

4. **History** Name three reasons immigrants came to the United States during the late 1800s and early 1900s.

5. **History** Why did immigrants have to pass through Ellis Island?

6. **Geography** Why did many immigrants settle in ethnic neighborhoods?

7. **History** People from what group moved to Harlem in large numbers in the early 1900s?

8. **Economy** Why did workers form labor unions?

Vocabulary

Choose the correct word to complete each sentence.

tenement, p. 217
heritage, p. 224
strike, p. 234

9. Immigrants brought their _____ with them to the United States.

10. Workers wanted to be paid more money, so they went on _____.

11. Families crowded into small apartments in a _____.

1846
Potato Famine

1892
Ellis Island opens

1904
Subway opens

1909
Garment workers strike

1845   1855   1865   1875   1885   1895   1905   1915

Apply Skills

Identify Primary and Secondary Sources Read the document below. Use your knowledge of primary sources to answer each question.

> We were checked again for eyesight, our ears, our heart with a stethoscope. We all passed the examination, and then we were told to stay in one place until we took the ferry to Battery Park. It was from the ferry I remember seeing the liberty statue. I had seen pictures of it in different books in Italy. I thought it was a beautiful monument, one of the most beautiful things I've seen.
> —Mario Vina

12. How can you tell this is a primary source?

   A. It mentions Battery Park.

   B. The writer gets examined.

   C. The writer was from Italy.

   D. The passage includes "we" and "I."

13. What can you learn from this source?

   A. the causes of immigration

   B. the importance of a ferry

   C. what it was like at Battery Park

   D. an immigrant's experience arriving in the United States

Timeline

Use the timeline above to answer the question.

14. How many years after Ellis Island opened did garment workers go on strike?

Critical Thinking

Write a short paragraph to answer each question below.

15. Compare and Contrast How were the challenges immigrants faced in their homelands similar to and different from the challenges they faced in New York City?

16. Cause and Effect Why did people build skyscrapers in New York City?

Activities

Art Activity Find out more about Ellis Island. Create a drawing of the immigration station.

Writing Activity Use the Internet or library books to research how large tenements were and how many people lived in them. Write a story about an immigrant living in a tenement apartment.

 Get help with your writing at www.eduplace.com/nycssp/

239

Fun with Social Studies

Musical History

Match the historical "artist" to the song title that best describes him or her.

Name	Artist
Follow the North Star	D. Clinton
From the Great Lakes to NYC	S. Anthony
Steam Rolling on the River	K. Mullany
We Want the Vote	R. Fulton
Workers Unite for Your Rights	F. Douglass

Picture This!

 VOCABULARY

Can you figure out which words are shown? Each word fits one of the clues on the right.

 **se** + 🌻SEEDS   a very tall building

🥫 + **al**   to leave the nation to which a state belongs

 ☁️ + 🖌️   a poorly built apartment building

 💵 + **e** + 🍬   a waterway made by people

Now Showing

What historic events or places do these movie posters describe?

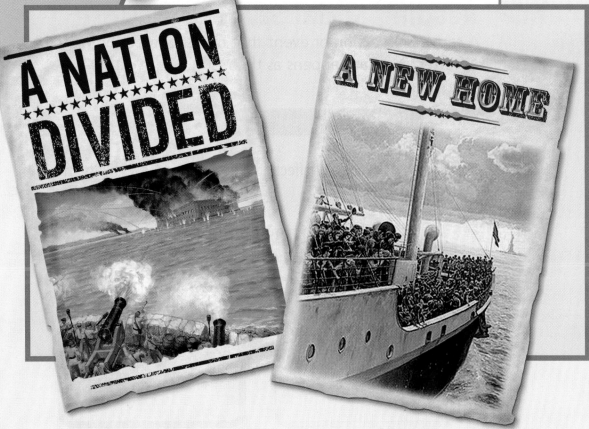

A NATION DIVIDED

A NEW HOME

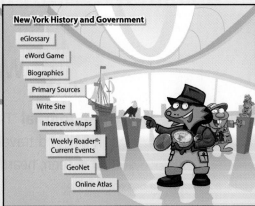

Review for Understanding

Reading Social Studies

A **cause** is an action or event that makes something happen. An **effect** is what happens as the result of the cause.

 Cause and Effect

1. Complete this cause-and-effect graphic organizer to show that you understand immigration.

Immigration

| Immigrants came to New York City | ➡ | |

 Write About the Big Idea

2. **Write a Journal** Think about what it might have been like to leave your home and travel to a new country in the late 1800s. What might you have seen, heard, and done? Write a journal entry detailing the experience.

Vocabulary and Main Idea

Write a sentence to answer each question.

3. Why did New Yorkers want to build a **canal** to connect New York City to the Great Lakes?

4. In what ways did **abolitionists** work for reform?

5. Why did the southern states want to **secede** in 1861?

6. How did **discrimination** affect many immigrants?

7. Name three **ethnic groups** that settled in New York City.

8. Why did some workers go on **strike** in the early 1900s?

Critical Thinking

Write a short paragraph to answer each question.

9. **Draw Conclusions** Why did many southerners want slavery to continue?

10. **Summarize** Describe the growth of New York City in the late 1800s and early 1900s.

Apply Skills

Read each source below. Use what you have learned to answer each question.

July 21st. After fighting all day, the Union soldiers came running back to Washington. I was amazed. Now people are saying that the war will last a long time.

On July 21, 1861, one of the first major battles of the Civil War took place at Bull Run in Virginia.

11. What clue word tells you that the writer of one of the quotes was part of the event?

   A. I
   B. people
   C. first
   D. battles

12. Which quote is probably from a secondary source?

   A. quote 1
   B. quote 2
   C. both
   D. neither

Unit 5 Activities

 ## Unit Writing Activity

Write a Report Work with a classmate to interview someone about his or her immigrant experience, or the immigrant experience of one of his or her ancestors.

■ Write a list of questions to ask the person you will be interviewing.

■ Take notes and use them to write a report about the experiences of the immigrant.

 ## Unit Project

Create a 3-D Timeline Work in a group to create a three-dimensional timeline of the history of New York City in the 1800s and 1900s.

■ Choose five events from the unit to show on your timeline.

■ Write the dates and captions for the events on large cards.

■ Tape the timeline to the floor, and use art materials to build three-dimensional models to illustrate the events.

Read More

■ *A Picnic in October* by Eve Bunting. Harcourt.
■ *The Brooklyn Bridge: A Wonders of the World Book* by Elizabeth Mann. Mikaya Press.
■ *Journey to Ellis Island: How My Father Came to America* by Carol Bierman. Hyperion/Madison.

 visit www.eduplace.com/nycssp/

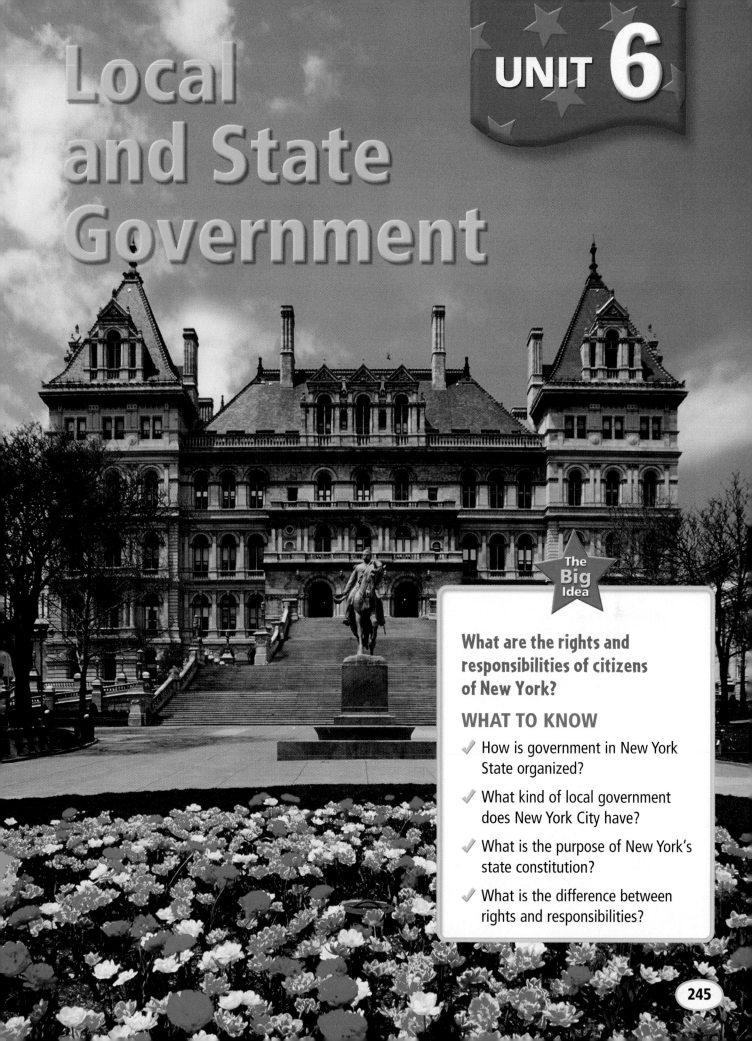

Local and State Government

The Big Idea

What are the rights and responsibilities of citizens of New York?

WHAT TO KNOW

✔ How is government in New York State organized?

✔ What kind of local government does New York City have?

✔ What is the purpose of New York's state constitution?

✔ What is the difference between rights and responsibilities?

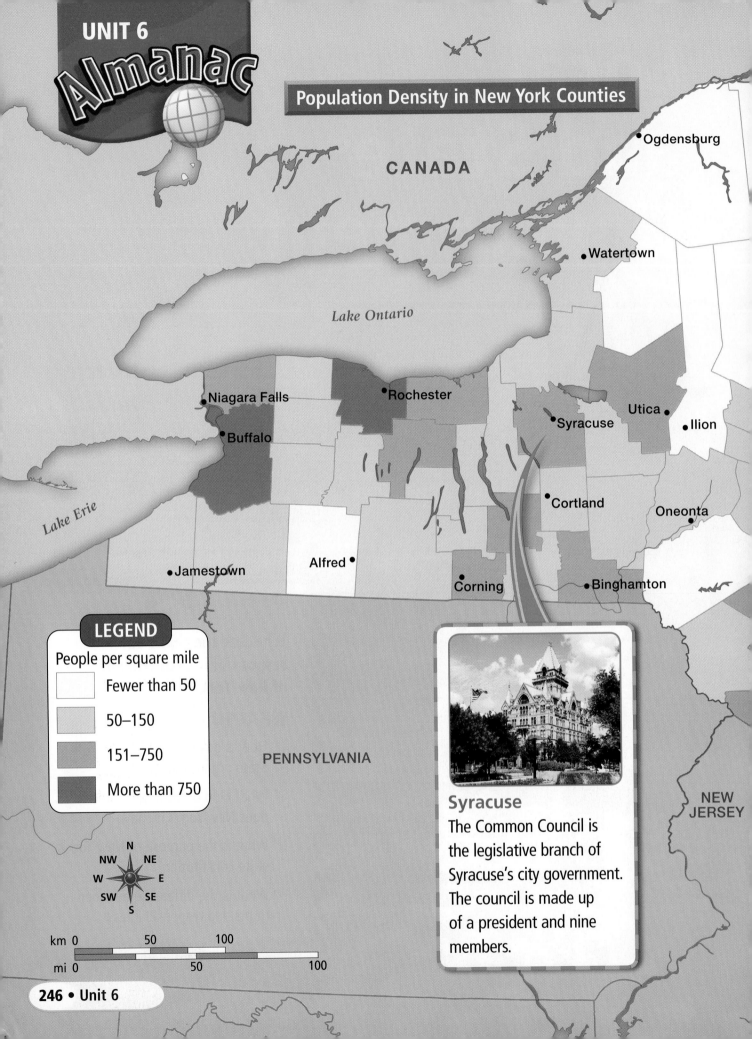

UNIT 6
Almanac

Population Density in New York Counties

CANADA

•Ogdensburg

•Watertown

Lake Ontario

•Niagara Falls

•Rochester

•Syracuse

Utica•

•Ilion

•Buffalo

Lake Erie

•Cortland

Oneonta•

•Jamestown

Alfred •

•Corning

•Binghamton

LEGEND

People per square mile

	Fewer than 50
	50–150
	151–750
	More than 750

PENNSYLVANIA

NEW JERSEY

N
NW — NE
W — E
SW — SE
S

km 0   50   100
mi 0   50   100

Syracuse
The Common Council is the legislative branch of Syracuse's city government. The council is made up of a president and nine members.

VERMONT

- Lake Placid
- Glens Falls
- Schenectady
- ★ Albany
- Poughkeepsie
- New York City

NEW HAMPSHIRE

MASSACHUSETTS

RHODE ISLAND

CONNECTICUT

Albany

New York State's government meets in Albany.

New York City

New York City is the largest city in New York State and in the United States.

ATLANTIC OCEAN

New York City

New York City Land Area

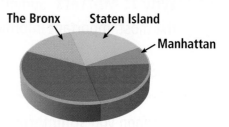

The Bronx   Staten Island

Manhattan

The area of New York City is 303 square miles.

Queens	109 sq. mi
Brooklyn	71 sq. mi
Staten Island	58 sq. mi
The Bronx	42 sq. mi
Manhattan	23 sq. mi

New York City Population, 2006

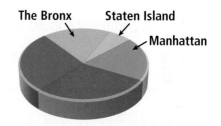

The Bronx   Staten Island

Manhattan

The population of New York City is 8,250,567 people.

Brooklyn	2,523,047 people
Queens	2,264,661 people
Manhattan	1,612,630 people
The Bronx	1,371,353 people
Staten Island	478,876 people

Compare Manhattan and Staten Island in both area and population. Which borough has higher population density?

Reading Social Studies

⊙ Summarize

Why It Matters Summarizing can help you understand and remember the most important information in a paragraph or passage.

Learn the Skill

When you **summarize** information, you give a short description in your own words about what you have read.

```
┌──────────────────────┐
│  Important fact from  │  ⟹
│     the reading       │        ┌──────────────┐
└──────────────────────┘        │              │
                                 │   Summary    │
┌──────────────────────┐        │              │
│  Important fact from  │  ⟹    └──────────────┘
│     the reading       │
└──────────────────────┘
```

- A summary should only include the most important ideas.
- Always use your own words when you summarize.

Practice the Skill

Read the paragraphs below. Write a summary for the second one.

Facts There are many museums in New York City, but the largest one is the Metropolitan Museum of Art. The Met, as it is often called, opened in 1872.

Summary (The Metropolitan Museum of Art, which opened in 1872, is the largest museum in New York City.)

New York City has several baseball and football teams, but only one basketball team—the New York Knicks. The Knicks were started in 1946. They have many fans across the country.

Apply the Skill

Read the paragraphs, and answer the questions.

The New York Public Library

The New York Public Library is one of the world's best-known library systems. It is made up of nearly 90 libraries spread across Manhattan, the Bronx, and Staten Island. Its collections include books, videos, compact discs, maps, and more. The library has more than 50 million items in its collections.

It does not cost anything to check items out of the library. However, the library still needs to buy new materials, pay its employees, and keep up its branches. Part of the money that keeps the library running comes from donations. In 1886, Samuel J. Tilden, a former governor of New York, donated more than two million dollars to help start the library.

Most of the New York Public Library's money comes from taxes paid by New Yorkers. They include taxes on property, taxes on what people earn, sales taxes, and others. For example, when you buy a book, you pay a sales tax. Every year, all the money from taxes is collected and put into a fund. The money in this fund is used to pay for all city services, including the library.

Summarize

1. How is the New York Public Library organized?

2. What role do donations have in supporting the library?

3. How do taxes New Yorkers pay help the library?

New York Government

City Hall, New York City

Study Skills

SKIM AND SCAN

Skimming and scanning are tools that help you quickly learn the main ideas of a lesson.

- To skim, quickly read the lesson title and the section titles. Look at the visuals, or images, and read the captions. Use this information to identify the main topics.

- To scan, look quickly through the text for specific details, such as key words or facts.

SKIM	SCAN
Lesson Title: New York City's Government	**Key Words and Facts:** • New York City has five boroughs: the Bronx, Brooklyn, Manhattan, Queens, and Staten Island.
Main Idea: New York City's mayor and city council work together to govern the five boroughs.	
Section Titles: City Leaders; Serving the City	• The mayor creates the city's budget.
Visuals: A Growing Borough; City Hall	

Vocabulary Preview

legislative branch

New York State's **legislative branch** includes members of the Senate and the Assembly. These leaders make laws for the whole state. **page 255**

judicial branch

Judges are leaders of New York's **judicial branch.** They make decisions about whether laws have been followed. **page 255**

Reading Strategy

Question Use this strategy as you read the lessons in this chapter. Stop and ask yourself questions. Do you need to go back and reread?

executive branch

The governor is the head of New York State's **executive branch.** This leader carries out laws for the state.
page 255

budget

New York City's leaders meet to agree on a **budget.** The budget tells how they will spend the money the city collects.
page 261

 visit www.eduplace.com/nycssp/

Branches of Government

WHAT TO KNOW
How is government in New York State organized?

VOCABULARY

legislative branch
executive branch
judicial branch
checks and balances
mayor

READING SKILL
Summarize List facts you can use to summarize how New York's government works.

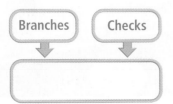

Branches   Checks

Before You Read You know that on a sports team, different players work together. Everyone follows the game's rules. Citizens also need to work together and follow the rules to create a fair government.

The State Constitution

Main Idea The United States Constitution and New York's constitution are alike in many ways.

The United States Constitution and New York's constitution share many things. Each describes how to organize government. They both give people the right to choose their leaders. People do this by voting. To vote is to make an official choice. Both constitutions also have a Bill of Rights that lists rights and freedoms. New York's constitution is also like the United States Constitution in the way it divides the government into three branches.

A Law for Everyone New York's constitution unites its diverse population under one government.

New York's Three Branches of Government

Legislative Branch
Assembly members make laws.

Executive Branch
The governor's office makes sure laws are enforced.

Judicial Branch
Justices on the Court of Appeals decide questions about laws.

SKILL Reading Charts What branch of government enforces laws?

State Leaders

The New York State government is made up of three branches, or parts. The **legislative branch** is responsible for making state laws. New York's legislative branch includes two groups of representatives: the Senate and the Assembly. The senators and assembly members discuss and pass the laws that affect everyone in the state.

Another branch in the state government is the executive branch. The **executive branch** is responsible for enforcing, or carrying out, the state's laws. The governor is the head of the executive branch. The governor has the power to approve new laws. He or she can also veto, or reject, laws.

The judicial branch is the third part of New York's government. The **judicial branch** makes decisions about the meaning of laws and whether laws have been followed. Judges, or justices, lead this branch. There are many courts in New York's judicial system, but the Court of Appeals is the highest court.

New York's constitution gives each branch of government different powers so that they can watch over each other. This system, called **checks and balances,** keeps any one branch from becoming too powerful.

✓ READING CHECK SUMMARIZE What is the job of the legislative branch?

Local Governments

Main Idea Local governments make laws and provide services in New York communities.

New Yorkers depend on local governments to run their cities, towns, and counties. Local governments pay for police and fire protection. They often run schools, hospitals, libraries, and parks.

Like the state government, local governments have many parts. Most city governments are led by an elected mayor and a council. A **mayor** is an elected official that leads a city. Other officials, such as city managers, are chosen by elected leaders to help run the government.

In city governments, the mayor acts as the executive branch and the city council acts as the legislative branch. The mayor leads the city council and plans how the city will spend money. The council approves the spending plan and makes new city laws.

Another kind of local government is the county government. County governments make decisions about matters that affect the whole county, such as fixing roads between cities. New York State is divided into 62 counties. Many counties are governed by a group of officials called a board of supervisors. Voters in a county elect representatives to serve on the board.

SKILL Reading Maps What county is farthest west?

New York Counties

Special Districts

States also have types of local government called special districts. A district is a single part of a city or other geographic area. Special districts are set up to provide government services to one or more counties in the state. Special districts in New York include court districts, voting districts, and school districts.

School districts in New York are organized by county. Voters in each school district elect school board members. Unlike the rest of the state, New York City does not have a school board. Its schools are run by a department of education.

READING CHECK SUMMARIZE What are special districts?

School Districts New York State has nearly 700 school districts.

SUMMARY

New York's constitution organizes the state government into three branches. Each branch has its own jobs to do. Local governments provide services for their residents.

Lesson Review

❶ **WHAT TO KNOW** How is government in New York State organized?

❷ **VOCABULARY** Fill in the blank with the words that best complete the sentence.

judicial branch   checks and balances

executive branch

New York's state courts make up the

_____.

❸ **CRITICAL THINKING: Draw Conclusions** Why do you think the executive branch is not allowed to make laws?

❹ **ART ACTIVITY** Use the Internet or library resources to find out about the people who work for your county. Then make an information pamphlet for people who are new to your county.

❺ **READING SKILL** Complete the graphic organizer to summarize information.

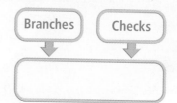

Branches   Checks

Organizing Government

When you have a tough task, sometimes it helps to share it with others. Governing a country as large and varied as the United States is a big job. To make it easier, the work is divided among national, state, and local governments. Those levels are also divided into different branches. Each branch can limit the power of the others. With the work divided, the government can do its many jobs, and no single part has all the power.

National and State Governments

Important Jobs The state and national governments each do important work for the people of New York. Look at the diagram to see which jobs the state has.

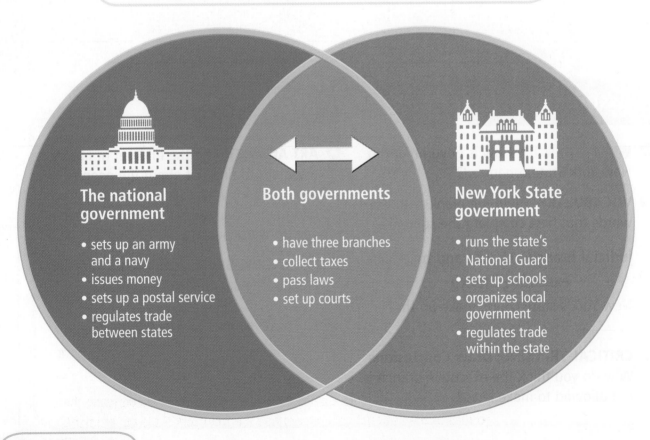

The national government

- sets up an army and a navy
- issues money
- sets up a postal service
- regulates trade between states

Both governments

- have three branches
- collect taxes
- pass laws
- set up courts

New York State government

- runs the state's National Guard
- sets up schools
- organizes local government
- regulates trade within the state

Checks and Balances

Sharing Power This diagram shows some of the ways that each branch of New York's state government can limit the power of the other two branches.

The governor approves or vetoes laws passed by the state legislature.

If two-thirds of the Senate and State Assembly agree, the state legislature can pass a law even if the governor has vetoed it.

The governor chooses the judges for the state's court system.

The Court of Appeals can declare the governor's actions unconstitutional.

Governor

State Legislature

Court of Appeals

The state Senate must approve the judges chosen by the governor.

The Court of Appeals can declare a law passed by New York's legislature unconstitutional.

Activities

1. **THINK ABOUT IT** With a partner, think up a motto or slogan for New York's state government that says something important about its system of three branches.

2. **WRITE ABOUT IT** Write a paragraph about the similarities between the duties of the national government and the New York State government.

New York City's Government

▶ **WHAT TO KNOW**
What kind of local government does New York City have?

▶ **VOCABULARY**
borough
budget

◎ **READING SKILL**
Categorize As you read, list information about two city officials.

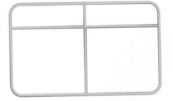

A Growing Borough
Brooklyn is home to more people than any other New York City borough.

Before You Read The clubs at your school need leaders to organize and make their group the best it can be. New York also has leaders who help the city meet the challenges every big city faces.

City Leaders

Main Idea New York City's mayor and city council work together to govern the five boroughs.

New York City is home to more than eight million people. It is the largest city in the United States. With so many people living there, New York City's government has a huge job.

New York City officials work together to govern the city's five boroughs. A **borough** is an area of a city with its own leaders. New York City's boroughs are the Bronx, Brooklyn, Manhattan, Queens, and Staten Island.

City Hall This building in Manhattan is home to New York City's executive and legislative branches.

Serving the City

Cities, towns, and counties use different types of local government to meet their needs. New York City has a mayor-council form of government. City residents elect a mayor every four years. The mayor of New York City is in charge of the executive branch. Leaders of the city's departments, such as the parks commission and the police department, are chosen by the mayor.

The mayor creates the city's budget for the year. A **budget** is a spending plan that shows how much money the city has and how that money will be spent. The mayor writes the budget to show how the city will provide services to its citizens. It is also the mayor's job to approve laws passed by the city council.

The city council is the city's legislative branch. It represents people from all areas of New York City. Fifty-one men and women are on the city council, one for each of the city's council districts.

Members of the city council make laws and important decisions that affect the lives of New Yorkers. The city council must approve the mayor's budget. It also decides how the city's land should be used. The city council makes laws that say where people can build new homes and businesses. Making sure that people in New York receive important services, such as recycling and trash collection, is another job of the city council.

✓ **READING CHECK** CATEGORIZE What jobs do the mayor and city council both work on?

Breaking Ground In 2006, Bronx Borough President Alfonso Carríon, Jr., (right) was joined by the mayor, the governor, and the owner of the New York Yankees to break ground for a new Yankee Stadium in the Bronx.

New York City Officials

Main Idea Many officials help New York City run smoothly.

A large number of officials share the job of governing New York City. Their work makes it possible for the government to offer services that support and protect New Yorkers.

The comptroller keeps track of New York City's money and makes sure it is spent wisely. The public advocate heads the city council and runs its meetings. When city council members cannot agree, the public advocate helps them make a decision.

The five boroughs each elect their own city officials, too. These officials are called borough presidents.

Borough presidents help the mayor make the city budget. Each borough president also appoints people to the borough's community board. This board gives the borough president advice about using land and improving services.

One government service New Yorkers use every day is transportation. The city provides its citizens with buses and subways so that people can move quickly around the city. New York City also supports public libraries. The city has more than 80 public libraries that loan books, magazines, and newspapers.

Many New Yorkers depend on city health services to keep them safe and well. Community clinics provide affordable medicine and health advice. New York City's fire departments and police departments assist people during emergencies. They also teach safety to help citizens avoid fire and crime.

Paying for Services

It costs New York City a lot of money to offer so many services to its residents. The government collects taxes from citizens to pay for the services. People pay part of what they earn to the city. They also pay a sales tax. That is money that the city collects when you buy a book, a baseball, or other goods. The New York City government also collects taxes from the sale of land in the city.

✓ READING CHECK MAIN IDEA AND DETAILS
What are two sources of money for New York City's government?

SUMMARY

The mayor and city council run New York's local government. They work with borough presidents and other officials to offer services to citizens. The government collects taxes to pay for the services it provides.

Supporting Services The sales tax paid on goods bought in New York City helps bring in money for local services such as schools, roads, and police.

Lesson Review

❶ **WHAT TO KNOW** What kind of local government does New York City have?

❷ **VOCABULARY** Write a short paragraph explaining what a city **budget** is used for.

❸ **CRITICAL THINKING: Evaluate** Which government official do you think has the most important job in New York City? Why?

❹ **SPEAKING ACTIVITY** What service would you like that New York City does not offer? Prepare a speech that tells what service you need and why. Explain how the city could pay for it.

❺  **READING SKILL** Complete the graphic organizer to categorize information.

New York Leaders

In a democracy, when people want to make a difference, they can. For many years, however, not everyone was allowed to take part in our government. Brave individuals have stepped up to change that. Here are some pioneer public officials from the Empire State who took that bold first step.

Herman Badillo

Herman Badillo knows a lot about running. Badillo has run the New York City marathon more than ten times! As a leader, Badillo runs for office. In 1970, he became the nation's first member of Congress to have been born in Puerto Rico. He has also served as the Bronx Borough President and as deputy mayor of New York City.

Betty W. Ellerin

In 1985, Ellerin became the first woman to serve on New York's Supreme Court. Fourteen years later, she was the first woman to serve as head justice of the court. By the time Ellerin retired, she had received many awards, and even had one award named for her.

Fiorello Raffaele La Guardia

La Guardia was the first Italian American elected to the United States Congress. He was later elected mayor of New York City. As mayor, La Guardia became famous for helping the city build tunnels and bridges. He also raised money for schools, hospitals, parks, and highways. One of New York City's airports is named after him.

Constance Baker Motley

When she was young, Constance Baker Motley was once turned away from a public beach because of her skin color. She didn't let that treatment discourage her, though. In 1964, Motley became the first black woman elected to the New York Senate. She was also the first black woman to become a United States judge.

Activities

1. **TALK ABOUT IT** To which branch of government does each leader belong?

2. **RESEARCH IT** Research one of the leaders in this feature to learn about his or her accomplishments. Prepare an outline that organizes the information you gather.

Skillbuilder

Make Decisions

▶ **VOCABULARY**
consequence

The government makes decisions that affect your school. All decisions have consequences. A **consequence** is an effect. You also can make decisions that affect what happens in your school. When you make a decision, try to spend time thinking it through.

Learn the Skill

Step 1: Identify the problem and decision that you must make.

Step 2: Think of all of the possible decisions you could make to solve your problem. Remember to respect other people's ideas, even if you disagree with them.

Step 3: Think about the consequences of each decision. It is important that you think about both the good and the bad consequences, so you make the most informed decision.

Step 4: Make your decision by choosing the option that best helps you reach your goal. Then take action to meet that goal.

Decision to be made:
How do we get more computers in the school library?

Option 1:
Write an assembly member to see if we can get money from the state.

Option 2:
Raise money ourselves.

Consequences:
Learn more about state government.

Our school would have to be chosen to get the money.

Consequences:
It would take a lot of work.

It would be quicker.

Final Decision:
Raise the money ourselves.

Practice the Skill

Think about the decision you made to bring your lunch today or to buy your lunch at school. How did you make that decision? What things did you think about?

Apply the Skill

Choose an issue that the people in your school must make a decision about. It might be a decision students have to make, or it might be a decision parents and teachers have to make. Use the steps you have learned to think about all of the choices and each choice's consequences. Then write a paragraph about your decision and why you made it.

Visual Summary

1–3. ✏️ Write a description for each item below.

State Government

_____
_____
_____
_____

Local Government

_____
_____
_____
_____

New York City Government

_____
_____
_____
_____

Facts and Main Ideas

Answer each question below.

4. **History** What system was created to make sure a government branch does not get too much power?

5. **Government** What is the highest court in New York State?

6. **Government** Who are the city officials responsible for governing New York City?

7. **Government** Which branch of state government includes the Senate and the Assembly?

8. **Government** Which group of city officials appoints members to community boards?

Vocabulary

Choose the correct word from the list below to complete each sentence.

judicial branch, p. 255
mayor, p. 256
borough, p. 260

9. The _____ makes decisions about laws.

10. In New York City, the _____ leads the city government.

11. Each _____ of New York City has its own president.

Make Decisions Read the paragraph below. Then use what you have learned about making a decision to answer each question.

> Mike Johnson has moved to New York City. A few months ago, he registered to vote. Now Mike is deciding whether to vote for Jan Rivera or Ted Thompson.

12. Mike needs more information. Which of the following could best help Mike decide for whom to vote?

   A. learning what Rivera and Thompson want for the city

   B. talking to a worker for Rivera

   C. talking to a worker for Thompson

   D. asking his neighbors who they plan to vote for

13. Rivera wants to raise taxes to build bike paths. What would be a consequence if Rivera won the election?

   A. Mike could not ride his bike to work.

   B. Mike would probably pay more taxes.

   C. More cars would be on city streets.

   D. Parking places for cars would be hard to find.

Write a short paragraph to answer each question below.

14. **Compare and Contrast** How is New York City's government similar to and different from other city governments?

15. **Analyze** Why is it important for each borough to have its own president?

Activities

HANDS ON

Art Activity Design a bulletin board that teaches about the duties of New York City officials, such as the mayor, comptroller, public advocate, and borough president.

Writing Activity Write a letter to the governor about services provided by the state that are important to you and your family.

Go Digital Get help with your writing at www.eduplace.com/nycssp/

Citizenship

Flag Day Parade, City Hall Park, New York City

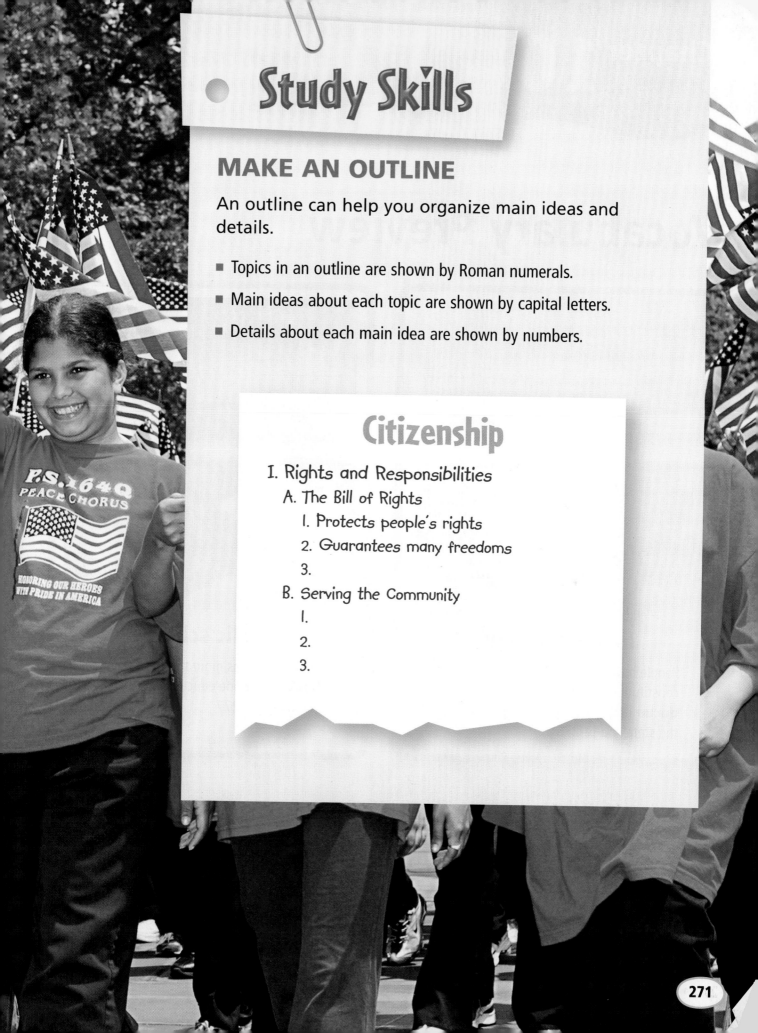

Study Skills

MAKE AN OUTLINE

An outline can help you organize main ideas and details.

- Topics in an outline are shown by Roman numerals.
- Main ideas about each topic are shown by capital letters.
- Details about each main idea are shown by numbers.

Citizenship

I. Rights and Responsibilities
  A. The Bill of Rights
    1. Protects people's rights
    2. Guarantees many freedoms
    3.
  B. Serving the Community
    1.
    2.
    3.

Vocabulary Preview

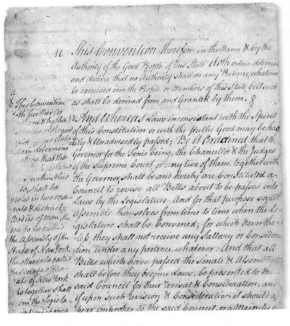

living document

People have amended New York's constitution many times. It is a **living document** because it changes along with the state. **page 276**

public schools

New York City has more than 1,000 **public schools** to provide education to the city's children. **page 277**

Reading Strategy

Summarize Use this strategy to help you understand important information in this chapter. Note the most important information and then put it into your own words.

responsibility

When you have a **responsibility,** people depend on you. Without responsible citizens, rules and laws would not be followed. **page 281**

patriotism

Patriotism is love for one's country. The flag is a symbol of patriotism. **page 283**

Go Digital visit www.eduplace.com/nycssp/

273

New York's Constitution

1777–Today

▶ **WHAT TO KNOW**
What is the purpose of New York's state constitution?

▶ **VOCABULARY**
living document
public school

⊘ **READING SKILL**
Compare and Contrast
As you read, list similarities and differences between New York's constitution and the United States Constitution.

New York constitution	United States Constitution

Before You Read How do you know how to behave in class? Your teacher might have a list of rules for everyone to follow. The people of New York follow rules, too. The rules are set by the state government.

A Plan for Government

Main Idea New York's constitution shares many of the ideas found in the United States Constitution.

Constitutions are documents people create to organize governments. The United States has a constitution with rules for the national government. Each state has a constitution for its own government, too. New York's current constitution was adopted in 1894. It was revised, or changed, in 1938.

State constitutions share many rules and ideas with the United States Constitution. For example, all states divide their government into different branches. The branches work together to keep the state safe and orderly, and to solve problems.

New York Constitution
The state's first constitution was written in 1777.

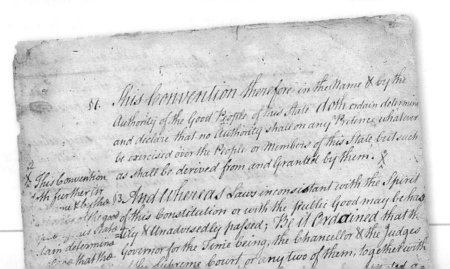

New York State Capitol Leaders of the state government meet in this building in Albany.

Government in Action

New York's constitution calls for a legislative branch to write the state's laws. The legislative branch is made up of the State Assembly and the Senate. The Assembly has 150 members. There are 62 people in the Senate.

The governor, who runs the executive branch, carries out the laws passed by the legislature. He or she also manages departments, such as the state police.

The judicial branch is made up of courts and judges that make sure state laws are followed. One court decides what should happen when people break laws. Another court, the Civil Court, handles arguments between people over money and property.

Safeguarding Liberties

Like the national constitution, the New York constitution protects the liberties New Yorkers enjoy each day. It promises adult citizens of the state the right to vote. It says that people can follow any religion they choose, or none at all.

The state constitution also protects people's freedom to write and say what they want. It protects the right to speak out against the government if people disagree with it. If people are accused of breaking the law, the constitution guarantees them a fair trial.

✓ READING CHECK COMPARE AND CONTRAST
Which branch of the state government makes sure state laws are followed?

A Living Document

Main Idea The constitution changes over time as the state changes.

As time passes, the things people need or expect from government can change. Laws that were written hundreds of years ago may no longer be useful. New Yorkers add amendments to the state constitution to change it.

New York's constitution has been amended many times. For example, some amendments have changed the terms of office for senators and other leaders. Others have protected rights. Because amendments change the meaning of the constitution, it continues to grow. For this reason, people call New York's constitution a **living document.**

Voting on Change New York's citizens help decide whether amendments are added to the state constitution by voting for or against them.

Amendments to the Constitution

One way to change the constitution is for the state legislature to suggest an amendment. The Senate and the Assembly must then approve the amendment. A convention can also be called to amend, or change, the constitution. Amendments proposed by conventions must be approved by New York voters. As New York's constitution has grown and changed, more people have been included as participants in government. Today, all adult citizens are guaranteed the right to vote.

1801	Number of state senators increased from 24 to 32.
1821	Voting rights extended to male citizens over the age of 21 who owned property, were in the military, or worked on highways.
1846	The terms of senators changed from four years to two.
1894	Present state constitution adopted.
1938	Women take part in New York's constitutional convention for the first time.

Amendments to the Constitution This chart shows how New York's government has changed over time.

Government Makes a Difference

Life in New York would be very different without a constitution or a government to make laws and provide services. There would be no state police officers to keep the peace or enforce laws. Streets and parks would get dirty without public workers to clean them. There also would be no public schools. **Public schools** are schools provided by the government.

Taking care of New York and its citizens is a big job. Government leaders must work with residents and organizations to make New York a healthy and safe place to live.

✓ READING CHECK DRAW CONCLUSIONS Why are governments necessary?

SUMMARY

New York's constitution organizes the state's government and protects individual liberties. The constitution is a living document that can be amended. New York needs a government to provide services and keep people safe.

Education State government helps organize New York's education system.

Lesson Review

1777 New York's first constitution

1894 New York's current constitution

| 1750 | 1800 | 1850 | 1900 |

1 **WHAT TO KNOW** What is the purpose of New York's state constitution?

2 **VOCABULARY** Use **living document** in a sentence about New York's constitution.

3 **TIMELINE SKILL** How many years before the adoption of the current New York Constitution was the state's first constitution written?

4 **RESEARCH ACTIVITY** Research the history of an amendment to New York's constitution. Find out why people wanted it. Write a brief summary of what you find.

5 **READING SKILL** Complete the graphic organizer to compare and contrast information.

New York constitution	United States Constitution

Graph and Chart Skills

Read a Table

When learning about a subject, such as the government, you might want to put information in a table. A table is a type of chart in which facts are organized in columns and rows. Tables make it easier to find and remember information.

▶ **VOCABULARY**
table

Learn the Skill

Step 1: Read the title to learn what the whole table shows.

Step 2: Look at how the table is set up. In this table, the information is arranged in columns and rows. You can see that each column has a heading. The headings name two types of information.

Step 3: Read down a column to find information about that heading. Read across each row to put together the information in the columns. Each row in the table below gives information about a change made to New York's constitution.

Amendments to the New York State Constitution

Year of Change	Effect of the Change
1821	Male citizens 21 and older who owned property, had served in the military, or had worked on highways were allowed to vote.
1846	Senators' terms changed from four years to two years.

Practice the Skill

Use the table on page 278 to answer these questions.

1 Whose voting rights were protected beginning in 1821?

2 In what year were senators' terms changed to two years?

3 How many years were senators allowed to serve before 1846?

Apply the Skill

Read this paragraph about amendments made to the Constitution of the United States. Write the information as it would appear in a table like the one on page 278.

The Constitution of the United States has been amended 27 times. Many amendments have had important effects on people's lives. For example, the Thirteenth Amendment ended slavery in the United States. It was passed in 1865, at the end of the Civil War. In 1920, the Nineteenth Amendment guaranteed women's right to vote. With these amendments, more people were protected by the Constitution.

Rights and Responsibilities

▶ **WHAT TO KNOW**
What is the difference between rights and responsibilities?

▶ **VOCABULARY**
responsibility
citizenship
patriotism

READING SKILL
Main Idea and Details As you read, list one right of a citizen in each of the circles below.

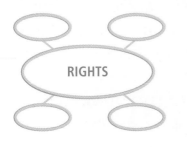

RIGHTS

Before You Read Have you ever elected a class president? Choosing a class president is practicing your right and duty as a member of a class.

The Bill of Rights

Main Idea The Bill of Rights helps protect people's rights.

People in the United States often say they live in a free country. What they mean is that our government works to protect our rights. The early leaders of our country believed that these rights were very important. They added the Bill of Rights to the Constitution to make sure people's rights were protected.

The Bill of Rights guarantees many freedoms. One is the freedom of speech. Americans have the right to express their opinions, even if they disagree with something our government has done. The Bill of Rights also protects freedom of religion.

Taking Part Students from Auburn hold a convention, or gathering, to elect student government leaders.

Trial by Jury
Trials in New York have either six or twelve jurors who serve on a jury.

Judge

Jurors

Knowing About Rights

Students and adults have rights. One of students' most important rights is the right to a good education. New York law says that all students may attend school from age 5 until they graduate from high school or turn 21.

Students also have a right to equal opportunities. Until 1972, girls did not have the same opportunity as boys to play sports in school. Today, laws protect the rights of both girls and boys to play sports in public schools.

People age 18 and older have the right to vote in elections. Adults also have a right to equal job opportunities. This means that everyone who has the skills for a job has an equal chance to be hired. Adults who are accused of crimes have a right to a trial by jury. A jury is a group of citizens chosen to decide whether a law has been broken.

Knowing Our Responsibilities

United States citizens enjoy many rights. They also have responsibilities. A **responsibility** is a duty. Citizens have the responsibility to obey the law and to participate in government.

Adult citizens can participate in many ways. They can vote. They pay taxes so that the government has money for services. They can serve on a jury when asked.

All citizens, even those too young to vote, can participate in government. They can work to change laws. All citizens have the responsibility to respect other people and other people's property. No one should take something that belongs to another person without permission.

✓ READING CHECK MAIN IDEA AND DETAILS
What is one right protected by the Bill of Rights?

281

Serving the Community

Main Idea Good citizens help their communities.

Governments and communities work best when citizens help others. People who do this show good citizenship. **Citizenship** is being a citizen and working for the common good. Doing things that improve a community is called community service. Picking up litter around your neighborhood or schoolyard is one example of a community service.

Adults can volunteer, or work without pay, at schools. Some adults, such as firefighters and police officers, work in jobs that help and protect the people in the community.

Good Citizens of New York City

In 2007, the New York Junior League helped fix up Seward Park, which needed many repairs. People in the community joined in the effort. Now Seward Park is a safe, fun, and beautiful place for kids to learn and play.

When the World Trade Center in New York City was attacked by enemies of the United States on September 11, 2001, the citizens of New York came together to help the victims and their families. **Rudy Giuliani,** the New York mayor at that time, said that he remembers how that day

66 brought about . . . acts of courage, generosity, decency, [and] unity. 99

Good Citizens After September 11, 2001, people from New York and across the country prepared food for rescue workers.

Celebrating Your Country

Good citizenship includes celebrating national holidays. On these days, citizens remember events and people important to the country. Citizens show patriotism during holidays. **Patriotism** is when a person shows his or her love for a country.

Most people do not go to school or work on the ten federal holidays. On other special days, such as Patriot Day, people usually do not take a day off. Patriot Day began because of the events on September 11, 2001. On this day, all United States citizens remember the people who died in these attacks and the people who worked to save them.

✔ **READING CHECK** MAIN IDEA AND DETAILS
What are three ways people can be good citizens?

Federal Holidays	
New Year's Day	January 1
Martin Luther King Jr. Day	third Monday in January
Presidents' Day	third Monday in February
Memorial Day	last Monday in May
Independence Day	July 4
Labor Day	first Monday in September
Columbus Day	second Monday in October
Veterans Day	November 11
Thanksgiving Day	fourth Thursday in November
Christmas Day	December 25

SUMMARY

All citizens have rights and responsibilities. By helping others, people can be good citizens. The government in the United States works best when citizens practice their responsibilities and respect each other's rights.

Lesson Review

❶ **WHAT TO KNOW** What is the difference between rights and responsibilities?

❷ **VOCABULARY** Use the word **citizenship** in a sentence about community service.

❸ **MAIN IDEA** What freedom in the Bill of Rights allows people to express their opinions?

❹ **DRAMA ACTIVITY** Work with a partner to create a skit about a person who practices good citizenship skills and a person who does not.

❺ **READING SKILL** Complete the graphic organizer to show the main idea and details.

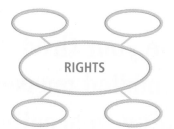

RIGHTS

National Symbols

★ ★ ★ ★ ★ ★ ★ ★ ★ ★ ★

Americans often feel proud when they see the stars and stripes of the United States flag waving high overhead. The flag and other national symbols make Americans think about the important ideas our nation represents. These ideas include freedom, democracy, and civil rights.

★ The Statue of Liberty ★

The people of the United States received the Statue of Liberty as a gift from the people of France in 1885. For millions of immigrants arriving in New York, "Lady Liberty" was the first thing they saw. It suggested they could find freedom and opportunity in America. The words below are engraved at the base of the statue.

> **"Give me your tired, your poor, Your huddled masses yearning to breathe free. . . ."**
>
> — from "The New Colossus" by Emma Lazarus

★ The Eagle ★

The Bald Eagle is our national bird. It symbolizes courage, strength, and independence. The eagle appears on coins and paper money, and also on the Great Seal of the United States. On the seal, an eagle holds an olive branch and an arrow in its left and right claws. The olive branch is a symbol of peace and the arrows symbolize strength in war.

★ The Flag of the United States ★

The nation's first official flag was created in 1777. It had 13 red and white stripes to stand for the 13 colonies that formed the United States. The flag also had 13 white stars on a blue background. Each time a new state joined the nation, a star was added. Today, the flag has 50 stars.

Look Closely The stripes on the flag have another meaning. They represent rays of light from the sun. Why do you think sunlight was chosen as a symbol?

Activities

1. **STEP INTO IT** Notice the torch in the Statue of Liberty's hand. Talk about what this shining light could mean.

2. **DRAW IT** Draw your own flag that represents New York City. Include symbols or colors that represent something important about the city.

 Visit Education Place for more primary sources. www.eduplace.com/nycssp/

Visual Summary

1–3. Write a description for each item below.

New York State Constitution

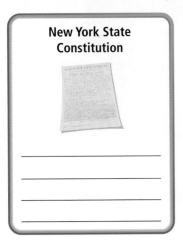

_____
_____
_____
_____

Government Services

_____
_____
_____
_____

Citizenship

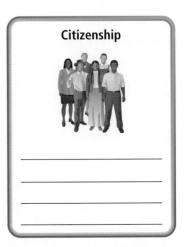

_____
_____
_____
_____

Facts and Main Ideas

Answer each question below.

4. **History** In what ways are New York's constitution and the United States Constitution similar?

5. **History** When was New York State's current constitution written?

6. **Government** Why do people describe New York's constitution as a living document?

7. **Citizenship** Name two ways a person can participate in government.

8. **Citizenship** What kinds of things can people do to help their community?

Vocabulary

Choose the correct word from the list below to complete the sentence.

public schools, p. 277
responsibility, p. 281
citizenship, p. 282

9. One _____ people have is to obey the laws in their state and country.

10. New York's government provides _____.

11. Taking part in community service shows good _____.

1777
New York's first constitution

1894
New York's current constitution

1938
New York's constitution revised

1750   1800   1850   1900   1950

Apply Skills

Read a Table Study the table below. Then use your table-reading skills to answer each question.

Citizens Take Responsibility in New York City

	Children	Adults
Right to Equality	boys and girls take equal part in sports	vote in elections
Responsibilities	attend school	serve on juries
Other Responsibilities	volunteer in the community	work in their community

12. What responsibility do adults have that children do not have?

   A. to participate in the community

   B. to attend school

   C. to serve on a jury

   D. to play sports

13. What is one responsibility children have?

   A. to vote in elections

   B. to volunteer in their community

   C. to serve on juries

   D. to stop attending school

Timeline

Use the timeline above to answer the following question.

14. How many years after New York's current constitution was adopted was it revised?

Critical Thinking

Write a short paragraph to answer each question below.

15. **Cause and Effect** What effects do amendments to the state constitution have on the document?

16. **Infer** What might happen if no one in a community practiced good citizenship?

Activities

HANDS ON **Citizenship Activity** Make a poster that shows one way you could volunteer in your community. Use words and pictures.

Writing Activity Write a persuasive essay explaining one right you believe all children should have. Give reasons for your choice.

Go Digital Get help with your writing at www.eduplace.com/nycssp/

287

Fun with Social Studies

Miss Information

New York's first constitution was written in 1777.

New York City provides many services for its citizens.

New York has three branches of government.

People age 10 and older have the right to vote in elections.

The governor is the leader of the judicial branch.

New York City is made up of three boroughs.

Miss Information is guiding a group of tourists through New York. Unfortunately, she's sharing a lot of incorrect information. Find the three mistakes.

Under Construction

abc VOCABULARY

Finish building the terms on the left by adding the word blocks on the right.

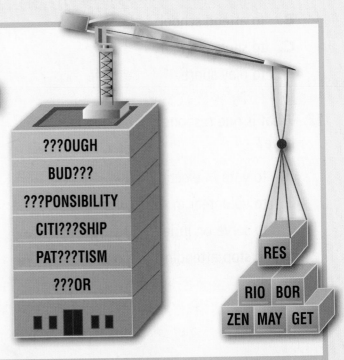

???OUGH
BUD???
???PONSIBILITY
CITI???SHIP
PAT???TISM
???OR

RES
RIO   BOR
ZEN   MAY   GET

Good Citizens

What right or responsibility is each student describing?

I am going to give a speech to my class about recycling.

I always follow traffic laws when I ride my bike.

I am going to join the girls soccer team at my school.

 Go Digital

Education Place®
www.eduplace.com

New York History and Government
- eGlossary
- eWord Game
- Biographies
- Primary Sources
- Write Site
- Interactive Maps
- Weekly Reader®: Current Events
- GeoNet
- Online Atlas

Visit Eduplace!

Log on to Eduplace to explore Social Studies online. Solve puzzles to watch the skateboarding tricks in eWord Game. Join Chester in GeoNet to see if you can earn enough points to become a GeoChampion, or just play Wacky Web Tales to see how silly your stories can get. Play now at www.eduplace.com/nycssp/

Reading Social Studies

When you **summarize** information, you give a short description in your own words about what you have read.

 Summarize

1. Complete this graphic organizer to summarize what you know about New York's government.

New York's Government

| New York City has many officials. | People participate in government. |

 Write About the Big Idea

2. **Make a Brochure** Teach others about citizenship in New York City. Create a brochure about the rights and responsibilities of New York citizens.

Vocabulary and Main Ideas

Write a sentence to answer each question.

3. What group forms New York City's **legislative branch**?

4. What is the responsibility of the **executive branch** of state government?

5. What duties do **borough** presidents have?

6. Why is it important for the **mayor** to create a yearly **budget**?

7. What can people do to practice good **citizenship** skills?

8. Name an example of **patriotism**.

Critical Thinking

Write a short answer for each question. Use details to support your answer.

9. **Summarize** Write a brief description of New York City's government and how it works.

10. **Compare and Contrast** In what ways are New York State's government and New York City's government similar, and in what ways are they different?

Apply Skills

Use the paragraph below and your decision-making skills to answer each question.

Susan wants to play soccer with her friends this afternoon. She can get a game started right after school, but she will have to do all her homework later. Or she could finish her homework first, then join the game.

11. What decision does Susan need to make?

   A. whether or not to play soccer

   B. whether or not to do homework

   C. whether to play soccer before or after doing homework

   D. whether or not to play soccer tomorrow

12. What is one consequence of Susan's playing soccer right after school?

   A. Susan will miss dinner.

   B. When she is ready to play, the game might be over.

   C. She will be finished with her homework before she plays soccer.

   D. She will have to do her homework later, and she might be tired.

Unit 6 Activities

 Unit Writing Activity

Write a Skit Write a skit in which the main characters work in different branches of the New York State government.

- There should be at least one character from each branch, such as a state senator, the governor, and a state judge.
- The characters should discuss a problem facing the state and decide how to fix it, given their different jobs.

 Unit Project

Plan a Website Work in a group to plan a website about government and citizenship.

- Organize information into categories, such as New York State's government, New York City's government, and the rights and responsibilities of citizens. These can be the pages that a computer user can link to from your home page.
- Include pictures of people, places, ideas, and events that are important in government. Visit a government website for ideas.
- Show what each page will look like.

Read More

- *Becoming a Citizen* by Sarah de Capua. Scholastic.
- *Rosy Cole's Worst Ever, Best Yet Tour of New York City* by Sheila Greenwald. Farrar/Kroupa.
- *New York* by Paige Weber. Enchanted Lion Books.

 visit www.eduplace.com/nycssp/

References

Citizenship Handbook

New York Governors R2

Primary Sources R3
   The Declaration of Independence R3
   The United States Constitution R6
   New York Constitution Excerpts R24

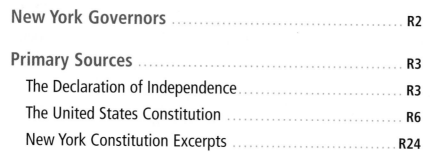

Resources

Five Themes of Geography R26

Geographic Terms R28

Atlas R30

Glossary R46

Index R50

Acknowledgments R62

New York Governors

State Governors

State Governors	Term	State Governors	Term
George Clinton	1777–1795	Grover Cleveland	1883–1884
John Jay	1795–1801	David B. Hill	1885–1891
George Clinton	1801–1804	Roswell P. Flower	1892–1894
Morgan Lewis	1804–1807	Levi P. Morton	1895–1896
Daniel D. Tompkins	1807–1817	Frank S. Black	1897–1898
John Tayler	1817	Theodore Roosevelt	1899–1900
DeWitt Clinton	1817–1822	Benjamin B. Odell, Jr.	1901–1904
Joseph C. Yates	1823–1824	Frank W. Higgins	1905–1906
DeWitt Clinton	1825–1828	Charles E. Hughes	1907–1910
Nathaniel Pitcher	1828	Horace White	1910
Martin Van Buren	1829	John Alden Dix	1911–1912
Enos T. Throop	1829–1832	William Sulzer	1913
William L. Marcy	1833–1838	Martin H. Glynn	1913–1914
William H. Seward	1839–1842	Charles S. Whitman	1915–1918
William C. Bouck	1843–1844	Alfred E. Smith	1919–1920
Silas Wright	1845–1846	Nathan L. Miller	1921–1922
John Young	1847–1848	Alfred E. Smith	1923–1928
Hamilton Fish	1849–1850	Franklin D. Roosevelt	1929–1932
Washington Hunt	1851–1852	Herbert H. Lehman	1933–1942
Horatio Seymour	1853–1854	Charles Poletti	1942
Myron H. Clark	1855–1856	Thomas E. Dewey	1943–1954
John A. King	1857–1858	W. Averall Harriman	1955–1958
Edwin D. Morgan	1859–1862	Nelson A. Rockefeller	1959–1973
Horatio Seymour	1863–1864	Malcolm Wilson	1973–1974
Reuben E. Fenton	1865–1868	Hugh L. Carey	1975–1982
John T. Hoffman	1869–1872	Mario M. Cuomo	1983–1994
John Adams Dix	1873–1874	George E. Pataki	1995–2006
Samuel J. Tilden	1875–1876	Eliot Spitzer	2007–2008
Lucius Robinson	1877–1879	David A. Paterson	2008–
Alonzo B. Cornell	1880–1882		

The Declaration of Independence

In Congress, July 4, 1776

The unanimous declaration of the thirteen United States of America

Introduction*

When, in the course of human events, it becomes necessary for one people to dissolve the political bonds which have connected them with another, and to assume, among the powers of the earth, the separate and equal station to which the laws of nature and of nature's God entitle them, a decent respect to the opinions of mankind requires that they should declare the causes which impel them to the separation.

Basic Rights

WE hold these truths to be self-evident: That all men are created equal, that they are endowed by their Creator with certain unalienable rights; that among these are life, liberty, and the pursuit of happiness; that, to secure these rights, governments are instituted among men, deriving their just powers from the consent of the governed; that whenever any form of government becomes destructive of these ends, it is the right of the people to alter or to abolish it, and to institute new government, laying its foundation on such principles, and organizing its powers in such form, as to them shall seem most likely to effect their safety and happiness. Prudence, indeed, will dictate that governments long established should not be changed for light and transient causes; and accordingly all experience hath shown that mankind are more disposed to suffer, while evils are sufferable, than to right themselves by abolishing the forms to which they are accustomed. But when a long train of abuses and usurpations, pursuing invariably the same object, evinces a design to reduce them under absolute despotism, it is their right, it is their duty, to throw off such government, and to provide new guards for their future security. Such has been the patient sufferance of these colonies; and such is now the necessity which constrains them to alter their former systems of government. The history of the present King of Great Britain is a history of repeated injuries and usurpations, all having in direct object the establishment of an absolute tyranny over these states. To prove this, let facts be submitted to a candid world.

Charges Against the King

HE has refused his assent to laws, the most wholesome and necessary for the public good.

HE has forbidden his governors to pass laws of immediate and pressing importance, unless suspended in their operation till his assent should be obtained; and, when so suspended, he has utterly neglected to attend to them.

HE has refused to pass other laws for the accommodation of large districts of people, unless those people would relinquish the right of representation in the legislature, a right inestimable to them, and formidable to tyrants only.

HE has called together legislative bodies at places unusual, uncomfortable, and distant from the depository of their public records, for the sole purpose of fatiguing them into compliance with his measures.

HE has dissolved representative houses repeatedly, for opposing, with manly firmness his invasions on the rights of the people.

*Titles have been added to the Declaration to make it easier to read. These titles are not in the original document.

In the Declaration of Independence, the colonists explained why they were breaking away from Britain. They believed they had the right to form their own country.

Members of the Continental Congress are shown signing the Declaration of Independence.

The opening part of the Declaration is very famous. It says that all people are created equal. Everyone has certain basic rights that are "unalienable." That means that these rights cannot be taken away. Governments are formed to protect these basic rights. If a government does not do this, then the people have a right to begin a new one.

Forming a new government meant ending the colonial ties to the king. The writers of the Declaration listed the wrongs of King George III to prove the need for their actions.

Colonists said the king had not let the colonies make their own laws. He had limited the people's representation in their assemblies.

The king had made colonial assemblies meet at unusual times and places. This made going to assembly meetings hard for colonial representatives.

In some cases the king stopped the assembly from meeting at all.

The king tried to stop people from moving to the colonies and into new western lands.

The king prevented the colonies from choosing their own judges. Instead, he sent over judges who depended on him for their jobs and pay.

The king kept British soldiers in the colonies, even though the colonists had not asked for them.

King George III

The king and Parliament had taxed the colonists without their consent. This was one of the most important reasons the colonists were angry at Britain.

The colonists felt that the king had waged war on them.

The king had hired German soldiers and sent them to the colonies to keep order.

HE has refused for a long time, after such dissolutions, to cause others to be elected; whereby the legislative powers, incapable of annihilation, have returned to the people at large for their exercise; the state remaining in the mean time, exposed to all the dangers of invasions from without and convulsions within.

HE has endeavored to prevent the population of these states; for that purpose obstructing the laws for the naturalization of foreigners; refusing to pass others to encourage their migration hither, and raising the conditions of new appropriations of lands.

HE has obstructed the administration of justice, by refusing his assent to laws for establishing judiciary powers.

HE has made judges dependent on his will alone, for the tenure of their offices, and the amount of payment of their salaries.

HE has erected a multitude of new offices, and sent hither swarms of officers to harass our people and eat out their substance.

HE has kept among us, in times of peace, standing armies, without the consent of our legislatures.

HE has affected to render the military independent of, and superior to, the civil power.

HE has combined with others to subject us to a Jurisdiction foreign to our constitution and unacknowledged by our laws, giving his assent to their acts of pretended legislation:

FOR quartering large bodies of armed troops among us;

FOR protecting them, by a mock trial, from punishment for any murders which they should commit on the inhabitants of these states;

FOR cutting off our trade with all parts of the world;

FOR imposing taxes on us without our consent;

FOR depriving us, in many cases, of the benefits of trial by jury;

FOR transporting us beyond seas, to be tried for pretended offenses;

FOR abolishing the free system of English laws in a neighboring province, establishing therein an arbitrary government, and enlarging its boundaries, so as to render it at once an example and fit instrument for introducing the same absolute rule into these colonies;

FOR taking away our charters, abolishing our most valuable laws, and altering fundamentally the forms of our governments;

FOR suspending our own legislatures, and declaring themselves invested with power to legislate for us in all cases whatsoever.

HE has abdicated Government here, by declaring us out of his protection and waging war against us.

HE has plundered our seas, ravaged our coasts, burned our towns, and destroyed the lives of our people.

HE is at this time transporting large armies of foreign mercenaries to complete the works of death, desolation, and tyranny, already begun with circumstances of cruelty and perfidy scarcely paralleled in the most barbarous ages, and totally unworthy the head of a civilized nation.

HE has constrained our fellow-citizens, taken captive on the high seas, to bear arms against their country, to become the executioners of their friends and brethren, or to fall themselves by their hands.

HE has excited domestic insurrections amongst us, and has endeavored to bring on the inhabitants of our frontiers, the merciless Indian savages, whose known rule of warfare is an undistinguished destruction of all ages, sexes, and conditions.

Response to the King

IN every stage of these oppressions we have petitioned for redress in the most humble terms; Our repeated petitions have been answered only by repeated injury. A prince, whose character is thus marked by every act which may define a tyrant, is unfit to be the ruler of a free people.

NOR have we been wanting in our attentions to our British brethren. We have warned them from time to time, of attempts by their legislature to extend an unwarrantable jurisdiction over us. We have reminded them of the circumstances of our emigration and settlement here. We have appealed to their native justice and magnanimity; and we have conjured them, by the ties of our common kindred, to disavow these usurpations, which, would inevitably interrupt our connections and correspondence. They, too, have been deaf to the voice of justice and of consanguinity. We must, therefore, acquiesce in the necessity which denounces our separation, and hold them, as we hold the rest of mankind, enemies in war, in peace, friends.

Independence

WE, therefore, the representatives of the United States of America, in General Congress Assembled, appealing to the Supreme Judge of the world for the rectitude of our intentions, do, in the name and by authority of the good people of these colonies, solemnly publish and declare, that these United Colonies are, and of right ought to be, FREE AND INDEPENDENT STATES; that they are absolved from all allegiance to the British crown, and that all political connection between them and the state of Great Britain is, and ought to be, totally dissolved; and that, as free and independent states, they have full power to levy war, conclude peace, contract alliances, establish commerce, and do all other acts and things which independent states may of right do. And for the support of this declaration, with a firm reliance on the protection of Divine Providence, we mutually pledge to each other our lives, our fortunes, and our sacred honor.

British soldiers became a symbol of British misrule to many colonists.

The colonists said that they had asked the king to change his policies, but he had not listened to them.

The writers declared that the colonies were free and independent states, equal to the world's other states. They had the powers to make war and peace and to trade with other countries.

The signers pledged their lives to the support of this Declaration. The Continental Congress ordered copies of the Declaration of Independence to be sent to all the states and to the army.

NEW HAMPSHIRE
Josiah Bartlett
William Whipple
Matthew Thornton

MASSACHUSETTS
John Hancock
John Adams
Samuel Adams
Robert Treat Paine
Elbridge Gerry

NEW YORK
William Floyd
Philip Livingston
Francis Lewis
Lewis Morris

RHODE ISLAND
Stephen Hopkins
William Ellery

NEW JERSEY
Richard Stockton
John Witherspoon
Francis Hopkinson
John Hart
Abraham Clark

PENNSYLVANIA
Robert Morris
Benjamin Rush
Benjamin Franklin
John Morton
George Clymer
James Smith
George Taylor
James Wilson
George Ross

DELAWARE
Caesar Rodney
George Read
Thomas McKean

MARYLAND
Samuel Chase
William Paca
Thomas Stone
Charles Carroll
  of Carrollton

NORTH CAROLINA
Willam Hooper
Joseph Hewes
John Penn

VIRGINIA
George Wythe
Richard Henry Lee
Thomas Jefferson
Benjamin Harrison
Thomas Nelson, Jr.
Francis Lightfoot Lee
Carter Braxton

SOUTH CAROLINA
Edward Rutledge
Thomas Heyward, Jr.
Thomas Lynch, Jr.
Arthur Middleton

CONNECTICUT
Roger Sherman
Samuel Huntington
William Williams
Oliver Wolcott

GEORGIA
Button Gwinnett
Lyman Hall
George Walton

Preamble The Preamble, or introduction, states the purposes of the Constitution. The writers wanted to strengthen the national government and give the nation a more solid foundation. The Preamble makes it clear that it is the people of the United States who have the power to establish or change a government.

Congress Section 1 gives Congress the power to make laws. Congress has two parts, the House of Representatives and the Senate.

Election and Term of Members Citizens elect the members of the House of Representatives every two years.

Qualifications Representatives must be at least 25 years old. They must have been United States citizens for at least seven years. They also must live in the state they represent.

Number of Representatives per State The number of representatives each state has is based on its population. The biggest states have the most representatives. Each state must have at least one representative. An enumeration, or census, must be taken every 10 years to find out a state's population. The number of representatives in the House is now fixed at 435.

George Washington watches delegates sign the Constitution.

The Constitution of the United States

Preamble*

We the people of the United States, in order to form a more perfect Union, establish justice, insure domestic tranquility, provide for the common defense, promote the general welfare, and secure the blessings of liberty to ourselves and our posterity, do ordain and establish this Constitution for the United States of America.

ARTICLE I
Legislative Branch

SECTION 1. CONGRESS

All legislative powers herein granted shall be vested in a Congress of the United States, which shall consist of a Senate and House of Representatives.

SECTION 2. HOUSE OF REPRESENTATIVES

1. **Election and Term of Members** The House of Representatives shall be composed of members chosen every second year by the people of the several States, and the electors in each State shall have the qualifications requisite for electors of the most numerous branch of the State Legislature.

2. **Qualifications** No person shall be a representative who shall not have attained to the age of twenty-five years, and been seven years a citizen of the United States, and who shall not, when elected, be an inhabitant of that State in which he shall be chosen.

3. **Number of Representatives per State** Representatives ~~and direct taxes~~** shall be apportioned among the several States which may be included within this Union, according to their respective numbers, ~~which shall be determined by adding to the whole number of free persons, including those bound to service for a term of years, and excluding Indians not taxed, three-fifths of all other persons.~~ The actual enumeration shall be made within three years after the first meeting of the Congress of the United States, and within every subsequent term of ten years, in such manner as they shall by law direct. The number of representatives shall not exceed one for every thirty thousand, but each State shall have at least one representative; ~~and until such enumeration shall be made, the State of New Hampshire shall be entitled to choose three, Massachusetts eight, Rhode Island and Providence Plantations one, Connecticut five, New York six, New Jersey four, Pennsylvania eight, Delaware one, Maryland six, Virginia ten, North Carolina five, South Carolina five, and Georgia three.~~

4. **Vacancies** When vacancies happen in the representation from any State, the executive authority thereof shall issue writs of election to fill such vacancies.

5. **Special Powers** The House of Representatives shall choose their speaker and other officers; and shall have the sole power of impeachment.

*The titles of the Preamble, and of each article, section, clause, and amendment have been added to make the Constitution easier to read. These titles are not in the original document.

**Parts of the Constitution have been crossed out to show that they are not in force any more. They have been changed by amendments or they no longer apply.

SECTION 3. SENATE

1. **Number, Term, and Selection of Members** *The Senate of the United States shall be composed of two senators from each State, chosen by the Legislature thereof, for six years; and each Senator shall have one vote.*

2. **Overlapping Terms and Filling Vacancies** *Immediately after they shall be assembled in consequence of the first election, they shall be divided as equally as may be into three classes. ~~The seats of the senators of the first class shall be vacated at the expiration of the second year, of the second class at the expiration of the fourth year, and of the third class at the expiration of the sixth year,~~ so that one-third may be chosen every second year; ~~and if vacancies happen by resignation, or otherwise, during the recess of the legislature of any State, the executive thereof may make temporary appointments until the next meeting of the legislature, which shall then fill such vacancies.~~*

3. **Qualifications** *No person shall be a senator who shall not have attained to the age of thirty years, and been nine years a citizen of the United States, and who shall not, when elected, be an inhabitant of that State for which he shall be chosen.*

4. **President of the Senate** *The Vice President of the United States shall be President of the Senate, but shall have no vote, unless they be equally divided.*

5. **Other Officers** *The Senate shall choose their other officers, and also a President pro tempore, in the absence of the Vice President, or when he shall exercise the office of the President of the United States.*

6. **Impeachment Trials** *The Senate shall have the sole power to try all impeachments. When sitting for that purpose, they shall be on oath or affirmation. When the President of the United States is tried, the Chief Justice shall preside: and no person shall be convicted without the concurrence of two-thirds of the members present.*

7. **Penalties** *Judgment in cases of impeachment shall not extend further than to removal from office, and disqualification to hold and enjoy any office of honor, trust, or profit under the United States: but the party convicted shall nevertheless be liable and subject to indictment, trial, judgement and punishment, according to law.*

SECTION 4. ELECTIONS AND MEETINGS

1. **Election of Congress** *The times, places and manner of holding elections for senators and representatives, shall be prescribed in each State by the legislature thereof; but the Congress may at any time by law make or alter such regulations, except as to the places of choosing Senators.*

2. **Annual Sessions** *The Congress shall assemble at least once in every year, ~~and such meeting shall be on the first Monday in December,~~ unless they shall by law appoint a different day.*

SECTION 5. RULES OF PROCEDURE

1. **Organization** *Each house shall be the judge of the elections, returns and qualifications of its own members, and a majority of each shall constitute a quorum to do business; but a smaller number may adjourn from day to day, and may be authorized to compel the attendance of absent members, in such manner, and under such penalties as each house may provide.*

Americans often use voting machines on election day.

Number, Term, and Selection of Members In each state, citizens elect two members of the Senate. This gives all states, whether big or small, equal power in the Senate. Senators serve six year terms. Originally, state legislatures chose the senators for their states. Today, however, people elect their senators directly. The Seventeenth Amendment made this change in 1913.

Qualifications Senators must be at least 30 years old and United States citizens for at least nine years. Like representatives, they must live in the state they represent.

President of the Senate The Vice President of the United States acts as the President, or chief officer, of the Senate. The Vice President votes only in cases of a tie.

Impeachment Trials If the House of Representatives impeaches, or charges, an official with a crime, the Senate holds a trial. If two-thirds of the senators find the official guilty, then the person is removed from office. The only President ever impeached was Andrew Johnson in 1868. He was found not guilty.

Election of Congress Each state decides where and when to hold elections. Today congressional elections are held in even-numbered years, on the Tuesday after the first Monday in November.

Annual Sessions The Constitution requires Congress to meet at least once a year. In 1933, the 20th Amendment made January 3rd the day for beginning a regular session of Congress.

Organization A quorum is the smallest number of members that must be present for an organization to hold a meeting. For each house of Congress, this number is the majority, or more than one-half, of its members.

Rules Each house can make rules for its members and expel a member by a two-thirds vote.

Journal The Constitution requires each house to keep a record of its proceedings. *The Congressional Record* is published every day. It includes parts of speeches made in each house and allows any person to look up the votes of his or her representative.

Pay and Protection Congress sets the salaries of its members, and they are paid by the federal government. No member can be arrested for anything he or she says while in office. This protection allows members to speak freely in Congress.

Restrictions Members of Congress cannot hold other federal offices during their terms. This rule strengthens the separation of powers and protects the checks and balances system set up by the Constitution.

Tax Bills A bill is a proposed law. Only the House of Representatives can introduce bills that tax the people.

Passing a Law A bill must be passed by the majority of members in each house of Congress. Then it is sent to the President. If the President signs it, the bill becomes a law. If the President refuses to sign a bill, and Congress is in session, the bill becomes law ten days after the President receives it.

The President can also veto, or reject, a bill. However, if each house of Congress repasses the bill by a two-thirds vote, it becomes a law. Passing a law after the President vetoed it is called overriding a veto. This process is an important part of the checks and balances system set up by the Constitution.

Orders and Resolutions Congress can also pass resolutions that have the same power as laws. Such acts are also subject to the President's veto.

2. *Rules* Each house may determine the rules of its proceedings, punish its members for disorderly behavior, and, with the concurrence of two-thirds, expel a member.

3. *Journal* Each house shall keep a journal of its proceedings, and from time to time publish the same, excepting such parts as may in their judgement require secrecy; and the yeas and nays of the members of either house on any question shall, at the desire of one-fifth of those present, be entered on the journal.

4. *Adjournment* Neither house, during the session of Congress, shall, without the consent of the other, adjourn for more than three days, nor to any other place than that in which the two houses shall be sitting.

SECTION 6. PRIVILEGES AND RESTRICTIONS

1. *Pay and Protection* The senators and representatives shall receive a compensation for their services, to be ascertained by law, and paid out of the treasury of the United States. They shall in all cases, except treason, felony and breach of the peace, be privileged from arrest during their attendance at the session of their respective houses, and in going to and returning from the same; and for any speech or debate in either house, they shall not be questioned in any other place.

2. *Restrictions* No senator or representative shall, during the time for which he was elected, be appointed to any civil office under the authority of the United States, which shall have been created, or the emoluments whereof shall have been increased during such time; and no person holding any office under the United States, shall be a member of either house during his continuance in office.

SECTION 7. MAKING LAWS

1. *Tax Bills* All bills for raising revenue shall originate in the House of Representatives; but the Senate may propose or concur with amendments as on other bills.

2. *Passing a Law* Every bill which shall have passed the House of Representatives and the Senate, shall, before it became a law, be presented to the President of the United States; if he approve, he shall sign it, but if not, he shall return it, with his objections, to that house in which it shall have originated, who shall enter the objections at large on their journal, and proceed to reconsider it. If after such reconsideration two-thirds of that house shall agree to pass the bill, it shall be sent, together with the objections, to the other house, by which it shall likewise be reconsidered, and if approved by two-thirds of that house, it shall become a law. But in all such cases the votes of both houses shall be determined by yeas and nays, and the names of the persons voting for and against the bill shall be entered on the journal of each house respectively. If any bill shall not be returned by the president within ten days (Sundays excepted) after it shall have been presented to him, the same shall be a law, in like manner as if he had signed it, unless the Congress by their adjournment prevent its return, in which case it shall not be a law.

3. *Orders and Resolutions* Every order, resolution, or vote to which the concurrence of the Senate and House of Representatives may be necessary (except on a question of adjournment) shall be presented to the President of the United States; and before the same shall take effect, shall be approved by him, or, being disapproved by him, shall be repassed by two-thirds of the Senate and House of Representatives, according to the rules and limitations prescribed in the case of a bill.

SECTION 8. POWERS DELEGATED TO CONGRESS

1. **Taxation** *The Congress shall have the power to lay and collect taxes, duties, imposts, and excises, to pay the debts and provide for the common defense and general welfare of the United States; but all duties, imposts and excises shall be uniform throughout the United States;*

2. **Borrowing** *To borrow money on the credit of the United States;*

3. **Commerce** *To regulate commerce with foreign nations, and among the several States, and with the Indian tribes;*

4. **Naturalization and Bankruptcy** *To establish an uniform rule of naturalization, and uniform laws on the subject of bankruptcies throughout the United States;*

5. **Coins and Measures** *To coin money, regulate the value thereof, and of foreign coin, and fix the standard of weights and measures;*

6. **Counterfeiting** *To provide for the punishment of counterfeiting the securities and current coin of the United States;*

7. **Post Offices** *To establish post offices and post roads;*

8. **Copyrights and Patents** *To promote the progress of science and useful arts by securing for limited times to authors and inventors the exclusive right to their respective writings and discoveries;*

9. **Courts** *To constitute tribunals inferior to the Supreme Court;*

10. **Piracy** *To define and punish piracies and felonies committed on the high seas, and offenses against the law of nations;*

11. **Declaring War** *To declare war, grant letters of marque and reprisal, and make rules concerning captures on land and water;*

12. **Army** *To raise and support armies, but no appropriation of money to that use shall be for a longer term than two years;*

13. **Navy** *To provide and maintain a navy;*

14. **Military Regulations** *To make rules for the government and regulation of the land and naval forces;*

15. **Militia** *To provide for calling forth the militia to execute the laws of the Union, suppress insurrections and repel invasions;*

16. **Militia Regulations** *To provide for organizing, arming and disciplining the militia, and for governing such part of them as may be employed in the service of the United States, reserving to the States respectively the appointment of the officers, and the authority of training the militia according to the discipline prescribed by Congress;*

17. **National Capital** *To exercise exclusive legislation in all cases whatsoever, over such district (not exceeding ten miles square) as may, by cession of particular states, and the acceptance of Congress, become the seat of the government of the United States, and to exercise like authority over all places purchased by the consent of the legislature of the State in which the same shall be, for the erection of forts, magazines, arsenals, dock-yards, and other needful buildings;—and*

18. **Necessary Laws** *To make all laws which shall be necessary and proper for carrying into execution the foregoing powers, and all other powers vested by this Constitution in the government of the United States, or in any department or officer thereof.*

Taxation Only Congress has the power to collect taxes. Federal taxes must be the same in all parts of the country.

Commerce Congress controls both trade with foreign countries and trade among states.

Naturalization and Bankruptcy Naturalization is the process by which a person from another country becomes a United States citizen. Congress decides the requirements for this procedure.

Coins and Measures Congress has the power to coin money and set its value.

Copyrights and Patents Copyrights protect authors. Patents allow inventors to profit from their work by keeping control over it for a certain number of years. Congress grants patents to encourage scientific research.

Declaring War Only Congress can declare war on another country.

Militia Today the Militia is called the National Guard. The National Guard often helps people after floods, tornadoes, and other disasters.

National Capital Congress makes the laws for the District of Columbia, the area where the nation's capital is located.

Necessary Laws This clause allows Congress to make laws on issues, such as television and radio, that are not mentioned in the Constitution.

Slave Trade This clause was another compromise between the North and the South. It prevented Congress from regulating the slave trade for 20 years. Congress outlawed the slave trade in 1808.

Habeas Corpus A writ of habeas corpus requires the government either to charge a person in jail with a particular crime or let the person go free. Except in emergencies, Congress cannot deny the right of a person to a writ.

Ports When regulating trade, Congress must treat all states equally. Also, states cannot tax goods traveling between states.

Regulations on Spending Congress controls the spending of public money. This clause checks the President's power.

Complete Restrictions The Constitution prevents the states from acting like individual countries. States cannot make treaties with foreign nations. They cannot issue their own money.

Partial Restrictions States cannot tax imports and exports without approval from Congress.

Other Restrictions States cannot declare war. They cannot keep their own armies.

Term of Office The President has the power to carry out the laws passed by Congress. The President and the Vice President serve four-year terms.

Electoral College A group of people called the Electoral College actually elects the President. The number of electors each state receives equals the total number of its representatives and senators.

SECTION 9. POWERS DENIED TO CONGRESS

1. **Slave Trade** ~~The migration or importation of such persons as any of the States now existing shall think proper to admit, shall not be prohibited by the Congress prior to the year 1808, but a tax or duty may be imposed on such importation, not exceeding ten dollars for each person.~~

2. **Habeas Corpus** The privilege of the writ of habeas corpus shall not be suspended, unless when in cases of rebellion or invasion the public safety may require it.

3. **Special Laws** No bill of attainder or ex post facto law shall be passed.

4. **Direct Taxes** ~~No capitation or other direct tax shall be laid, unless in proportion to the census or enumeration herein before directed to be taken.~~

5. **Export Taxes** No tax or duty shall be laid on articles exported from any State.

6. **Ports** No preference shall be given by any regulation of commerce or revenue to the ports of one State over those of another; nor shall vessels bound to, or from, one State, be obliged to enter, clear, or pay duties in another.

7. **Regulations on Spending** No money shall be drawn from the treasury, but in consequence of appropriations made by law; and a regular statement and account of the receipts and expenditures of all public money shall be published from time to time.

8. **Titles of Nobility and Gifts** No title of nobility shall be granted by the United States: and no person holding any office or profit or trust under them, shall, without the consent of the Congress, accept of any present, emolument, office, or title, of any kind whatever, from any king, prince, or foreign state.

SECTION 10. POWERS DENIED TO THE STATES

1. **Complete Restrictions** No State shall enter into any treaty, alliance, or confederation; grant letters of marque and reprisal; coin money; emit bills of credit; make anything but gold and silver coin a tender in payment of debts; pass any bill of attainder, ex post facto law, or law impairing the obligation of contracts, or grant any title of nobility.

2. **Partial Restrictions** No State shall, without the consent of the Congress, lay any imposts or duties on imports or exports, except what may be absolutely necessary for executing its inspection laws; and the net produce of all duties and imposts, laid by any State on imports or exports, shall be for the use of the treasury of the United States; and all such laws shall be subject to the revision and control of the Congress.

3. **Other Restrictions** No State shall, without the consent of Congress, lay any duty of tonnage, keep troops, or ships of war in time of peace, enter into any agreement or compact with another State, or with a foreign power, or engage in war, unless actually invaded, or in such imminent danger as will not admit of delay.

ARTICLE II
Executive Branch

SECTION 1. PRESIDENT AND VICE PRESIDENT

1. **Term of Office** The executive power shall be vested in a President of the United States of America. He shall hold his office during the term of four years, and together with the Vice President, chosen for the same term, be elected as follows:

2. **Electoral College** Each State shall appoint, in such manner as the legislature thereof may direct, a number of electors, equal to the whole number of senators and representatives to which the State may be entitled in the Congress; but no

senator or representative, or person holding an office of trust or profit under the United States, shall be appointed an elector.

3. **Election Process** ~~The electors shall meet in their respective States, and vote by ballot for two persons, of whom one at least shall not be an inhabitant of the same State with themselves. And they shall make a list of all the persons voted for, and of the number of votes for each; which list they shall sign and certify, and transmit sealed to the seat of the government of the United States, directed to the President of the Senate. The President of the Senate shall, in the presence of the Senate and House of Representatives, open all the certificates, and the votes shall then be counted. The person having the greatest number of votes shall be the President, if such number be a majority of the whole number of electors appointed, and if there be more than one who have such majority, and have an equal number of votes, then the House of Representatives shall immediately choose by ballot one of them for President; and if no person have a majority, then from the five highest on the list the said house shall in like manner choose the President. But in choosing the President, the votes shall be taken by States, the representation from each State having one vote; a quorum for this purpose shall consist of a member or members from two-thirds of the States, and a majority of all the States shall be necessary to a choice. In every case, after the choice of the President, the person having the greatest number of votes of the electors shall be the Vice President. But if there should remain two or more who have equal votes, the Senate shall choose from them by ballot the Vice President.~~

4. **Time of Elections** The Congress may determine the time of choosing the electors, and the day on which they shall give their votes; which day shall be the same throughout the United States.

5. **Qualifications** No person except a natural-born citizen, ~~or a citizen of the United States at the time of the adoption of this Constitution,~~ shall be eligible to the office of President; neither shall any person be eligible to that office who shall not have attained to the age of thirty-five years, and been fourteen years a resident within the United States.

6. **Vacancies** ~~In case of the removal of the President from office, or of his death, resignation, or inability to discharge the powers and duties of the said office, the same shall devolve on the Vice President, and the Congress may by law provide for the case of removal, death, resignation, or inability, both of the President and Vice President, declaring what officer shall then act as President, and such officer shall act accordingly, until the disability be removed, or a President shall be elected.~~

7. **Salary** The President shall, at stated times, receive for his services a compensation, which shall neither be increased nor diminished during the period for which he shall have been elected, and he shall not receive within that period any other emolument from the United States, or any of them.

8. **Oath of Office** Before he enter on the execution of his office, he shall take the following oath or affirmation:—"I do solemnly swear (or affirm) that I will faithfully execute the office of President of the United States, and will to the best of my ability, preserve, protect and defend the Constitution of the United States."

SECTION 2. POWERS OF THE PRESIDENT

1. **Military Powers** The President shall be commander in chief of the army and navy of the United States, and of the militia of the several States, when called into the actual service of the United States; he may require the opinion, in writing, of the principal officer in each of the executive departments, upon any subject relating to the duties of their respective offices, and he shall have power to

Election Process Originally, electors voted for two people. The candidate who received the majority of votes became President. The runner-up became Vice President. Problems with this system led to the 12th Amendment, which changed the electoral college system.

Today electors almost always vote for the candidate who won the popular vote in their states. In other words, the candidate who wins the popular vote in a state also wins its electoral votes.

Time of Elections Today we elect our President on the Tuesday after the first Monday in November.

Qualifications A President must be at least 35 years old, a United States citizen by birth, and a resident of the United States for at least 14 years.

Vacancies If the President resigns, dies, or is impeached and found guilty, the Vice President becomes President. The 25th Amendment replaced this clause in 1967.

Salary The President receives a yearly salary that cannot be increased or decreased during his or her term. The President cannot hold any other paid government positions while in office.

Oath of Office Every President must promise to uphold the Constitution. The Chief Justice of the Supreme Court usually administers this oath.

Military Powers The President is the leader of the country's military forces.

Treaties and Appointments The President can make treaties with other nations. However, treaties must be approved by a two-thirds vote of the Senate. The President also appoints Supreme Court Justices and ambassadors to foreign countries. The Senate must approve these appointments.

grant reprieves and pardons for offenses against the United States, except in cases of impeachment.

2. *Treaties and Appointments* He shall have power, by and with the advice and consent of the Senate, to make treaties, provided two-thirds of the Senators present concur; and he shall nominate, and by and with the advice and consent of the Senate, shall appoint ambassadors, other public ministers and consuls, judges of the Supreme Court, and all other officers of the United States, whose appointments are not herein otherwise provided for, and which shall be established by law: but the Congress may by law vest the appointment of such inferior officers, as they think proper, in the President alone, in the courts of law, or in the heads of departments.

3. *Temporary Appointments* The President shall have power to fill up all vacancies that may happen during the recess of the Senate, by granting commissions which shall expire at the end of their next session.

Duties The President must report to Congress at least once a year and make recommendations for laws. This report is known as the State of the Union address. The President delivers it each January.

SECTION 3. DUTIES

He shall from time to time give to the Congress information of the State of the Union, and recommend to their consideration such measures as he shall judge necessary and expedient; he may on extraordinary occasions, convene both houses, or either of them, and in case of disagreement between them with respect to the time of adjournment, he may adjourn them to such time as he shall think proper; he shall receive ambassadors and other public ministers; he shall take care that the laws be faithfully executed, and shall commission all the officers of the United States.

Impeachment The President and other officials can be forced out of office only if found guilty of particular crimes. This clause protects government officials from being impeached for unimportant reasons.

SECTION 4. IMPEACHMENT

The President, Vice President, and all civil officers of the United States, shall be removed from office on impeachment for, and conviction of, treason, bribery, or other high crimes and misdemeanors.

ARTICLE III
Judicial Branch

SECTION 1. FEDERAL COURTS

Federal Courts The Supreme Court is the highest court in the nation. It makes the final decisions in all of the cases it hears. Congress decides the size of the Supreme Court. Today it contains nine judges. Congress also has the power to set up a system of lower federal courts. All federal judges may hold their offices for as long as they live.

The judicial power of the United States shall be vested in one Supreme Court, and in such inferior courts as the Congress may from time to time ordain and establish. The judges, both of the Supreme and inferior courts, shall hold their offices during good behaviour, and shall, at stated times, receive for their services, a compensation, which shall not be diminished during their continuance in office.

SECTION 2. AUTHORITY OF THE FEDERAL COURTS

General Jurisdiction Jurisdiction means the right of a court to hear a case. Federal courts have jurisdiction over such cases as those involving the Constitution, federal laws, treaties, and disagreements between states.

1. *General Jurisdiction* The judicial power shall extend to all cases, in law and equity, arising under this Constitution, the laws of the United States, and treaties made, or which shall be made, under their authority; to all cases affecting ambassadors, other public ministers and consuls; to all cases of admiralty and maritime jurisdiction; to controversies to which the United States shall be a party; to controversies between two or more States; between a State and citizens of another State; between citizens of different States; between citizens of the same State claiming lands under grants of different States, and between a State, or the citizens thereof, and foreign states, citizens or subjects.

2. The Supreme Court *In all cases affecting ambassadors, other public ministers and consuls, and those in which a State shall be party, the Supreme Court shall have original jurisdiction. In all the other cases before mentioned, the Supreme Court shall have appellate jurisdiction, both as to law and fact, with such exceptions, and under such regulations as the Congress shall make.*

3. Trial by Jury *The trial of all crimes, except in cases of impeachment, shall be by jury; and such trial shall be held in the State where the said crimes shall have been committed; but when not committed within any state, the trial shall be at such place or places as the Congress may by law have directed.*

SECTION 3. TREASON

1. Definition *Treason against the United States shall consist only in levying war against them, or in adhering to their enemies, giving them aid and comfort. No person shall be convicted of treason unless on the testimony of two witnesses to the same overt act, or on confession in open court.*

2. Punishment *The Congress shall have power to declare the punishment of treason, but no attainder of treason shall work corruption of blood, or forfeiture except during the life of the person attainted.*

ARTICLE IV
Relations Among the States

SECTION 1. OFFICIAL RECORDS

Full faith and credit shall be given in each state to the public acts, records and judicial proceedings of every other State. And the Congress may by general laws prescribe the manner in which such acts, records, and proceedings shall be proved, and the effect thereof.

SECTION 2. PRIVILEGES OF THE CITIZENS

1. Privileges *The citizens of each State shall be entitled to all privileges and immunities of citizens in the several states.*

2. Return of a Person Accused of a Crime *A person charged in any State with treason, felony, or other crime, who shall flee from justice, and be found in another State, shall on demand of the executive authority of the State from which he fled, be delivered up, to be removed to the State having jurisdiction of the crime.*

3. Return of Fugitive Slaves ~~No person held to service or labor in one State, under the laws thereof, escaping into another, shall, in consequence of any law or regulation therein, be discharged from such service or labor, but shall be delivered up on claim of the party to whom such service or labor may be due.~~

The Supreme Court One of the Supreme Court's most important jobs is to decide whether laws that pass are constitutional. This power is another example of the checks and balances system in the federal government.

Trial by Jury The Constitution guarantees everyone the right to a trial by jury. The only exception is in impeachment cases, which are tried in the Senate.

Definition People cannot be convicted of treason in the United States for what they think or say. To be guilty of treason, a person must rebel against the government by using violence or helping enemies of the country.

Official Records Each state must accept the laws, acts, and legal decisions made by other states.

Privileges States must give the same rights to citizens of other states that they give to their own citizens.

Return of a Person Accused of a Crime If a person charged with a crime escapes to another state, he or she must be returned to the original state to go on trial. This act of returning someone from one state to another is called extradition.

Every American has a right to a trial by jury. Jurors' chairs are shown below.

SECTION 3. NEW STATES AND TERRITORIES

New States Congress has the power to create new states out of the nation's territories. All new states have the same rights as the old states. This clause made it clear that the United States would not make colonies out of its new lands.

1. **New States** New states may be admitted by the Congress into this Union; but no new State shall be formed or erected within the jurisdiction of any other State, nor any State be formed by the junction of two or more States, or parts of States, without the consent of the legislatures of the States concerned, as well as of the Congress.

2. **Federal Lands** The Congress shall have power to dispose of and make all needful rules and regulations respecting the territory or other property belonging to the United States; and nothing in this Constitution shall be so construed as to prejudice any claims of the United States, or of any particular State.

SECTION 4. GUARANTEES TO THE STATES

Guarantees to the State The federal government must defend the states from rebellions and from attacks by other countries.

The United States shall guarantee to every State in this Union a republican form of government, and shall protect each of them against invasion; and on application of the legislature, or of the executive (when the legislature cannot be convened) against domestic violence.

ARTICLE V
Amending the Constitution

Amending the Constitution An amendment to the Constitution may be proposed either by a two-thirds vote of each house of Congress or by a national convention called by Congress at the request of two-thirds of the state legislatures. To be ratified, or approved, an amendment must be supported by three-fourths of the state legislatures or by three-fourths of special conventions held in each state.

Once an amendment is ratified, it becomes part of the Constitution. Only a new amendment can change it. Amendments have allowed people to change the Constitution to meet the changing needs of the nation.

The Congress, whenever two-thirds of both houses shall deem it necessary, shall propose amendments to this Constitution, or, on the application of the legislatures of two-thirds of the several States, shall call a convention for proposing amendments, which, in either case, shall be valid to all intents and purposes, as part of this Constitution, when ratified by the legislatures of three-fourths of the several States, or by conventions in three-fourths thereof, as the one or the other mode of ratification may be proposed by the Congress; provided, ~~that no amendment which may be made prior to the year 1808, shall in any manner affect the first and fourth clauses in the ninth section of the first article;~~ and that no State, without its consent, shall be deprived of its equal suffrage in the Senate.

ARTICLE VI
General Provisions

Federal Supremacy The Constitution is the highest law in the nation. Whenever a state law and a federal law are different, the federal law must be obeyed.

Oaths of Office All state and federal officials must take an oath promising to obey the Constitution.

1. **Public Debt** All debts contracted and engagements entered into, before the adoption of this Constitution, shall be as valid against the United States under this Constitution, as under the Confederation.

2. **Federal Supremacy** This Constitution, and the laws of the United States which shall be made in pursuance thereof; and all treaties made, or which shall be made, under the authority of the United States, shall be the supreme law of the land; and the judges in every State shall be bound thereby, anything in the Constitution or laws of any State to the contrary notwithstanding.

3. **Oaths of Office** The senators and representatives before mentioned, and the members of the several State legislatures, and all executive and judicial officers, both of the United States, and of the several States, shall be bound by oath or affirmation to support this Constitution; but no religious test shall ever be required as a qualification to any office or public trust under the United States.

ARTICLE VII
Ratification

The ratification of the conventions of nine States shall be sufficient for the establishment of this Constitution between the States so ratifying the same.

Done in Convention by the unanimous consent of the States present the seventeenth day of September in the year of our Lord one thousand seven hundred and eighty-seven and of the independence of the United States of America the twelfth. In witness whereof we have hereunto subscribed our names.

George Washington, President and deputy from Virginia

DELAWARE
George Read
Gunning Bedford, Junior
John Dickinson
Richard Bassett
Jacob Broom

MARYLAND
James McHenry
Daniel of St. Thomas Jenifer
Daniel Carroll

VIRGINIA
John Blair
James Madison, Junior

NORTH CAROLINA
William Blount
Richard Dobbs Spaight
Hugh Williamson

SOUTH CAROLINA
John Rutledge
Charles Cotesworth
*   Pinckney*
Charles Pinckney
Pierce Butler

GEORGIA
William Few
Abraham Baldwin

NEW HAMPSHIRE
John Langdon
Nicholas Gilman

MASSACHUSETTS
Nathaniel Gorham
Rufus King

CONNECTICUT
William Samuel Johnson
Roger Sherman

NEW YORK
Alexander Hamilton

NEW JERSEY
William Livingston
David Brearley
William Paterson
Jonathan Dayton

PENNSYLVANIA
Benjamin Franklin
Thomas Mifflin
Robert Morris
George Clymer
Thomas FitzSimons
Jared Ingersoll
James Wilson
Gouverneur Morris

Ratification The Constitution went into effect as soon as nine of the 13 states approved it.

Each state held a special convention to debate the Constitution. The ninth state to approve the Constitution, New Hampshire, voted for ratification on June 21, 1788.

Delegates wait for their turn to sign the new Constitution.

Amendments to the Constitution

Basic Freedoms The government cannot pass laws that favor one religion over another. Nor can it stop people from saying or writing whatever they want. The people have the right to gather openly and discuss problems they have with the government.

Weapons and the Militia This amendment was included to prevent the federal government from taking away guns used by members of state militias.

Housing Soldiers The army cannot use people's homes to house soldiers unless it is approved by law. Before the American Revolution, the British housed soldiers in private homes without permission of the owners.

Search and Seizure This amendment protects people's privacy in their homes. The government cannot search or seize anyone's property without a warrant, or a written order, from a court. A warrant must list the people and the property to be searched and give reasons for the search.

Rights of the Accused A person accused of a crime has the right to a fair trial. A person cannot be tried twice for the same crime. This amendment also protects a person from self-incrimination, or having to testify against himself or herself.

Right to a Fair Trial Anyone accused of a crime is entitled to a quick and fair trial by jury. This right protects people from being kept in jail without being convicted of a crime. Also, the government must provide a lawyer for anyone accused of a crime who cannot afford to hire a lawyer.

Jury Trial in Civil Cases Civil cases usually involve two or more people suing each other over money, property, or personal injury. A jury trial is guaranteed in large lawsuits.

AMENDMENTS TO THE CONSTITUTION

AMENDMENT I (1791)*
Basic Freedoms

Congress shall make no law respecting an establishment of religion, or prohibiting the free exercise thereof; or abridging the freedom of speech, or of the press; or the right of the people peaceably to assemble, and to petition the government for a redress of grievances.

AMENDMENT II (1791)
Weapons and the Militia

A well-regulated militia, being necessary to the security of a free State, the right of the people to keep and bear arms, shall not be infringed.

AMENDMENT III (1791)
Housing Soldiers

No soldier shall, in time of peace, be quartered in any house, without the consent of the owner, nor in time of war, but in a manner to be prescribed by law.

AMENDMENT IV (1791)
Search and Seizure

The right of the people to be secure in their persons, houses, papers, and effects, against unreasonable searches and seizures, shall not be violated, and no warrants shall issue, but upon probable cause, supported by oath or affirmation, and particularly describing the place to be searched, and the persons or things to be seized.

AMENDMENT V (1791)
Rights of the Accused

No person shall be held to answer for a capital, or otherwise infamous crime, unless on a presentment or indictment of a grand jury, except in cases arising in the land or naval forces, or in the militia, when in actual service in time of war or public danger; nor shall any person be subject for the same offense to be twice put in jeopardy of life or limb; nor shall be compelled in any criminal case to be a witness against himself, nor be deprived of life, liberty, or property, without due process of law; nor shall private property be taken for public use without just compensation.

AMENDMENT VI (1791)
Right to a Fair Trial

In all criminal prosecutions, the accused shall enjoy the right to a speedy and public trial, by an impartial jury of the State and district wherein the crime shall have been committed, which district shall have been previously ascertained by law, and to be informed of the nature and cause of the accusation; to be confronted with the witnesses against him; to have compulsory process for obtaining witnesses in his favor, and to have the assistance of counsel for his defense.

AMENDMENT VII (1791)
Jury Trial in Civil Cases

In suits at common law, where the value in controversy shall exceed twenty dollars, the right of trial by jury shall be preserved, and no fact tried by a jury shall be otherwise reexamined in any court of the United States, than according to the rules of the common law.

*The date after each amendment indicates the year the amendment was ratified.

AMENDMENT VIII (1791)
Bail and Punishment

Excessive bail shall not be required, nor excessive fines imposed, nor cruel and unusual punishments inflicted.

AMENDMENT IX (1791)
Powers Reserved to the People

The enumeration in the Constitution, of certain rights, shall not be construed to deny or disparage others retained by the people.

AMENDMENT X (1791)
Powers Reserved to the States

The powers not delegated to the United States by the Constitution, nor prohibited by it to the States, are reserved to the States respectively, or to the people.

AMENDMENT XI (1795)
Suits Against States

The judicial power of the United States shall not be construed to extend to any suit in law or equity, commenced or prosecuted against one of the United States by citizens of another State, or by citizens or subjects of any foreign State.

AMENDMENT XII (1804)
Election of the President and Vice President

The electors shall meet in their respective States and vote by ballot for President and Vice President, one of whom, at least, shall not be an inhabitant of the same State with themselves; they shall name in their ballots the person voted for as President, and in distinct ballots the person voted for as Vice President, and they shall make distinct lists of all persons voted for as President, and of all persons voted for as Vice President, and of the number of votes for each, which lists they shall sign and certify, and transmit sealed to the seat of the government of the United States, directed to the President of the Senate; the President of the Senate shall, in the presence of the Senate and House of Representatives, open all the certificates and the votes shall then be counted; the person having the greatest number of votes for President, shall be the President, if such number be a majority of the whole number of electors appointed; and if no person have such majority, then from the persons having the highest numbers not exceeding three on the list of those voted for as President, the House of Representatives shall choose immediately, by ballot, the President. But in choosing the President, the votes shall be taken by States, the representation from each State having one vote; a quorum for this purpose shall consist of a member or members from two-thirds of the States, and a majority of all the States shall be necessary to a choice. And if the House of Representatives shall not choose a President whenever the right of choice shall devolve upon them, before the fourth day of March next following, then the Vice President shall act as President, as in case of the death or other constitutional disability of the President. The person having the greatest number of votes as Vice President, shall be the Vice President, if such number be a majority of the whole number of electors appointed, and if no person have a majority, then from the two highest numbers on the list, the Senate shall choose the Vice President; a quorum for the purpose shall consist of two-thirds of the whole number of senators, and a majority of the whole number shall be necessary to a choice. But no person constitutionally ineligible to the office of President shall be eligible to that of Vice President of the United States.

Bail and Punishment Courts cannot treat people accused of crimes in ways that are unusually harsh.

Powers Reserved to the People The people keep all rights not listed in the Constitution.

Powers Reserved to the States Any rights not clearly given to the federal government by the Constitution belong to the states or the people.

Suits Against the States A citizen from one state cannot sue the government of another state in a federal court. Such cases are decided in state courts.

Election of the President and Vice President Under the original Constitution, each member of the Electoral College voted for two candidates for President. The candidate with the most votes became President. The one with the second highest total became Vice President.

The 12th Amendment changed this system. Members of the electoral college distinguish between their votes for the President and Vice President. This change was an important step in the development of the two party system. It allows each party to nominate its own team of candidates.

The Twelfth Amendment allowed parties to nominate teams of candidates, as this campaign poster shows.

This etching shows a group of former slaves celebrating their emancipation.

Abolition This amendment ended slavery in the United States. It was ratified after the Civil War.

Citizenship This amendment defined citizenship in the United States. "Due process of law" means that no state can deny its citizens the rights and privileges they enjoy as United States citizens. The goal of this amendment was to protect the rights of the recently freed African Americans.

Number of Representatives This clause replaced the Three-Fifths Clause in Article 1. Each state's representation is based on its total population. Any state denying its male citizens over the age of 21 the right to vote will have its representation in Congress decreased.

Penalty of Rebellion Officials who fought against the Union in the Civil War could not hold public office in the United States. This clause tried to keep Confederate leaders out of power. In 1872, Congress removed this limit.

Government Debt The United States paid all of the Union's debts from the Civil War. However, it did not pay any of the Confederacy's debts. This clause prevented the southern states from using public money to pay for the rebellion or from compensating citizens who lost their enslaved persons.

AMENDMENT XIII (1865)
End of Slavery

SECTION 1. ABOLITION

Neither slavery nor involuntary servitude, except as a punishment for crime whereof the party shall have been duly convicted, shall exist within the United States, or any place subject to their jurisdiction.

SECTION 2. ENFORCEMENT

Congress shall have power to enforce this article by appropriate legislation.

AMENDMENT XIV (1868)
Rights of Citizens

SECTION 1. CITIZENSHIP

All persons born or naturalized in the United States, and subject to the jurisdiction thereof, are citizens of the United States and of the State wherein they reside. No State shall make or enforce any law which shall abridge the privileges or immunities of citizens of the United States; nor shall any State deprive any person of life, liberty, or property, without due process of law; nor deny to any person within its jurisdiction the equal protection of the laws.

SECTION 2. NUMBER OF REPRESENTATIVES

Representatives shall be apportioned among the several States according to their respective numbers, counting the whole number of persons in each State, excluding Indians not taxed. But when the right to vote at any election for the choice of electors for President and Vice President of the United States, representatives in Congress, the executive and judicial officers of a State, or the members of the legislature thereof, is denied to any of the male inhabitants of such State, being twenty-one years of age, and citizens of the United States, or in any way abridged, except for participation in rebellion, or other crime, the basis of representation therein shall be reduced in the proportion which the number of such male citizens shall bear to the whole number of male citizens twenty-one years of age in such State.

SECTION 3. PENALTY FOR REBELLION

No person shall be a senator or representative in Congress, or elector of President and Vice President, or hold any office, civil or military, under the United States, or under any State, who, having previously taken an oath, as a member of Congress, or as an officer of the United States, or as a member of any State legislature, or as an executive or judicial officer of any State, to support the Constitution of the United States, shall have engaged in insurrection or rebellion against the same, or given aid or comfort to the enemies thereof. But Congress may by a vote of two-thirds of each house, remove such disability.

SECTION 4. GOVERNMENT DEBT

The validity of the public debt of the United States, authorized by law, including debts incurred for payment of pensions and bounties for services in suppressing insurrection or rebellion, shall not be questioned. But neither the United States nor any State shall assume or pay any debt or obligation incurred in aid of insurrection or rebellion against the United States, or any claim for the loss or emancipation of any slave; but all such debts, obligations and claims shall be held illegal and void.

SECTION 5. ENFORCEMENT

The Congress shall have power to enforce, by appropriate legislation, the provisions of this article.

AMENDMENT XV (1870)
Voting Rights

SECTION 1. RIGHT TO VOTE

The right of citizens of the United States to vote shall not be denied or abridged by the United States or by any State on account of race, color, or previous condition of servitude.

SECTION 2. ENFORCEMENT

The Congress shall have power to enforce this article by appropriate legislation.

AMENDMENT XVI (1913)
Income Tax

The Congress shall have power to lay and collect taxes on incomes, from whatever sources derived, without apportionment among the several States, and without regard to any census or enumeration.

AMENDMENT XVII (1913)
Direct Election of Senators

SECTION 1. METHOD OF ELECTION

The Senate of the United States shall be composed of two senators from each State, elected by the people thereof, for six years; and each senator shall have one vote. The electors in each State shall have the qualifications requisite for electors of the most numerous branch of the State legislatures.

SECTION 2. VACANCIES

When vacancies happen in the representation of any State in the Senate, the executive authority of such State shall issue writs of election to fill such vacancies: Provided, that the legislature of any State may empower the executive thereof to make temporary appointments until the people fill the vacancies by election as the legislature may direct.

SECTION 3. EXCEPTION

~~This amendment shall not be so construed as to affect the election or term of any Senator chosen before it becomes valid as part of the Constitution.~~

AMENDMENT XVIII (1919)
Ban on Alcoholic Drinks

SECTION 1. PROHIBITION

~~After one year from the ratification of this article the manufacture, sale, or transportation of intoxicating liquors within, the importation thereof into, or the exportation thereof from the United States and all territory subject to the jurisdiction thereof for beverage purposes is hereby prohibited.~~

SECTION 2. ENFORCEMENT

~~The Congress and the several States shall have concurrent power to enforce this article by appropriate legislation.~~

Right to Vote No state can deny its citizens the right to vote because of their race. This amendment was designed to protect the voting rights of African Americans.

Income Tax Congress has the power to tax personal incomes.

Direct Election of Senators In the original Constitution, the state legislatures elected senators. This amendment gave citizens the power to elect their senators directly. It made senators more responsible to the people they represented.

The Prohibition movement used posters like this to reach the public.

Prohibition This amendment made it against the law to make or sell alcoholic beverages in the United States. This law was called prohibition. Fourteen years later, the 21st Amendment ended Prohibition.

Ratification The amendment for Prohibition was the first one to include a time limit for ratification. To go into effect, the amendment had to be approved by three-fourths of the states within seven years.

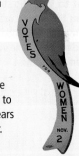

Women's Suffrage This amendment gave the right to vote to all women 21 years of age and older.

This 1915 banner pushed the cause of women's suffrage.

Beginning of Terms The President and Vice President's terms begin on January 20th of the year after their election. The terms for senators and representatives begin on January 3rd. Before this amendment, an official defeated in November stayed in office until March.

Presidential Succession A President who has been elected but has not yet taken office is called the President-elect. If the President-elect dies, then the Vice President-elect becomes President. If neither the President-elect nor the Vice President-elect can take office, then Congress decides who will act as President.

President Kennedy delivers his inaugural address in 1961.

SECTION 3. RATIFICATION

~~This article shall be inoperative unless it shall have been ratified as an amendment to the Constitution by the legislatures of the several States, as provided in the Constitution, within seven years from the date of the submission hereof to the States by Congress.~~

AMENDMENT XIX (1920)
Women's Suffrage

SECTION 1. RIGHT TO VOTE

The right of citizens of the United States to vote shall not be denied or abridged by the United States or by any State on account of sex.

SECTION 2. ENFORCEMENT

The Congress shall have power to enforce this article by appropriate legislation.

AMENDMENT XX (1933)
Terms of Office

SECTION 1. BEGINNING OF TERMS

The terms of the President and Vice-President shall end at noon on the 20th day of January, and the terms of senators and representatives at noon on the 3rd day of January, of the years in which such terms would have ended if this article had not been ratified; and the terms of their successors shall then begin.

SECTION 2. SESSIONS OF CONGRESS

The Congress shall assemble at least once in every year, and such meeting shall begin at noon on the 3rd day of January, unless they shall by law appoint a different day.

SECTION 3. PRESIDENTIAL SUCCESSION

If, at the time fixed for the beginning of the term of the President, the President-elect shall have died, the Vice President-elect shall become President. If a President shall not have been chosen before the time fixed for the beginning of his term, or if the President-elect shall have failed to qualify, then the Vice President-elect shall act as President until a President shall have qualified; and the Congress may by law provide for the case wherein neither a President-elect nor a Vice President-elect shall have qualified, declaring who shall then act as President, or the manner in which one who is to act shall be selected, and such person shall act accordingly until a President or Vice President shall have qualified.

SECTION 4. ELECTIONS DECIDED BY CONGRESS

The Congress may by law provide for the case of the death of any of the persons from whom the House of Representatives may choose a President whenever the right of choice shall have devolved upon them, and for the case of the death of any of the persons from whom the Senate may choose a Vice President whenever the right of choice shall have devolved upon them.

SECTION 5. EFFECTIVE DATE

~~Sections 1 and 2 shall take effect on the 15th day of October following the ratification of this article.~~

SECTION 6. RATIFICATION

This article shall be inoperative unless it shall have been ratified as an amendment to the Constitution by the legislatures of three-fourths of the several States within seven years from the date of its submission.

AMENDMENT XXI (1933)
End of Prohibition

SECTION 1. REPEAL OF EIGHTEENTH AMENDMENT

The eighteenth article of amendment to the Constitution of the United States is hereby repealed.

SECTION 2. STATE LAWS

The transportation or importation into any State, territory, or possession of the United States for delivery or use therein of intoxicating liquors, in violation of the laws thereof, is hereby prohibited.

SECTION 3. RATIFICATION

This article shall be inoperative unless it shall have been ratified as an amendment to the Constitution by conventions in the several States, as provided in the Constitution, within seven years from the date of the submission hereof to the States by the Congress.

End of Prohibition This amendment repealed, or ended, the 18th Amendment. It made alcoholic beverages legal once again in the United States. However, states can still control or stop the sale of alcohol within their borders.

AMENDMENT XXII (1951)
Limit on Presidential Terms

SECTION 1. TWO-TERM LIMIT

No person shall be elected to the office of the President more than twice, and no person who has held the office of President, or acted as President, for more that two years of a term to which some other person was elected President shall be elected to the office of the President more than once. But this article shall not apply to any person holding the office of President when this article was proposed by the Congress, and shall not prevent any person who may be holding the office of President, or acting as President, during the term within which this article becomes operative from holding the office of President or acting as President during the remainder of such term.

SECTION 2. RATIFICATION

This article shall be inoperative unless it shall have been ratified as an amendment to the Constitution by the legislatures of three-fourths of the several States within seven years from the date of its submission to the States by the Congress.

Two-Term Limit George Washington set a precedent that Presidents should not serve more than two terms in office. However, Franklin D. Roosevelt broke the precedent. He was elected President four times between 1932 and 1944. Some people feared that a President holding office for this long could become too powerful. This amendment limits Presidents to two terms in office.

AMENDMENT XXIII (1961)
Presidential Votes for Washington, D.C.

SECTION 1. NUMBER OF ELECTORS

The District constituting the seat of government of the United States shall appoint in such manner as the Congress may direct:

A number of electors of President and Vice President equal to the whole number of senators and representatives in Congress to which the District would be entitled if it were a State, but in no event more than the least populous State; they shall be in addition to those appointed by the States, but they shall be considered, for the purposes of the election of President and Vice President, to be elec-

Presidential Votes for Washington, D.C. This amendment gives people who live in the nation's capital a vote for President. The electoral votes in Washington D.C., are based on its population. However, it cannot have more votes than the state with the smallest population. Today, Washington, D.C. has three electoral votes.

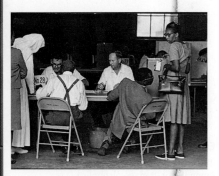

African Americans vote in Selma, Alabama, in 1966.

Ban on Poll Taxes A poll tax requires a person to pay a certain amount of money to register to vote. These taxes were used to stop poor African Americans from voting. This amendment made any such taxes illegal in federal elections.

Vacancy in the Vice Presidency If the Vice President becomes President, he or she may nominate a new Vice President. This nomination must be approved by both houses of Congress.

Disability of the President This section tells what happens if the President suddenly becomes ill or is seriously injured. The Vice President takes over as Acting President. When the President is ready to take office again, he or she must tell Congress.

tors appointed by a State; and they shall meet in the District and perform such duties as provided by the twelfth article of amendment.

SECTION 2. ENFORCEMENT

The Congress shall have power to enforce this article by appropriate legislation.

AMENDMENT XXIV (1964)
Ban on Poll Taxes

SECTION 1. POLL TAXES ILLEGAL

The right of citizens of the United States to vote in any primary or other election for President or Vice President, for electors for President or Vice President, or for senator or representative in Congress, shall not be denied or abridged by the United States or any State by reason of failure to pay any poll tax or other tax.

SECTION 2. ENFORCEMENT

The Congress shall have power to enforce this article by appropriate legislation.

AMENDMENT XXV (1967)
Presidential Succession

SECTION 1. VACANCY IN THE PRESIDENCY

In case of the removal of the President from office or of his death or resignation, the Vice President shall become President.

SECTION 2. VACANCY IN THE VICE PRESIDENCY

Whenever there is a vacancy in the office of the Vice President, the President shall nominate a Vice President who shall take office upon confirmation by a majority vote of both houses of Congress.

SECTION 3. DISABILITY OF THE PRESIDENT

Whenever the President transmits to the President pro tempore of the Senate and the Speaker of the House of Representatives his written declaration that he is unable to discharge the powers and duties of his office, and until he transmits to them a written declaration to the contrary, such powers and duties shall be discharged by the Vice President as Acting President.

SECTION 4. DETERMINING PRESIDENTIAL DISABILITY

Whenever the Vice President and a majority of either the principal officers of the executive departments or of such other body as Congress may by law provide, transmit to the President pro tempore of the Senate and the Speaker of the House of Representatives their written declaration that the President is unable to discharge the powers and duties of his office, the Vice President shall immediately assume the powers and duties of the office as Acting President.

Thereafter, when the President transmits to the President pro tempore of the Senate and the Speaker of the House of Representatives his written declaration that no inability exists, he shall resume the powers and duties of his office unless the Vice President and a majority of either the principal officers of the executive departments or of such other body as Congress may by law provide, transmit within four days to the President pro tempore of the Senate and the Speaker of the House of Representatives their written declaration that the President is unable to discharge the powers and duties of his office. Thereupon Congress shall decide the issue, assembling within 48 hours for that purpose if not in session. If the

Congress, within 21 days after receipt of the latter written declaration, or, if Congress is not in session, within 21 days after Congress is required to assemble, determines by two-thirds vote of both houses that the President is unable to discharge the powers and duties of his office, the Vice President shall continue to discharge the same as Acting President; otherwise, the President shall resume the powers and duties of his office.

AMENDMENT XXVI (1971)
Voting Age

SECTION 1. RIGHT TO VOTE

The right of citizens of the United States, who are 18 years of age or older, to vote shall not be denied or abridged by the United States or by any state on account of age.

Right to Vote This amendment gave the vote to everyone 18 years of age and older.

SECTION 2. ENFORCEMENT

The Congress shall have power to enforce this article by appropriate legislation.

AMENDMENT XXVII (1992)
Congressional Pay

No law, varying the compensation for the services of the senators and representatives, shall take effect, until an election of representatives shall have intervened.

Limit on Pay Raises This amendment prohibits a Congressional pay raise from taking effect during the current term of the Congress that voted for the raise.

The voting age was lowered to 18 in 1971.

New York Constitution Excerpts

 *The Constitution of the State of New York*

Preamble

We The People of the State of New York, grateful to Almighty God for our Freedom, in order to secure its blessings, DO ESTABLISH THIS CONSTITUTION.

Article 1

Bill of Rights

SECTION 1

No member of this state shall be disfranchised [denied a right], or deprived of any of the rights or privileges secured to any citizen thereof, unless by the law of the land, or the judgment of his or her peers . . .

Article 1

Bill of Rights

SECTION 3

The free exercise and enjoyment of religious profession and worship, without discrimination or preference, shall forever be allowed in this state to all humankind . . .

Article 1

Bill of Rights

SECTION 8

Every citizen may freely speak, write and publish his or her sentiments [thoughts] on all subjects . . . and no law shall be passed to restrain or abridge the liberty of speech or of the press.

Article 1

Bill of Rights

SECTION 9.1

No law shall be passed abridging [limiting] the rights of the people peaceably [peacefully] to assemble and to petition the government, or any department thereof . . .

Article 1

Bill of Rights

SECTION 11

No person shall be denied the equal protection of the laws of this state or any subdivision thereof. No person shall, because of race, color, creed or religion, be subjected to any discrimination in his or her civil rights by any other person . . .

Article 11

Education

SECTION 1

The legislature shall provide for the maintenance and support of a system of free common schools, wherein all the children of this state may be educated.

Article 1

Conservation

SECTION 4

The policy of the state shall be to conserve and protect its natural resources and scenic beauty and encourage the development and improvement of its agricultural lands for the production of food and other agricultural products.

The Five Themes of Geography

Learning about places is an important part of history and geography. Geography is the study of Earth's surface and the way people use it. When geographers study Earth and its geography, they often think about five main themes, or topics. Keeping these themes in mind as you read will help you think like a geographer.

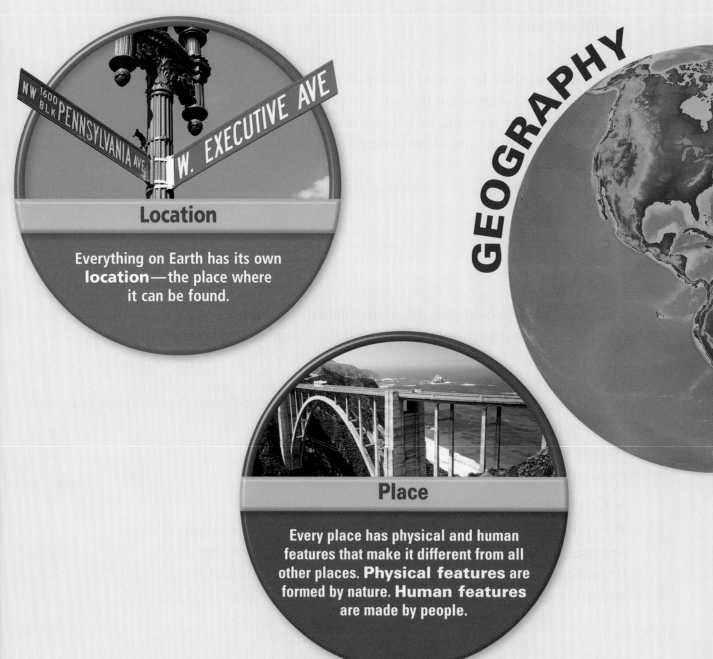

Location

Everything on Earth has its own **location**—the place where it can be found.

Place

Every place has physical and human features that make it different from all other places. **Physical features** are formed by nature. **Human features** are made by people.

GEOGRAPHY

Human-Environment Interactions

People and their surroundings interact, or affect each other. People's activities may change the environment. The environment may affect people. Sometimes people must change how they live to fit into their surroundings.

Movement

People, goods, and ideas move every day. They move in your state, our country, and around the world.

THEMES

Regions

Areas of Earth with main features that make them different from other areas are called regions. A **region** can be described by its physical features or its human features.

Geographic Terms

basin
a round area of land surrounded by higher land

bay
part of a lake or ocean that is partially enclosed by land

canyon
a valley with steep cliffs shaped by erosion

cape
a piece of land that points out into a body of water

coast
the land next to a sea or ocean

coastal plain
a flat area of land near an ocean

delta
land that is formed by soil deposited near the mouth of a river

desert
a dry region with little vegetation

fault
a break or crack in the earth's surface

▲ **glacier**
a large ice mass that pushes soil and rocks as it moves

hill
a raised area of land

island
an area of land surrounded by water

isthmus
a narrow piece of land connecting two larger land areas

lake
a large body of water surrounded by land

mountain
a raised mass of land with steep slopes

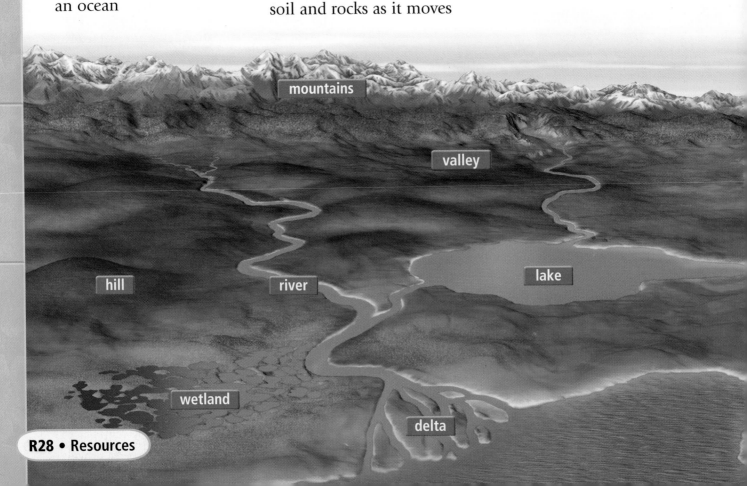

mountains

valley

hill

river

lake

wetland

delta

ocean
a large body of salt water that covers much of Earth's surface

peninsula
a strip of land surrounded by water on three sides

plain
a large area of flat land

plateau
an area of land that rises above nearby land and which may be flat or hilly

port
a sheltered part of a lake or ocean where ships can dock

prairie
a flat area of grassland with few trees

rain forest
a thick forest that receives heavy rainfall throughout the year

river
a body of water that flows from a high area to a lower area

river basin
an area that is drained by a river

tectonic plate
a huge slab of rock in Earth's crust that can cause earthquakes and volcanoes when it moves

tributary
a river or stream that flows into another river

valley
a low area of land between hills or mountains

▲ **volcano**
an opening in Earth's surface through which melted rock and gases escape

wetland
an area that is soaked with water, such as a marsh or a swamp

plateau

cape

bay

peninsula

plain

coastal plain

Atlas

The World: Political

ALB.	—Albania
AZER.	—Azerbaijan
BOS. & HERZ.	—Bosnia & Herzegovina
CEN. AFR. REP.	—Central African Republic
DEM. REP. OF CONGO	—Democratic Republic of Congo
FR.	—France
IT.	—Italy
KOS.	—Kosovo
LIECH.	—Liechtenstein
LUX.	—Luxembourg
MONT.	—Montenegro
NETH.	—Netherlands
N.Z.	—New Zealand
N. KOREA	—North Korea
REP. OF CONGO	—Republic of Congo
SERB.	—Serbia
SLOV.	—Slovenia
S. KOREA	—South Korea
SWITZ.	—Switzerland
U.A.E.	—United Arab Emirates
U.K.	—United Kingdom
U.S.	—United States

ARCTIC OCEAN

RUSSIA

ASIA

EUROPE

ICELAND

Area of Index

KAZAKHSTAN

MONGOLIA

GEORGIA
ARMENIA
TURKEY
AZER.
UZBEKISTAN
KYRGYZSTAN
TURKMENISTAN
TAJIKISTAN
CHINA

N. KOREA
S. KOREA

JAPAN

PACIFIC
OCEAN

TUNISIA
CYPRUS
LEBANON
SYRIA
IRAQ
JORDAN
AFGHANISTAN

MOROCCO
ISRAEL
IRAN
KUWAIT
PAKISTAN
NEPAL
BHUTAN

ALGERIA
LIBYA
EGYPT
BAHRAIN
QATAR
SAUDI
ARABIA
U. A. E.
OMAN
INDIA
BANGLADESH
MYANMAR

WESTERN
SAHARA
(Morocco)

TAIWAN

CAPE
VERDE

MAURITANIA

AFRICA

MALI
NIGER
CHAD
SUDAN
ERITREA
YEMEN

LAOS
THAILAND

VIETNAM

Northern
Mariana
Islands
(U.S.)

MARSHALL
ISLANDS

SENEGAL
GAMBIA
GUINEA BISSAU
GUINEA
SIERRA
LEONE
LIBERIA
BURKINA
FASO
GHANA
TOGO
BENIN
IVORY
COAST
NIGERIA
CEN.AFR.
REP.
DJIBOUTI
ETHIOPIA
CAMBODIA
PHILIPPINES
BRUNEI

Guam (U.S.)
FEDERATED STATES
OF MICRONESIA

KIRIBATI

EQU.
GUINEA
CAMEROON
SOMALIA
SRI LANKA
MALAYSIA
PALAU
NAURU

SAO TOME
AND PRINCIPE
GABON
REP. OF
CONGO
DEM.
REP.
OF
CONGO
UGANDA
RWANDA
BURUNDI
KENYA
MALDIVES
SINGAPORE
INDONESIA
PAPUA
NEW
GUINEA
SOLOMON
ISLANDS

TANZANIA

EAST
TIMOR

TUVALU

ANGOLA
MALAWI
ZAMBIA
MOZAMBIQUE
COMOROS

INDIAN
OCEAN

VANUATU

FIJI

ZIMBABWE

NAMIBIA
BOTSWANA
MADAGASCAR
MAURITIUS
Reunion
(Fr.)

New
Caledonia
(Fr.)

SWAZILAND
LESOTHO
SOUTH AFRICA

km 0   1000   2000
mi 0   1000   2000

AUSTRALIA

ATLANTIC
OCEAN

NEW
ZEALAND

SOUTHERN OCEAN

ANTARCTICA

Atlas

FINLAND

SWEDEN

NORWAY

RUSSIA

ESTONIA
LATVIA
LITHUANIA

km 0   150   300
mi 0   150   300

NORTH
SEA

DENMARK

RUSSIA

BELARUS

UNITED
KINGDOM

NETH.

GERMANY

POLAND

IRELAND

BELGIUM
LUX.
CZECH
REPUBLIC
UKRAINE

ATLANTIC
OCEAN

FRANCE
LIECH.
SWITZ.
SAN
MARINO
AUSTRIA
SLOVAKIA
HUNGARY
SLOV.
CROATIA
BOS. &
HERZ.
SERB.
MONT.
MOLDOVA
ROMANIA

MONACO

KOS.

Corsica
(Fr.)
ITALY
MACEDONIA
ALB.
BULGARIA

PORTUGAL

ANDORRA
Balearic
Islands
(Sp.)
Sardinia
(It.)

GREECE

TURKEY

SPAIN

Sicily (It.)

GIBRALTAR
(U.K.)
MEDITERRANEAN SEA

MOROCCO
ALGERIA
TUNISIA

The World: Physical

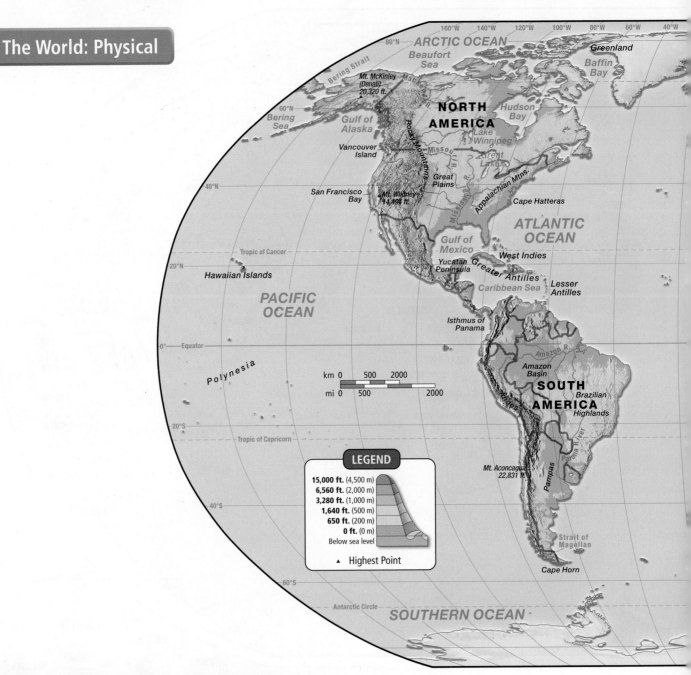

ARCTIC OCEAN
Beaufort Sea
Greenland
Baffin Bay
Bering Strait
Mt. McKinley (Denali) 20,320 ft.
NORTH AMERICA
Hudson Bay
Bering Sea
Gulf of Alaska
Rocky Mountains
Lake Winnipeg
Great Lakes
Vancouver Island
Missouri R.
San Francisco Bay
Mt. Whitney 14,494 ft.
Great Plains
Appalachian Mtns.
Cape Hatteras
ATLANTIC OCEAN
Mississippi R.
Tropic of Cancer
Gulf of Mexico
West Indies
Hawaiian Islands
Yucatan Peninsula
Greater Antilles
PACIFIC OCEAN
Caribbean Sea
Lesser Antilles
Isthmus of Panama
Equator
Amazon R.
Amazon Basin
SOUTH AMERICA
Brazilian Highlands
Polynesia
Andes
Paraná River
Tropic of Capricorn
Mt. Aconcagua 22,831 ft.
Pampas
Strait of Magellan
Cape Horn
Antarctic Circle
SOUTHERN OCEAN

km 0 500 2000
mi 0 500 2000

LEGEND

15,000 ft. (4,500 m)
6,560 ft. (2,000 m)
3,280 ft. (1,000 m)
1,640 ft. (500 m)
650 ft. (200 m)
0 ft. (0 m)
Below sea level

▲ Highest Point

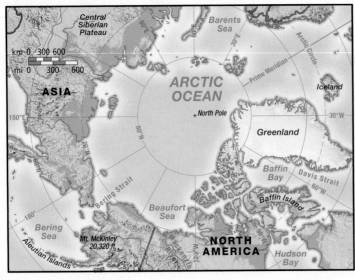

Central Siberian Plateau
Barents Sea
ASIA
Arctic Circle
Prime Meridian
km 0 300 600
mi 0 300 600
ARCTIC OCEAN
Iceland
North Pole
Greenland
Bering Strait
Baffin Bay
Davis Strait
Baffin Island
Beaufort Sea
Bering Sea
Mt. McKinley 20,320 ft.
Aleutian Islands
NORTH AMERICA
Hudson Bay

ARCTIC OCEAN

Barents
Sea

Central
Siberian
Plateau

EUROPE

North
Sea

Northern European Plain

Iceland

ASIA

Ob River

Yenisey River

Volga River

Sea of
Okhotsk

Kamchatka
Peninsula

60°N

Danube

Alps

Pyrenees

Mt. Elbrus
18,510 ft.

Aral
Sea

Lake
Baikal

Amur River

Sea
of
Japan

40°N

PACIFIC
OCEAN

Atlas Mtns.

Strait of
Gibraltar

Black Sea

Caucasus
Mountains

Caspian Sea

Gobi Desert

Mediterranean Sea

SAHARA

SAHEL

Plateau
of Tibet

Himalaya Mountains

Mt. Everest
29,035 ft.

Huang He

East
China
Sea

Tropic of Cancer

Yangtze

20°N

Micronesia

Niger River

AFRICA

Arabian
Sea

Bay of
Bengal

South
China
Sea

Philippine Islands

Congo River

Lake
Victoria

Nile River

Great
Rift
Valley

Mt. Kilimanjaro
19,340 ft.

Sumatra

Borneo

Equator

Java

New Guinea

Melanesia

0°

INDIAN
OCEAN

Strait of
Sunda

Madagascar

Great Sandy
Desert

Coral
Sea

20°S

Kalahari
Desert

Tropic of Capricorn

AUSTRALIA

Nullarbor
Plain

Darling River

Tasman
Sea

ATLANTIC
OCEAN

Prime Meridian

Cape of
Good Hope

Mt. Kosciusko
7,310 ft.

North Island

South Island

60°S

SOUTHERN OCEAN

Antarctic Circle

ANTARCTICA

20°W 0° 20°E 40°E 60°E 80°E 100°E 120°E 140°E 160°E

Arctic Circle

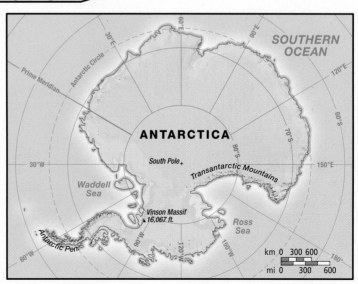

SOUTHERN
OCEAN

60°E

30°E

Antarctic Circle

80°E

Prime Meridian

120°E

ANTARCTICA

60°S

30°W

South Pole +

70°S

Transantarctic Mountains

150°E

Waddell
Sea

80°S

30°W

Vinson Massif
16,067 ft.

Ross
Sea

Antarctic Pen.

120°W

90°W

150°W

60°W

km 0 300 600

mi 0 300 600

160°E

Political

GREENLAND
(DENMARK)

Hudson
Bay

Labrador
Sea

CANADA

60°N

Great
Lakes

Ottawa ⊛

UNITED STATES

⊛ Washington, D.C.

ATLANTIC
OCEAN

40°N

Great
Salt
Lake

Gulf of
Mexico

BAHAMAS

Havana

Tropic of Cancer

Hawaii (U.S.)

MEXICO

Mexico City ⊛

CUBA

HAITI

DOMINICAN REPUBLIC

20°N

BELIZE

Kingston

U.S. VIRGIN ISLANDS

GUATEMALA

Belmopan

Santo

ST. KITTS AND NEVIS

JAMAICA

Domingo

ST. LUCIA

Guatemala City

Tegucigalpa

Port-Au-

BARBADOS

EL SALVADOR

Managua

Prince

San Salvador

San José

GRENADA

HONDURAS

Panama

Caracas

NICARAGUA

City

VENEZUELA

Georgetown

Paramaribo

COSTA RICA

Bogotá

Cayenne

PANAMA

FRENCH GUIANA

PACIFIC
OCEAN

COLOMBIA

SURINAME

(FRANCE)

Equator

Galápagos Is.
(Ecuador)

ECUADOR

Quito ⊛

GUYANA

0°

Lima

BRAZIL

PERU

⊛ Brasília

La Paz

French Polynesia
(France)

BOLIVIA

⊛ Sucre

20°S

Tropic of Capricorn

PARAGUAY

CHILE

Asunción ⊛

N

W ⊕ E

URUGUAY

S

Santiago ⊛

Buenos Aires ⊛ ⊛ Montevideo

40°S

ARGENTINA

LEGEND

⊛   National capital

Falkland Islands
(U.K.)

National border

km 0   500   1000

mi 0   500   1000

South Georgia
(U.K.)

60°S

140°W   120°W   100°W   80°W   60°W   40°W

R34 • Resources

Western Hemisphere Map Labels

ARCTIC OCEAN

Beaufort Sea

Baffin Bay

Bering Strait

Yukon R.

Mackenzie R.

Mt. McKinley (Denali) 20,320 ft. (6,194 m)

Davis Strait

Bering Sea

Gulf of Alaska

Coast Mountains

ROCKY MOUNTAINS

Hudson Bay

CANADIAN SHIELD

Labrador Sea

NORTH AMERICA

Great Lakes

Coast Ranges

Great Salt Lake

Range and Basin

Missouri R.

Mississippi R.

APPALACHIAN MOUNTAINS

ATLANTIC OCEAN

GREAT PLAINS

Death Valley 282 ft. (-86 m)

Mt. Whitney 14,495 ft. (4,418 m)

Rio Grande

Coastal Plain

Gulf of Mexico

Bahamas

Cuba

Hispaniola

Puerto Rico

Tropic of Cancer

Hawaiian Islands

Caribbean Sea

Lake Nicaragua

Lake Maracaibo

PACIFIC OCEAN

Line Islands

Equator

Galápagos Islands

Amazon R.

AMAZON BASIN

Marquesas

ANDES

Society Islands

SOUTH AMERICA

Cook Islands

Tropic of Capricorn

Atacama Desert

Mt. Aconcagua 22,834 ft. (6,960 m)

Rio de la Plata

Valdés Peninsula -131 ft. (-40 m)

Falkland Islands

Strait of Magellan

South Georgia

LEGEND

15,000 ft. (4,500 m)
6,560 ft. (2,000 m)
3,280 ft. (1,000 m)
1,640 ft. (500 m)
650 ft. (200 m)
0 ft. (0 m)
Below sea level

▲ Highest Point

N W E S

km 0 500 1000
mi 0 500 1000

80°N 60°N 40°N 20°N 0° 20°S 40°S 60°S

160°W 140°W 120°W 100°W 80°W 60°W 40°W

Atlas: Physical

GREENLAND

80°N
40°W

WASHINGTON
★ Seattle
★ Olympia
...land
Columbia R.
★ Salem

OREGON

IDAHO
★ Boise
Pocatello
Snake River

Helena ★
MONTANA
• Billings

WYOMING
Casper •

Cheyenne ★

W N E S

Sacramento ★
San Francisco

Reno •
★ Carson City

NEVADA

Salt Lake City ★
Provo •

UTAH

COLORADO
Denver ★
Colorado Springs •
Pueblo •

**PACIFIC
OCEAN**

CALIFORNIA

Las Vegas •

Colorado River

• Los Angeles

ARIZONA

Santa Fe ★
Albuquerque •

• San Diego

★ Phoenix

**NEW
MEXICO**

• Tucson

El Paso

LEGEND
⊛ National capital
★ State capital
• Major city
— National boundary
⋯ State boundary

Rio Grande

Gulf of California

MEXICO

Kauai
HAWAII
Niihau
Oahu
Honolulu
Kailua
Molokai
Lanai
Maui
Kahoolawe
PACIFIC OCEAN
Hilo
Hawaii

km 0 50 100
mi 0   50 100

CANADA

NORTH DAKOTA
★ Bismarck
• Fargo

MINNESOTA

SOUTH DAKOTA
★ Pierre
• Sioux Falls
Minneapolis
• St. Paul

Lake Superior

WISCONSIN
Madison ★
• Milwaukee

MICHIGAN
Grand Rapids •
Lansing ★

Lake Michigan
Lake Huron

St. Lawrence River

NEW HAMPSHIRE
VERMONT

MAINE
★ Augusta
• Portland
Concord ★
• Manchester

Burlington •
Montpelier ★

NEW YORK
Albany ★
• Rochester
• Buffalo

L. Ontario

MASSACHUSETTS
Boston ★
Providence ★
RHODE ISLAND
CONNECTICUT

Hartford ★
New Haven •

IOWA
Cedar Rapids •
Des Moines ★
Omaha ★

NEBRASKA
★ Lincoln

Chicago •

ILLINOIS
Springfield ★

Missouri R.

OHIO
Columbus ★

Cleveland •

Lake Erie

Detroit •

INDIANA
Indianapolis ★

Cincinnati •

PENNSYLVANIA
Harrisburg ★
Pittsburgh •

Newark •
New York •

Trenton ★
Philadelphia •

NEW JERSEY
Dover ★
DELAWARE

Annapolis ★
Washington, D.C. ⊛

MARYLAND

KANSAS
Kansas City •
Topeka ★

Kansas City •
Jefferson City ★

St. Louis •

MISSOURI

Louisville •

KENTUCKY
Frankfort ★

Ohio R.

WEST VIRGINIA
Charleston ★

Baltimore •

Richmond ★
Norfolk •

VIRGINIA

OKLAHOMA
Tulsa •
Oklahoma City ★

Fort Smith •

ARKANSAS
Little Rock ★

Memphis •

TENNESSEE
Nashville •

Mississippi River

NORTH CAROLINA
Greensboro •
Raleigh ★

Columbia ★
SOUTH CAROLINA
Charleston •

TEXAS
• Dallas

Austin ★
• Houston
• San Antonio

LOUISIANA
Jackson ★

MISSISSIPPI

Baton Rouge ★
• New Orleans

Birmingham •
Montgomery ★

ALABAMA

Mobile •

GEORGIA
Atlanta ★

Savannah •

ATLANTIC OCEAN

Tallahassee ★

Jacksonville •

FLORIDA
Tampa •

Miami •

BAHAMAS

Gulf of Mexico

km 0 100 200 300 400 500
mi 0 100 200 300 400 500

CUBA

United States: Physical

ARCTIC OCEAN

70N

RUSSIA

Brooks Range

Bering Strait

Yukon R.

Mt. McKinley
(Denali)
20,320 ft. ▲

Alaska Range

CANADA

60N

Bering
Sea

170W

Gulf of
Alaska

Aleutian
Islands

160W

Kodiak Is.

150W

140W

km 0   250   500
mi 0   250   500

110W

COAST RANGE

CASCADE RANGE

Mt. Rainer
14,410 ft.

Columbia R.

Mt. Hood
11,239 ft.

COLUMBIA PLATEAU

BITTERROOT RANGE

Missouri River

Snake River

Yellowstone River

ROCKY MOUNTAINS

BIGHORN MTNS.

Black Hills

Badlands

GREAT PLAINS

Mt. Shasta
14,162 ft.

Sacramento R.

CENTRAL VALLEY

SIERRA NEVADA

San Joaquin R.

BASIN
AND
RANGE

WASATCH RANGE

Green River

35N

San Francisco
Bay

Mt. Whitney
14,494 ft.

Death Valley
282ft. below sea level

Colorado River

Pikes Peak
14,110 ft.

PACIFIC
OCEAN

Mojave
Desert

Grand
Canyon

Painted
Desert

Colorado
Plateau

SANGRE DE CRISTO MTNS.

CONTINENTAL DIVIDE

Channel
Islands

30N

LEGEND

15,000 ft. (4,500 m)
6,560 ft. (2,000 m)
3,280 ft. (1,000 m)
1,640 ft. (500 m)
650 ft. (200 m)
0 ft. (0 m)
Below sea level

▲ Highest Point

Sonoran
Desert

Gila River

Llano

Estacado

Rio Grande

Pecos River

Edwa
Plate

25N

160W

Kauai

155W

Niihau

Oahu

Molokai

Lanai

Maui

Kahoolawe

Mauna Kea
13,796 ft.

20N

PACIFIC OCEAN

Hawaii

Mauna Loa
13,678 ft.

Gulf of California

MEXICO

Tropic of Cancer

km 0   50   100
mi 0   50   100

115W

110W

105W

CANADA

Mesabi Range

Lake Superior

St. Lawrence River

Mt. Washingto 6,288 ft.

White Mtns.

Adirondack Mountains

Connecticut R.

Lake Michigan

Lake Huron

L. Ontario

ALLEGHENY PLATEAU

Catskill Mtns.

Hudson R.

Nantu Martha' Vineyar

Lake Erie

Long Island

Mississippi River

Sand Hills

Des Moines River

Missouri River

Delaware River

Susquehanna River

Platte River

CENTRAL PLAINS

Delaware Bay

Wabash River

Ohio R.

Chesapeake Bay

OZARK PLATEAU

Arkansas River

Mt. Mitchell 6,684 ft.

Cumberland Plateau

Tennessee R.

A P P A L A C H I A N   M O U N T A I N S

BLUE RIDGE MOUNTAINS

FALL LINE

ATLANTIC COASTAL PLAIN

Mississippi River

OUACHITA MOUNTAINS

Red River

ATLANTIC OCEAN

Savannah R.

Oconee R.

Sabine River

Tombigbee R.

Alabama R.

Chattahoochee River

Altameha R.

Brazos River

Pearl River

PLAIN

Colorado River

COASTAL

GULF

Mobile Bay

Pensacola Bay

Galveston Bay

Tampa Bay

Gulf of Mexico

Everglades

BAHAMAS

Florida Keys

km 0   100   200   300   400   500

mi 0   100   200   300   400   500

Tropic of Cancer

CUBA

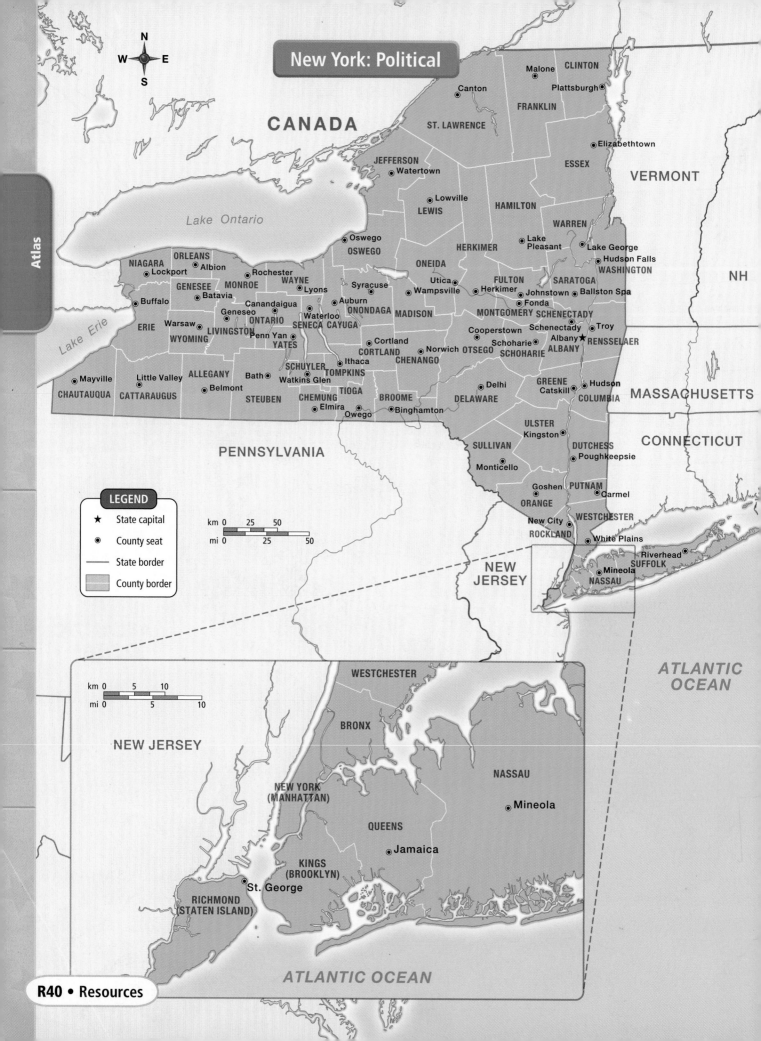

New York: Political

CANADA

W N E S

CLINTON
Malone •
Plattsburgh •

FRANKLIN

Canton •

ST. LAWRENCE

• Elizabethtown

ESSEX

VERMONT

JEFFERSON
• Watertown

LEWIS
• Lowville

HAMILTON

WARREN

Lake Ontario

OSWEGO
• Oswego

HERKIMER

Lake • Pleasant

• Lake George
• Hudson Falls

WASHINGTON

NH

ORLEANS
• Albion

NIAGARA
• Lockport

MONROE
• Rochester

WAYNE
• Lyons

ONEIDA
• Utica
• Wampsville

FULTON
• Herkimer
• Johnstown
• Fonda

SARATOGA
• Ballston Spa

GENESEE
• Batavia

SENECA **CAYUGA**
• Auburn

• Syracuse

ONONDAGA

MADISON

MONTGOMERY

SCHENECTADY
• Schenectady

• Troy

Buffalo •

ERIE

Warsaw •
WYOMING

LIVINGSTON
• Geneseo

ONTARIO
• Canandaigua

Waterloo •

Penn Yan •
YATES

Cooperstown •

Schoharie •
SCHOHARIE

Albany ★
RENSSELAER

ALBANY

Lake Erie

CHAUTAUQUA
• Mayville

CATTARAUGUS
Little Valley •

ALLEGANY
• Belmont

SCHUYLER
TOMPKINS
Watkins Glen •
• Ithaca

Cortland •
CORTLAND

CHENANGO
Norwich •

OTSEGO

GREENE
Catskill •

• Hudson

COLUMBIA

MASSACHUSETTS

Bath •

STEUBEN

CHEMUNG
Elmira •

TIOGA
Owego •

BROOME
• Binghamton

DELAWARE
• Delhi

PENNSYLVANIA

SULLIVAN
• Monticello

ULSTER
Kingston •

DUTCHESS
• Poughkeepsie

CONNECTICUT

LEGEND

★ State capital
⊙ County seat
— State border
▭ County border

km 0   25   50
mi 0   25   50

ORANGE
Goshen •

PUTNAM
• Carmel

New City •
ROCKLAND

WESTCHESTER
• White Plains

NEW JERSEY

Riverhead •
SUFFOLK

• Mineola
NASSAU

ATLANTIC OCEAN

---

km 0   5   10
mi 0   5   10

NEW JERSEY

WESTCHESTER

BRONX

NASSAU

NEW YORK (MANHATTAN)

• Mineola

QUEENS

KINGS (BROOKLYN)
St. George •

Jamaica •

RICHMOND (STATEN ISLAND)

ATLANTIC OCEAN

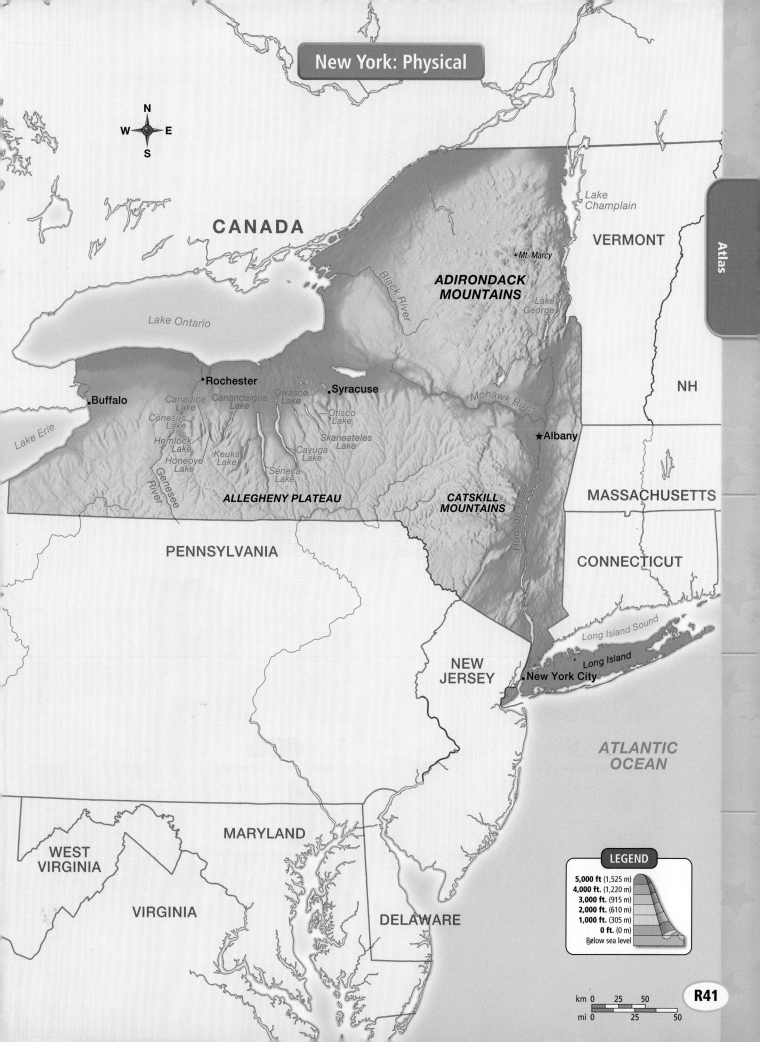

New York: Physical

N
W E
S

CANADA

Lake Ontario

Lake Champlain

VERMONT

Mt. Marcy

ADIRONDACK
MOUNTAINS

Black River

*Lake
George*

•Rochester

•Syracuse

*Owasco
Lake*

Mohawk River

NH

Canadice
Lake

Canandaigua
Lake

*Otisco
Lake*

★Albany

•Buffalo

Conesus
Lake

Skaneateles
Lake

Hemlock
Lake

Keuka
Lake

Cayuga
Lake

Lake Erie

Honeoye
Lake

Seneca
Lake

MASSACHUSETTS

*Genesee
River*

ALLEGHENY PLATEAU

CATSKILL
MOUNTAINS

CONNECTICUT

PENNSYLVANIA

Hudson River

Long Island Sound

Long Island

NEW
JERSEY

•New York City

ATLANTIC
OCEAN

WEST
VIRGINIA

MARYLAND

VIRGINIA

DELAWARE

LEGEND

5,000 ft. (1,525 m)
4,000 ft. (1,220 m)
3,000 ft. (915 m)
2,000 ft. (610 m)
1,000 ft. (305 m)
0 ft. (0 m)
Below sea level

km 0   25   50

mi 0   25   50

New York: Precipitation

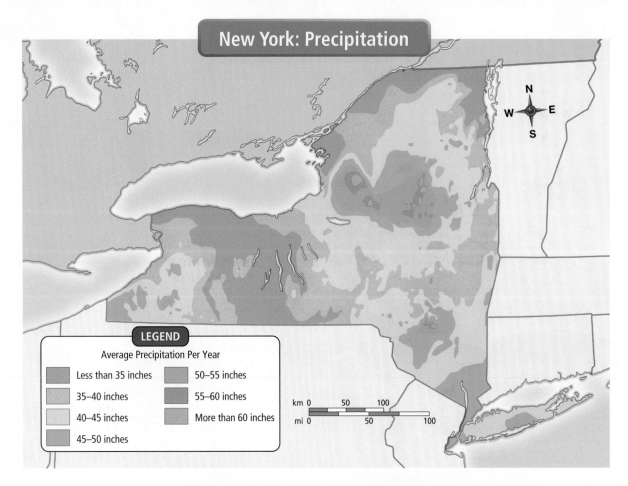

LEGEND

Average Precipitation Per Year

- Less than 35 inches
- 35–40 inches
- 40–45 inches
- 45–50 inches
- 50–55 inches
- 55–60 inches
- More than 60 inches

km 0 50 100
mi 0 50 100

New York: Temperature

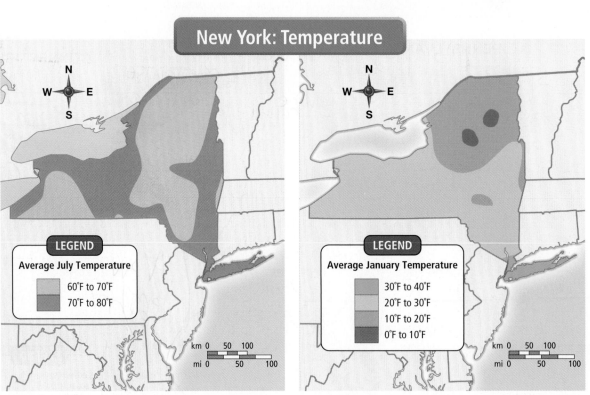

LEGEND

Average July Temperature

- 60°F to 70°F
- 70°F to 80°F

km 0 50 100
mi 0 50 100

LEGEND

Average January Temperature

- 30°F to 40°F
- 20°F to 30°F
- 10°F to 20°F
- 0°F to 10°F

km 0 50 100
mi 0 50 100

Major Roads and Airports

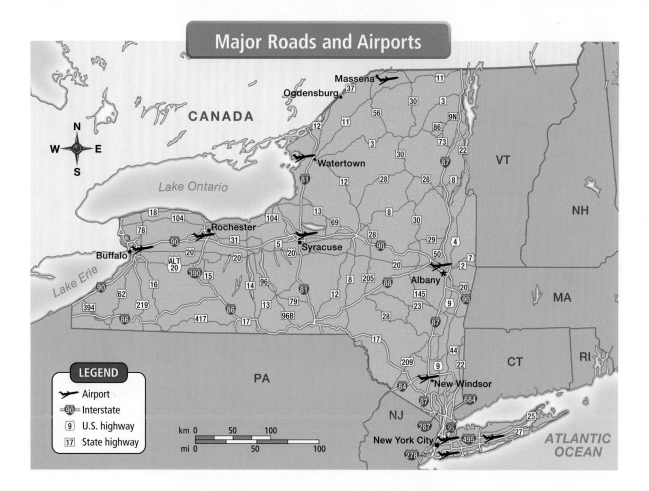

CANADA

Massena ✈
Ogdensburg 37

11

30 3

56 9N
86
73
22

VT

NH

12 11
3
30

Watertown ✈
81 12 28 28 8

13 8 30

Lake Ontario

18 104
78
90 104 69
20 31 5
ALT 20
390 15
16
90 62
394 219
86
417
417 13 79
96B 205 88 23
14 96 81 8
12
17

Rochester ✈
Syracuse ✈
28 90 20 29 50 4
145 9
87 44 22

Albany ★
7 2 20 90
209 9
84 87
287 95

MA

CT RI

PA

NJ

New Windsor ✈
684 25
27
495 ATLANTIC OCEAN
New York City ✈
278

LEGEND
✈ Airport
90 Interstate
9 U.S. highway
17 State highway

km 0   50   100
mi 0   50   100

Buffalo ✈
Lake Erie

Atlas

New York: State Parks

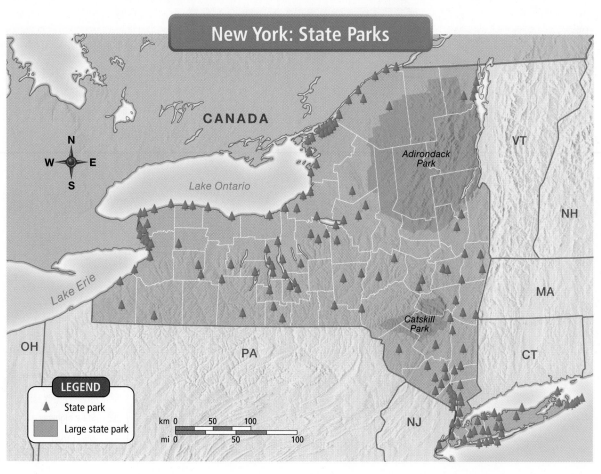

CANADA

Lake Ontario

VT

NH

Adirondack Park

Lake Erie

MA

OH

PA

Catskill Park

CT

NJ

ATLANTIC

LEGEND
🔺 State park
⬛ Large state park

km 0   50   100
mi 0   50   100

R43

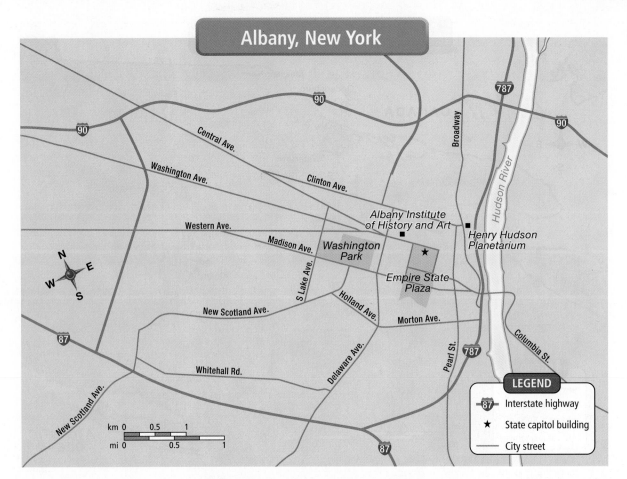

Albany, New York

90 • 787 • 90 • 90 • 87 • 787 • 87

Central Ave.
Washington Ave.
Clinton Ave.
Broadway
Hudson River
Western Ave.
Madison Ave.
Albany Institute of History and Art
Henry Hudson Planetarium
S Lake Ave.
Washington Park
Empire State Plaza
New Scotland Ave.
Holland Ave.
Morton Ave.
Whitehall Rd.
Delaware Ave.
Pearl St.
Columbia St.
New Scotland Ave.

LEGEND
87   Interstate highway
★   State capitol building
——   City street

km 0   0.5   1
mi 0   0.5   1

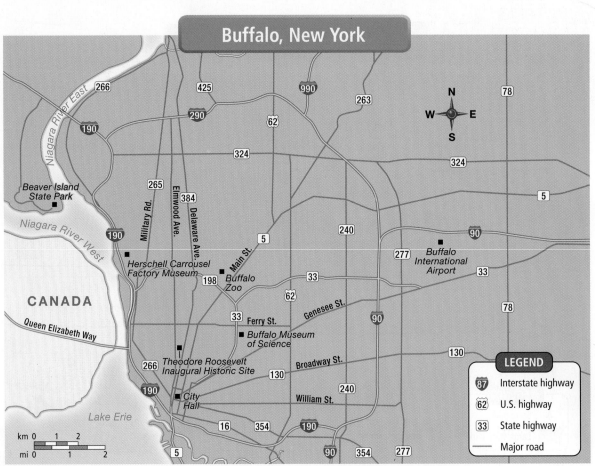

Buffalo, New York

266 • 425 • 990 • 263 • 78
190 • 290 • 62
324 • 324
265 • 5
384
Niagara River East
Beaver Island State Park
Niagara River West
Military Rd.
Elmwood Ave.
Delaware Ave.
Main St.
5
240
277
Buffalo International Airport
90
33
Herschell Carrousel Factory Museum
198
Buffalo Zoo
33
62
CANADA
33 Ferry St.
Genesee St.
78
Queen Elizabeth Way
Buffalo Museum of Science
130
Theodore Roosevelt Inaugural Historic Site
266
130
Broadway St.
190
City Hall
240
Lake Erie
William St.
16 354 190
5
90 354 277

LEGEND
87   Interstate highway
62   U.S. highway
33   State highway
——   Major road

km 0   1   2
mi 0   1   2

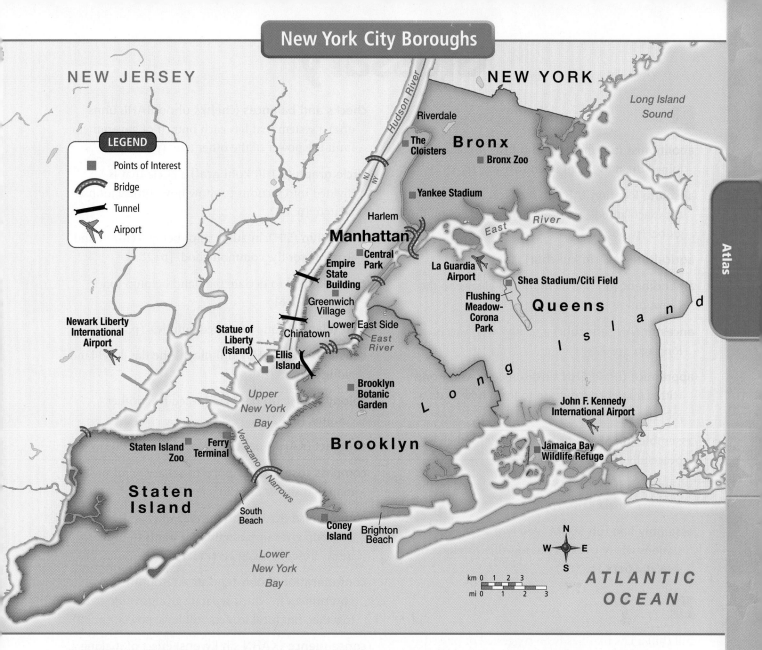

New York City Boroughs

NEW JERSEY

NEW YORK

Long Island Sound

Hudson River

Riverdale

Bronx

The Cloisters

Bronx Zoo

Yankee Stadium

Harlem

East River

Manhattan

Central Park

La Guardia Airport

Empire State Building

Shea Stadium/Citi Field

Greenwich Village

Flushing Meadow-Corona Park

Queens

Lower East Side

East River

Chinatown

Newark Liberty International Airport

Statue of Liberty (island)

Ellis Island

Brooklyn Botanic Garden

Long Island

John F. Kennedy International Airport

Upper New York Bay

Staten Island Zoo

Ferry Terminal

Brooklyn

Jamaica Bay Wildlife Refuge

Verrazano Narrows

Staten Island

South Beach

Coney Island

Brighton Beach

Lower New York Bay

ATLANTIC OCEAN

LEGEND
- ◼ Points of Interest
- Bridge
- Tunnel
- ✈ Airport

km 0 1 2 3
mi 0 1 2 3

N W E S

Borough	Origin of Name
The Bronx	For Mr. and Mrs. Bronck (the Broncks), a Danish man and his Dutch wife, the first settlers there to buy land from Native Americans
Brooklyn	For a town in the Netherlands
Manhattan	From the Lenape word for "island"
Queens	For Queen Catherine, who was Queen of England when the English took control of New Netherland in 1664
Staten Island	From the Dutch word for "state" or "government"; the Dutch government took over the island in 1637

Glossary

Glossary

abolitionist (ab uh LIH shuhn ihst) someone who joined the movement to end slavery. (p. 197)

absolute location (AB suh loot loh KAY shuhn) the exact latitude and longitude of a place on the globe. (p. 66)

agriculture (AG rih kul chur) farming. (p. 38)

amendment (uh MEND muhnt) a change to the Constitution. (p. 165)

ancestor (AN sehs tohr) a relative who was born long ago. (p. 37)

apprentice (uh PREHN tihs) someone who works with a master craftsperson to learn how to do a job. (p. 113)

assemble (uh SEHM buhl) to come together peacefully in a group. (p. 165)

assembly (uh SEHM blee) a group elected by the people to make laws. (p. 77)

assembly line (uh SEHM blee lyn) a series of work stations where workers put together products one step at a time. (p. 191)

bill (bil) a law that has been suggested or passed. (p. 165)

borough (BOHR oh) an area of a city with its own leaders. (p. 260)

budget (BUHJ iht) a plan for spending money. (p. 261)

canal (kuh NAL) a waterway made by people. (p. 191)

cash crop (kash krop) a crop that people grow and sell to earn money. (p. 107)

century (SEHN chuh ree) a period of 100 years. (p. 162)

checks and balances (chehks uhnd BAHL uhns ehz) a system that lets each branch of government limit the power of the other two. (p. 255)

circle graph (SUHR kuhl graf) a circle that is divided into sections to show how information is related. (p. 82)

citizenship (SIHT ih zuhn ship) being a citizen and working for the common good. (p. 282)

claim (klaym) to declare that land belongs to a country. (p. 61)

clan (klan) a group of related families. (p. 37)

coastal plain (KOHST uhl playn) the flat, level land along a coast. (p. 15)

colony (KAHL uh nee) land ruled by another country. (p. 62)

compact (KAHM pakt) an agreement. (p. 103)

compass rose (KUHM puhs rohz) a symbol on a map that shows direction. (p. 21)

compromise (KAHM pruh myz) when a person or group gives up something it wants in order to move closer to an agreement. (p. 206)

confederation (kuhn fehd ur AY shuhn) a government in which separate groups work together, but local leaders still have power. (p. 30)

consequence (KAHN sih kwens) effect of making a decision. (p. 266)

constitution (kahn stih TOO shuhn) a plan for running a government. (p. 156)

continent (KAHN tuh nuhnt) a very large landmass. (p. 12)

convention (kuhn VEHN shuhn) a meeting that brings many people together for a common purpose. (p. 198)

culture (KUHL chur) the way of life that people create for themselves and pass on to their children. (p. 40)

decade (DEHK ayd) a period of 10 years. (p. 162)

delegate (DEHL ih giht) someone chosen to speak or act for others. (p. 157)

democracy (dih MAHK ruh see) a system in which the people hold the power of government. (p. 158)

discrimination (dih skrihm uh NAY shuhn) the unfair treatment of other people based upon their differences. (p. 217)

diversity (dih VUR sih tee) variety among the people in a group. (p. 72)

draft (draft) when the government chooses people who have to serve in the military. (p. 202)

economy (ih KAHN uh mee) the way people use an area's resources. (p.104)

emancipation (ih MAN suh pay shuhn) the freeing of enslaved people. (p. 196)

enforce (ehn FAWRS) to carry out laws. (p. 255)

environment (ehn VY ruhn muhnt) the water, land, and air that surround us. (p. 10)

ethnic group (EHTH nik groop) a group of people who share a race, nationality, religion, or culture. (p. 222)

executive branch (ig ZEHK yuh tihv branch) the part of the government that is responsible for enforcing, or carrying out, laws. (p. 255)

fall line (fahl lyn) the place where rivers from higher land flow to lower land and often form waterfalls. (p. 101)

famine (FAM ihn) a widespread shortage of food. (p. 215)

federal (FEHD ur uhl) a type of government in which states and the central government share power. (p. 157)

founder (FOWN duhr) a person who starts something. (p. 68)

glacier (GLAY shur) a huge, slow-moving sheet of ice. (p. 14)

governor (GUHV ur nur) the official in charge of a colony (p. 62)

hemisphere (HEHM ih sfeer) one half of Earth's surface. (p. 12)

heritage (HAYR ih tij) something passed down from one generation to the next, such as language, traditions, food, or skills. (p. 224)

immigrant (IHM ih gruhnt) a person who leaves one country to live in another country. (p. 112)

immigration (ihm ih GRAY shuhn) the movement of people to a new country. (p. 215)

independence (ihn duh PEHN duhns) freedom from being ruled by another country. (p. 126)

interdependent (ihn tur dih PEHN duhnt) depending on each other. (p. 218)

judicial branch (joo DIHSH ul branch) the part of the government that decides the meaning of laws and whether laws have been followed. (p. 255)

labor union (LAY bur YOON yuhn) a group organized to protect workers' rights. (p. 234)

landform (LAND fohrm) a natural feature of Earth's surface. (p. 14)

latitude (LAT ih tood) distance north or south of the equator, measured by lines that circle the globe parallel to the equator. (p. 66)

legend (LEHJ uhnd) a table or list on a map that shows what the symbols on the map mean. (p. 21)

legislative branch (LEHJ ih slay tihv branch) the part of the government that is responsible for making laws. (p. 255)

living document (LIHV ihng DOHK yuh muhnt) a document, such as a constitution, that changes over time. (p. 276)

longhouse (LAWNG hows) a long, narrow house in which several families could live. (p. 30)

longitude (LAHN jih tood) distance east or west of the prime meridian, measured by lines that run between North and South poles. (p. 66)

Loyalist (LOI uh lihst) a colonist who wanted British rule. (p. 132)

maize (mayz) a form of corn (p. 31)

map scale (MAP skayl) the part of a map that compares distance on a map to distance in the real world. (p. 21)

mayor (MAY uhr) an elected official who leads a city. (p. 256)

melting pot (MEHL ting paht) a place where people from different backgrounds come together to form a diverse society. (p. 214)

mercantilism (MEHR kuhn tuh lihzm) a system in which a government controlled the economy of its colonies to grow rich from trade. (p. 108)

merchant (MUHR chuhnt) a person who buys and sells goods. (p. 115)

migrate (MY grayt) to move from one region and settle in another. (p. 223)

militia (muh LIHSH uh) a group of citizens who fight in an emergency. (p. 126)

natural resources (NACH ur ul REE sohr sihz) things from the environment that people use. (p. 38)

Patriot (PAY tree uht) a colonist who wanted independence from Britain. (p. 132)

patriotism (PAY tree uh tihz uhm) when a person shows his or her love for a country. (p. 283)

patroon (puh TROON) a landowner who was granted land in exchange for bringing settlers to New Netherland. (p. 69)

plantation (plan TAY shuhn) a large farm on which crops are grown by workers who live there. (p.107)

plateau (pla TOH) an area that rises above the nearby land. (p. 15)

point of view (poynt uhv vyoo) the way someone thinks about a person, a situation, or an event. (p. 130)

primary source (PRY mehr ee sawrs) a firsthand account of an event. (p. 220)

proprietor (proh PRY eht uhr) a person who owned and controlled the land of a colony (p. 106)

protest (PROH tehst) to speak out against something. (p. 125)

public school (PUHB lihk SKOOL) a school provided by the government. (p. 277)

ratification (raht if ih KAY shuhn) approval. (p.158)

region (REE juhn) an area that has one or more features in common. (p. 11)

report (rih PORHT) a presentation of information that has been researched. (p. 116)

representative (rehp rih ZEHN tuh tihv) a person who is chosen to speak for others. (p. 124)

reservation (rehz ur VAY shuhn) land set aside for Native Americans by the United States government. (p. 190)

reservoir (REHZ ur vwahr) a place where water is collected and stored for use. (p. 232)

responsibility (rih spahn suh BIHL ih tee) a duty that someone is expected to fulfill. (p. 281)

retreat (rih TREET) to turn back. (p. 133)

revise (rih VYZ) to change. (p. 274)

revolution (rehv uh LOO shuhn) a war fought to overthrow a government. (p. 126)

right (ryt) a freedom protected by law. (p. 77)

route (root) a road or waterway that travelers follow. (p. 60)

secede (sih SEED) to leave the nation to which a state belongs. (p. 201)

secondary source (SEHK uhn dehr ee sawrs) an account of an event recorded by someone who was not present at the event. (p. 220)

self-government (sehlf GUHV urn muhnt) the power of the people to make laws for themselves. (p.103)

sewer (SOO ur) an underground pipe for carrying waste. (p. 232)

skyscraper (SKY skray pur) a very tall building. (p. 231)

slavery (SLAY vuh ree) a cruel system in which one person owns another. (p. 69)

steamboat (STEEM boht) a boat powered by a steam engine. (p. 194)

strike (stryk) when workers refuse to work as a way to force business owners to improve their working conditions. (p. 234)

suffrage (SUHF rihj) the right to vote. (p. 198)

surrender (suh REHN dur) to give up. (p. 135)

table (TAY buhl) a chart in which facts are organized in columns and rows. (p. 278)

tax (taks) a fee people pay to the government for services. (p. 77)

technology (tehk NAHL uh jee) the use of scientific knowledge. (p. 70)

telegraph (TEHL ih graf) a machine that sends electric signals over wires. (p. 195)

tenement (TEHN uh muhnt) a poorly built apartment building. (p. 217)

tolerance (TAHL ur uhns) respect for other people's differences. (p. 72)

tradition (truh DIH shun) a way of life that has been followed for a long time. (p. 29)

turnpike (TURN pyk) a road that travelers pay to use. (p. 194)

veto (VEE toh) to reject. (p. 255)

volunteer (vawl uhn TEER) someone who chooses to do work without pay. (p. 203)

W

wigwam (WIHG wahm) a house made of a wood frame and covered with hides or woven reeds. (p. 28)

Index

Page numbers in italics with *m* before them refer to maps.

 A

Abolitionists, 197
  American Anti-Slavery Society, 169, 197
  Cornish, Samuel Eli, 168–169, 197
  Douglass, Frederick, 197
  Freedom's Journal, 169, 197
  in New York, 197
  North Star, The, 197
  Russwurm, John, 197
  Tappan, Arthur, 197
  Tappan, Lewis, 197
  Truth, Sojourner, 197
  Tubman, Harriet, 200
  Underground Railroad, 197
  Weeksville, New York, 197
Absolute location, 66
Adams, Abigail, 166
Adams, John, 166
Adirondack Mountains, 10, 14, 15
Adirondack Upland, 15
Africa, 69, 72, 108
  enslaved Africans, 69
  trade and, 69, 108, 111
African Americans
  abolitionists, 197
  African Burial Ground, 81
  in American Revolution, 136
  in the Civil War, 202
  Cornish, Samuel Eli, 168–169, 197
  cultural contributions, 223, 224
  daily lives, 80–81, 107
  Douglass, Frederick, 197
  Equiano, Olaudah, 166
  Fields, the, 81
  Fraunces, Samuel, 136
  Glover, Savion, 224
  in Harlem, 223
  lack of inclusiveness in Constitution, 166–167
  Lamb, Pompey, 136
  Meal Market, 81
  migration, 202, 216, 223
  Motley, Constance Baker, 265
  in New Netherland, 69, 77
  in New York City, 80–81, 136, *m228–229*
  in New York colony, 77, 114, 136
  population, 78, 80
  Randolph, Asa Philip, 237
  rights, 77, 114, 167
  Russwurm, John, 197
  in Southern Colonies, 107
  Truth, Sojourner, 197
  Tubman, Harriet, 200
  See also Enslaved Africans.
African Burial Ground, 81
Africans, 69
  See also African Americans *and* Enslaved Africans.
Agriculture, 27, 38, 107
  See also Farming.

Alaska, 28
Albany, New York, 11, 61, 62, 135, 247, *mR44*
Alexander, Mary Provoost, 115
Algonquian War, 62
Algonquians, 28–31, 36
  clothing, 29
  conflicts, 62
  daily life, 29
  fishing, 29
  houses, 28
  hunting land, 62
  interaction with Dutch, 62
  interaction with explorers, 61
  trade, 29, 61
  traditions, 29
Allen, Ethan, 126
Amendments, 155, 165–167, 276, 278–279
American Anti-Slavery Society, 169, 197
American Indians. *See* Native Americans.
American Revolution, 126–127, 132–137, 190
  African Americans in, 136
  Allen, Ethan, 126
  Arnold, Benedict, 126, 135
  Battle of Lexington and Concord, 126
  Battle of Long Island, 133
  Battle of Oriskany, 135
  Battle of Princeton, 134
  Battle of Saratoga, 123, 135
  Battle of Trenton, 134
  Battle of Yorktown, 93, 136, 168
  Brant, Joseph, 135
  British army, 133, 134, 135
  British navy, 133, 134
  in Boston, 133
  in Brooklyn, 133
  Burgoyne, John, 135
  Clinton, George, 136, 139
  Continental Army, 126, 133, 134, 136, 137, 139
  Corbin, Margaret, 123, 137
  Cornplanter (John O'Bail), 138
  Cornwallis, Charles, 136
  Declaration of Independence, 127, 128–129, 160, 198
  Fort Ticonderoga, 126, *m126*
  Fort Washington, 137
  Fraunces, Samuel, 136
  Gates, Horatio, 135
  Haudenosaunee in, 132, 136, 138
  Herkimer, Nicholas, 136
  Howe, William, 133
  Hudson River, 135
  Lamb, Pompey, 136
  Loyalists, 132, 135–136, 138
  Ludington, Sybil, 134
  in Manhattan, 133, 136
  militias, 134
  Native Americans in, 132, 136, 138
  in New York City, 132, 133, 136
  in New York State, 132, 133, *m133*, 134, 135, 136
  O'Bail, John (Cornplanter), 138
  Patriots, 132, 134, 136–137, 139

  St. Leger, Barry, 135
  Schuyler, Philip, 126
  Washington, George, 126, 133, 134, 136, 138, 159
  women in, 134, 137
American symbols, 284–285
Amsterdam, 71
Ancestor, defined, 37
Animal signs, 37
Anthony, Susan B., 198–199
Appalachian Plateau, 15
Apples, 105, 106
Appoint, 262
Apprentices, defined, 99, 113
Archaeologists, 32–33
Armies
  British, 108, 133, 134, 135
  Continental, 126, 133, 134, 136, 137, 139
Arnold, Benedict, 126, 135
Articles of Confederation, 157
Asia, 28
  route to, 60, 61, 92
Asian immigration, 183
Assemble, 165
Assembly, defined, 59, 77, 114
  in New York State, 255, 259, 275
Assembly lines, 100, 191
Atlantic Coastal Plain, 15
Atlantic Ocean, 53, 108
Atlas, R30–R45

 B

Badillo, Herman, 264
Baker, S. Josephine, 232
Bald eagle, 285. *See also* Eagle *and* National symbols.
Banking, 218
Bar graphs
  City Populations, 1740s, 93
  City Populations Today, 93
  Crossing the Atlantic Through the Years, 53
  Famous New York City Skyscrapers, 231
  Immigrants in Manhattan, 1900–1950, 228
  Immigration to New York State, 1860, 183
  Immigration to New York State Today, 183
  Mountains in New York, 3
  New York–England Trade, 110
  Population Growth of New York City, 78
  Rivers in New York, 3
Barley, 105, 106
Basketball
  New York Knicks, 248
Batteries, 55, 106
Battery Park, 55
Battles
  American Revolution, 93, 123, 126, 133, *m133*, 134, 135, 136
  Lexington and Concord, 126
  Long Island, 133

Index

Oriskany, 135
Princeton, 134
Saratoga, 123, 135
Trenton, 134
Yorktown, 93, 136, 168
Bays, 64, 101
Beans, 31, 38
Beaver hats, 63
Bifocal glasses, 106
Big Tree Treaty, 190
Bill, defined, 165
Bill of Rights, 155, 165–166, 172, 280
First Amendment, 165, 172
freedom of religion, 275, 280
freedom of speech, 275, 280
Zenger trial, 115, 164
Biography Features
Badillo, Herman, 264
Champlain, Samuel de, 65
Clinton, George, 139
Cornish, Samuel Eli, 169
Cornplanter, 138
Ellerin, Betty W., 264
Hamilton, Alexander, 168
Hudson, Henry, 65
Jay, John, 139
La Guardia, Fiorello, 265
Mohawk ironworkers, 43
Motley, Constance Baker, 265
Mullany, Kate, 237
Parker, Ely S., 42
Randolph, Asa Philip, 237
Schneiderman, Rose, 236
Shenandoah, Joanne, 43
Verrazano, Giovanni da, 64
Bodies of water, 16, 19
Boerum Hill, 43
Boroughs, 260
the Bronx, 17, 260, 264
Brooklyn, 78, 112, 133, 186, 260
Manhattan, 65, 70, 74, 112, 133, 136, 223, 224, 260
presidents, 262, 264
Queens, 222, 260
Staten Island, 15, 17, 260
Boston, Massachusetts, 93, 125, 126, 133
Boston Tea Party, 125
Brady, Mathew, 204–205
Branches of government, 158, 254–255, 274–275
Brant, Joseph, 135
Brazil, 112
Breede Wegh, *m71*
Bridges, 75, 265
Britain, 124, 125, 132, 139
army, 133, 134, 135
Burgoyne, John, 135
Cornwallis, Charles, 136
government, 124
Howe, William, 133
immigration from, 183
Loyalists, 132, 135–136
navy, 108, 133, 134
St. Leger, Barry, 135
tax laws, 124, 125
war with France, 124, 139
See also England.
British immigration, 183
Broadway, *m71*

Bronx, 17, 260, 264
Badillo, Herman, 264
Carrión, Alfonso, Jr., 262
Brooklyn, 186, 260
American Revolution in, 133
colonial, 78, 112
Native Americans in, 78
Brooklyn Bridge, 226
Brooklyn ferry, 112
Budget, defined, 253, 261
Buffalo, New York, 11, 192, *mR44*
Building codes, 232
Burgoyne, John, 135
Businesses, 105, 106, 113, 115

Calendars, 125
Canada, 13, 62, 65, 136
Canals, 71, *m71,* 188, *m192–193,* 194
Canawagus, New York, 138
Cannons, *m126*
Capital, 149, 157, 163
Caribbean, 69, 108, 111
Caribbean immigration, 223
Carnegie Hall Tower, 230
Carrión, Alfonso, Jr., 262
Cartier, Jacques, 61
Cash crops, 99, 107
indigo, 99, 107, 111
rice, 107
tobacco, 107
Categorize, 76, 260
Catskill Mountains, 15
Cattle, 105
Cause and effect, 124, 190, 184–185, 214, 222
Cayuga Indians, 30
Celebrations, 225, 227
Century, 162
Ceremonies, 40
Champlain, Samuel de, *m52–53,* 53, 61, 65
Chart and Graph Skills
Make a Table, 278–279
Make a Timeline, 162–163
Read a Circle Graph, 82–83
Charter of Liberties, 77
Charts and graphs
Amendments to New York's Constitution, 276
Amendments to the New York State Constitution, 278
Changes in Immigration, 1880–1920, 215
Checks and Balances, 259
Citizens Take Responsibility in New York City, 287
City Populations, 1740s, 93
City Populations Today, 93
Colonial New York Trade, 110
Crossing the Atlantic Through the Years, 53
Famous New York City Skyscrapers, 231
Federal Holidays, 283
Immigrants in Manhattan, 1900–1950, 228

Immigration to New York State, 1860, 183
Immigration to New York State Today, 183
Make Decisions, 266
Middle Colonies, 106
Mountains in New York, 3
National and State Governments, 258
New England Colonies, 105
New York by the Numbers, 19
New York City Land Area, 247
New York City Population, 2006, 247
New York–England Trade, 110
New York's Three Branches of Government, 255
Population Growth, 1800s, 149
Population Growth of New York City, 78
Population Growth Today, 149
Population of New York City, 1900, 222
Rivers in New York, 3
Seasonal Ceremonies, 40
Southern Colonies, 107
Traded Goods, 111
Values, Practices, Traditions, 171
Workers in New York, 1700s, 83
Checks and balances, 158, 255, 259
Child labor laws, 234
China, 60
Chinese immigration, 183, 228
Chinatown, 223, 227
Chrysler Building, 231
Church of England, 102
Circle graphs, 82
Changes in Immigration, 1880–1920, 215
New York City, 1900, 222
New York City Land Area, 247
New York City Population, 2006, 247
Workers in New York, 1700s, 83
Cities
colonial, 93, 105, 106
See also New York City.
Citizenship, 268, 270, 282
Citizenship Skills
Make Decisions, 266–267
Resolve Conflicts, 206–207
Understand Point of View, 130–131
City council, 251, 261
Civil rights, 172
Civil War, 200–203, 204–205, 207
African Americans in, 202
Brady, Mathew, 204–205
causes, 200–201
Confederacy, 201–203, 207
Draft Riots, 202
effects, 203
Emancipation Proclamation, 202, 203
Lincoln, Abraham, 201
New York in, 202, 205
photography in, 204–205
secession, 201
Union, 201–203, 207
women in, 189, 203
Claim, defined, 61
Clans, 37
Classify, 132
Clermont, 194

Clinton, DeWitt, 192
Clinton, George, 136, 139
Cloth, 108, 111, 125
Coastal plain, 15
Cod, 105
Colonies, 58, 62
    characteristics, 100–101, 104–107
    Dutch, 62, 63, 68–73, 74–75
    English, 63, 76–79, 100–103, 104–109,
      112–115, 124–127
    French, 69
    reasons for settlement, 102–103
Columbus, Christopher, 53, 60
Common good, 160
Communication, 195
Community service, 282
Compact, defined, 98, 103
Compare and contrast, 94–95, 104, 144,
    200, 274
Compass rose, 21
Compromise, defined, 206
Comptroller, 262
Conclusions, defined, 54
Concord, Massachusetts, 126
Confederacy, 201–203, 207
Confederation, 26, 30
Congress, 128
    First Continental Congress, 126, 139
    Second Continental Congress, 126
    United States Congress, 264, 265
Connecticut, 134
Connecticut River, 62
Consequence, defined, 266
Constitution, New York State, 150, 154,
    156, 162, 254–255, 272
    foundation for a new government,
      160
Constitution, United States, 150, 154,
    157–159, 162
    amendments, 165–167
    Bill of Rights, 155, 165–166, 172, 280
    branches of government, 158, 254–255,
      274–275
    checks and balances, 158, 255, 259
    democracy, 158, 166
    federal government, 157, 158
    foundation for a new government,
      160
    as a framework, 157
    lack of inclusiveness, 166–167
    living document, 272, 276
    Preamble, 160
    ratification, 155, 158–159
    rights, 158, 164
    rule of law, 158
    slavery in, 203
    Zenger trial, 115, 164
Constitution Day, 171
Constitutional Convention, 154, 157,
    160–161, 162, 163
    delegates, 157
Continent, 8, 12
Continental Army, 126, 133, 134, 136,
    137, 139
Continental Congress
    First, 126, 139
    Second, 126, 128
Contributions of immigrants
    celebrations, 225
    culture, 224–226

    food, 225
    language, 224–225
    murals, 226
    music, 224
    recreation, 224–225
    skills, 226
    traditions, 224–225
Convention, 198. *See also* Constitutional
    Convention *and* Seneca Falls
    Convention.
Corbin, Margaret, 123, 137
Corn, 105, 106
Cornish, Samuel Eli, 168–169, 197
Cornplanter (John O'Bail), 138
Cornwallis, Charles, 136
Cotton, 109, 193, 201
Court of Appeals, 255, 259
Courts, 77, 115, 255, 259, 264
    judicial branch, 252, 255
    juries, 77
    in New Netherland, 77
    in New York colony, 77, 115
    in New York State, 255, 259
Craftspeople, 105, 106
Crops, 108
    apples, 105, 106
    barley, 105, 106
    beans, 31, 38
    cash crops, 99, 107
    corn, 31, 38, 105, 106
    hay, 106
    indigo, 99, 107, 111
    oats, 106
    peaches, 106
    potatoes, 106
    rice, 107
    rye, 105
    squash, 31, 38
    tobacco, 107
    wheat, 105, 106
Crotty, Erin M., 15
Culture, 40, 224–226
    centers of, 106
    contributions of immigrants, 224–226
    in the Middle Colonies, 106
    in New England Colonies, 105
    in the Southern Colonies, 107
Czech immigration, 215, *m228–229*

Daily life
    of African Americans, 80–81, 107
    of children, 95, 105, 106, 107, 113
    on farms, 105, 106, 107
    of men, 113
    in the Middle Colonies, 106, 113
    in New Amsterdam, 70
    in New England Colonies, 105
    in New York colony, 113
    on plantations, 107
    in the Southern Colonies, 107
    of women, 113
Danbury, Connecticut, 134
Daughters of Liberty, 125
Decade, 162
Declaration of Independence, 127,
    128–129, 160, 198
    foundation for a new government,
      160

Declaration of Sentiments, 198
Delaware Indians. *See* Lenape.
Delaware River, 36, 62, 69, 134
Delegates, 154, 157
Democracy, 158, 166
**Differences between English and
    Dutch rule,** 113
Discrimination, 217
Diseases, 62, 216, 217, 232
District, 253, 257, 261. *See also* Special
    districts.
Diversity, 72
    in New Amsterdam, 69, 70, 72
    in New York City, 78, 214–215, 218,
      222–226
    in New York colony, 112
Division of labor, 39
Dominican Republic immigration, 183,
    225
Douglass, Frederick, 197
Draft, 202, 207
Draft Riots, 202
Draw conclusions, 54–55, 60, 88, 230
Duke of York, James, 77, 106
Dutch colonies, 62
    diversity, 72
    economy, 69, 70
    founders of, 68
    furs, 62, 63, 68, 69, 70
    government, 62, 76, 77
    growth of, 63, 68, 70, 72
    Native Americans and, 62, 68
    New Amsterdam, 68–72
    New Netherland, 59, 62–63, 68–69
    patroons, 69
    population, 63
    Rensselaerswyck, 69
    settlement, 62, *m62,* 68, 70
    slavery, 69
    surrender to English, 76
    tolerance, 59, 72
    See also New Amsterdam *and* New
      Netherland.
Dutch doors, 75
Dutch Reformed Church, 70
Dutch West India Company, 68
    control of trade, 69
    slave trade and, 69

Eagle, as national symbol, 285
Earth, 66
East River, 17
Economics
    banking, 218
    child labor laws, 234
    emergence of New York as an
      economic power, 191
    gold, 60, 102
    labor movement, 234
    reasons for settlement, 102
    resources, 98
    See also Trade.
Economy, 98, 104
    of the Middle Colonies, 106
    of New England Colonies, 98, 105
    of New Netherland, 69, 70
    of New York colony, 78, 106, 113
    of the Southern Colonies, 99, 107

Education, 70, 95, 105, 114, 151, 281
    public schools, 151, 272, 277
    Roelantsen, Adam, 70
Elders, 37, 39
Elect, 256
Elections
    colonial assembly, 77
    House of Burgesses, 107
    town meetings, 105
Electricity, 55, 106
Elk Lake, 10
Ellerin, Betty W., 264
Ellis Island, 212, 213, 216–217, 220
Emancipation, 196–197, 202, 203
    gradual emancipation law, 197
Emancipation Proclamation, 202, 203
Empire State Building, 231
Enforce, defined, 255
England, 103
    Church of England, 102
    colonies, 63, 76, 100–103, 104–109
    government, 108
    Greenwich, 66
    rule in New York, 76–79
    settlers from, 78
    trade, 108
English colonies, 63, 76, 100–103, 104–109
    farms, 78, 100
    Georgia, 100, 102
    government, 77, 105–107, 114
    growth of, 63, 106, 112
    Jamestown, 102, 116–117
    laws, 77, 114
    Middle Colonies, 100, *m101*, 102, 106
    New England Colonies, 101, *m101*, 102, 103, 105
    New York colony, 76–79, 100, 106, 113, 114
    population, 63, 78, 80, 93, 106
    reasons for settlement, 102–103
    rights, 77, 114, 115
    settlement, 100
    slavery, 80–81, 107, 113
    Southern Colonies, 101, *m101*, 107
    trade with England, 108–109, 110–111, 113, 126
    transportation, 100
    Virginia, 93, 102, 107, 136, 165
Enslaved Africans
    African Burial Ground, 81
    daily life, 80–81, 107, 113
    Fields, the, 81
    laws, 114, 197
    Meal Market, 81
    movement of, 69, 78, 107, 114
    in New York colony, 80–81, 113, 114
    rights, 114
    in Southern Colonies, 107
    work, 69, 107, 113
Environment, 10
    Native Americans and, 28–31, 38–40
Equality, 171
Equator, 12, 66, *m66*
Equiano, Olaudah, 166
Erie Canal, 181, 182, 188, *m192–193*, 194
    Buffalo, New York, 192
    Clinton, DeWitt, 192
    Hudson River, 188, 192
    impact of, 193
    Lake Erie, 188, 192

    lower shipping costs, 193
    New York City, 192–193
    Rome, New York, 192
    Stevens, John, 192
Erie–Ontario Lowland, 15
Establishment of colonies
    characteristics, 100–101, 104–107
    reasons for immigration, 102–103
    role of geography, 100–101
Ethnic groups, 215, 216, 222–226
    African, 69
    African American, 77, 78, 80–81, 107, 114, 136, 216, 223, *m228–229*
    Asian, 183
    British, 124–127, 132–137, 183
    Caribbean, 223
    Chinese, 183, 223, 227, *m228–229*
    Czech, 215, 228–229
    Dominican Republic, 183, 225
    Dutch, 61–63, 68–72, 112, 138
    English, 63, 69, 78, 112
    French, 69, 70, 78, *m228–229*
    German, 70, 78, 112, 134, 183, 215, *m228–229*
    Greek, *m228–229*
    Guyanese, 183, 222
    Hungarian, 215
    Indian, 218
    Irish, 78, 183, 184, 215, 224, *m228–229*
    Italian, 64, 215, *m228–229*
    Jewish, 72, 112, 216, 222, *m228–229*
    Mexican, 223
    Native American, 28-31, 32–33, 36–41, 42–43, 61, 64, 65, 78, 114, 132, 135, 136, 138
    Polish, 215, *m228–229*
    Puerto Rican, 218, 264
    Russian, 215, *m228–229*
    Scandinavian, *m228–229*
    Scottish, 78, 112
    Senegalese, 223
    Swedish, 69, 70, 112, 215
    Syrian, *m228–229*
    Turkish, 225, *m228–229*
Ethnic neighborhoods, 223, 228–229
Europe, 60, 72, 108, 111, 113
European immigration, 183, 212
Executive branch, 253, 255, 259, 275
Exploration, 60
    reasons for, 60
    routes, *m52–53*
    of New York State, *m52–53*, 61
    of North America, 60, 61, 64–65
    of Pacific coast, 92
Explorers, 60, 64–65
    Cartier, Jacques, 61
    Champlain, Samuel de, *m52–53*, 61, 65
    Columbus, Christopher, 53, 60
    Hudson, Henry, *m52–53*, 61, 65
    interaction with Native Americans, 64–65
    Verrazano, Giovanni da, *m52–53*, 61, 64

F

Factories, 191, 201
Fall line, defined, 101
Family life, 113

Famine, 215
Farming
    in English colonies, 78, 95, 100, 105, 106, 107
    in Middle Colonies, 106, 113
    in New Amsterdam, 70
    in New England Colonies, 105
    in New Netherland, 62, 70
    in New York colony, 78, 113
    slash-and-burn farming, 38
    wind and, 55
"Father of New York", 139
Federal government, 157, 158, 258, 274
Federal Hall, 159
Federal holidays, 283
Federalist Papers, 158
Fenner, New York, 55
Ferries, 112
Fields, the, 81
Finger Lakes, 16
Finished goods, 108, 110, 111
Fire department, 233
Fireplaces, 106
First Amendment, 165, 172
First Continental Congress, 126, 139
Fishing, 31, 38, 98, 101, 105, 108
Flag of the United States, 285
Flour, 193
Floyd, William, 126
Forced migration, 62, 69, 78, 107, 114, 136, 216
Forests, 101
Forest Hills, Queens, 222
Forts, 62, 78, 126, *m126*, 136, 137, 138
    French, 78
    Nassau, 62
    in New York, 62, 78, 126, *m126*, 136, 137, 138
    Stony Point, 136
    Ticonderoga, 126, *m126*
    Washington, 137
Foundations of government
    Declaration of Independence, 127, 128–129, 160, 198
    Mayflower Compact, 160
    New York State Constitution, 150, 154, 156, 160, 162, 254–255, 272
    United States Constitution, 150, 154, 157–159, 160, 162, 164, 165–167
Founders, defined, 68
France, 124
    American Revolution and, 135, 136
    Cartier, Jacques, 61
    Champlain, Samuel de, *m52–53*, 53, 61, 65
    explorers, 61, 65
    forts, 78
    Huguenots, 69
    immigration from, 69, 70, 78, *m228–229*
    settlers from, 78
    war between Britain and, 124, 139
Franklin, Benjamin, 106
Fraunces, Samuel, 136
Free Africans. *See* African Americans.
Freedom, 164, 165, 171
    of assembly, 165
    independence, 126
    of petition, 165
    political, 102
    of the press, 115, 164, 165

protected by government, 77
of religion, 69, 77, 102, 275, 280
rights, 77
of speech, 115, 275, 280
Freedom's Journal, 169, 197
French immigration, *m228–229*
Fulton, Robert, 194
Fun with Social Studies, 46–47, 86–87, 142–143, 176–177, 240–241, 288–289
Furniture, 108, 111, 113
Furs
beaver hats, *63*
New Netherland and, 62, 63, 68, 69, 70
trade of, 61, 62, 63, 68, 69, 70, 111

Ganondagan State Historic Site, 24–25
Gates, Horatio, 135
Generalize, 4–5, 10
Genesee River, 138
Geneseo, New York, 11
Geography
absolute location, 66
bodies of water, 16, 19
coast, 100, 101, 104
environment, 10
equator, 12, 66, *m66*
fall line, 101
features of New York City, 17, 18
features of New York State, 14–16, 18–19
hills, 100
influence on settlement, 62, 100, 101
landforms, 14–15, 18–19
of the Middle Colonies, 100
mountains, 101
of New England Colonies, 101
of the Southern Colonies, 101
waterfalls, 101
See also Rivers.
Georgia, 100, 102
German immigration, 183, 215, *m228–229*
Germany, 78, 112, 134
Giuliani, Rudy, 282
Glacier, 9, 14
Glass, 111, 125
Globe, 66, *m66*
Glover, Savion, 224
Gold, 60, 102
Goods, 68, 109, 113, 115
finished, 108, 110, 111
Government
Articles of Confederation, 157
assembly, 59, 77, 114
Bill of Rights, 155, 165–166, 172, 280
branches of government, 158, 254–255, 258–259, 274–275
Charter of Liberties, 77
checks and balances, 158, 255, 259
citizens' role in, 281–283
compact, 103
Constitutional Convention, 154, 157, 160–161, 162, 163
control of economy, 108
democracy, 158, 166
Dutch colonies, 62, 68–72, 76
elections, 77, 105, 107
English colonies, 77, 105–107, 114

executive branch, 253, 255, 259, 275
federal, 157, 158, 258, 274
governors, 58, 62, 68, 76, 77, 114, 115
House of Burgesses, 107
judicial branch, 252, 255
laws, 70, 77, 103, 105, 106, 107, 109, 114, 124, 125
legislative branch, 252, 255
Lenape, 37
local, 256–257, 258
Mayflower Compact, 103
in the Middle Colonies, 106
in New England Colonies, 105
in New Netherland, 62, 76, 77
in New York City, 260–261
in New York colony, 77, 106
in New York State, 245, 258–259
New York State constitution, 150, 154, 156, 160, 162, 255, 272
paying for, 263
plans of, 77, 103, 139 150, 154, 156, 157–159, 160, 162, 255, 272
proprietors, 106, 107
purpose of, 277
religion and, 105, 114
rights, 158, 164
rule of law, 158, 160
self-government, 103
services of, 262
in the Southern Colonies, 107
state, 254–255, 258–259
United States Constitution, 150, 154, 157–159, 160, 162, 164, 165–167
Governors, 58, 62
Clinton, George, 136, 139
Kieft, Willem, 62, 72
May, Cornelius, 62
Minuit, Peter, 68
of New Netherland, 58, 62, 68, 76, 77
of New York colony, 77, 114, 115
of New York State, 136, 139, 255, 259, 275
Nicolls, Richard, 77
proprietors and, 106
Stuyvesant, Peter, 58, 76, 77
Gradual emancipation laws, 197
Grant, Ulysses S., 42
Graphs. *See* Charts and graphs.
Great Lakes, 15, 16, 29
Greek immigration, *m228–229*
Green Corn Ceremony, 39
Greenwich, England, 66
Grim, David, 80–81
Growth
of cities, 93, 106
of Dutch colonies, 63, 68
of English colonies, 63, 106, 112
of New Netherland, 63, 68, 70, 72
of New York City, 93, 112, 214, 218, 228, 230–232
of New York colony, 93, 112
Gulf of Mexico, 29
Guyanese immigration, 183
Little Guyana, 222

Half Moon, 65
Hamilton, Alexander, 155, 156, 157, 158, 168

Hamilton, Andrew, 164
Harbors
in New Amsterdam, 70, 72, 76
New York Harbor, 61, 79, 111, 133
Harlem, Manhattan, 70, 223
Harlem River, 17
Harmon, Patience, 40
Haudenosaunee, 28, 30–31, 138
American Revolution and, 132, 136
Big Tree Treaty, 190
daily life, 30–31
farming, 30–31
five nations, 30
longhouses, 30
maize, 31
Red Jacket, 190
reservations, 190
villages, 30
Hay, 106
Heeren Gracht, *m71*
Hemisphere, 8, 12
Heritage, 183, 213, 224–226. *See also* Immigration.
Herkimer, Nicholas, 136
Historical sites, 24–25, 80–81
Holidays, 283
Patriot Day, 283
See also Federal holidays.
Holland Land Company, 190
House of Burgesses, 107
Howe, William, 133
Hudson, Henry, *m52–53,* 61, 65
Hudson River, 4, 11, 16, 15, 18, 36, 188, 192, 194
American Revolution and, 133, 134, 135
Dutch settlement, 62, 63
English settlement, 63
Erie Canal, 188, 192
exploration of, 61, 65
transportation, 70
Hudson River Valley, 6–7
American Revolution and, 135
Native Americans in, 62
settlement, 62
Hungarian immigration, 215, *m228–229*
Hunting, 38, 39
Huron Indians, 61

Identify Primary and Secondary Sources, 220–221
Immigration, 112, 211, 212, 214–219, 220, 222–227, 230–235
African American, 216, 223, *m228–229*
Asian, 183
British, 183
Caribbean, 223
celebrations, 225, 227
Chinese, 183, 223, 227, *m228–229*
contributions to New York City, 224–226
Czech, 215, 228–229
discrimination, 217
Dominican Republic, 183, 225
Dutch, 61–63, 68–72, 112, 138
effects on New York City, 222–227, 230–235

Ellis Island, 212, 213, 216–217, 220
English, 63, 69, 78, 112
ethnic groups, 215, 216, 222–226
ethnic neighborhoods, 223, 228–229
European, 183, 212
French, 69, 70, 78, m228–229
German, 70, 78, 112, 134, 183, 215, m228–229
Greek, m228–229
Guyanese, 183, 222
heritage, 212, 213, 224–226
Hungarian, 215, m228–229
immigrant experiences, 216–217
Indian, 218
Irish, 183, 184, 215, 224, m228–229
Italian, 215, m228–229
Jewish, 72, 112, 216, 222, m228–229
and labor unions, 212, 213, 234, 236–237
life in America, 217, 222–227
melting pot, 214
Mexican, 223
to New York City, 183, 214–219, 222–223
opportunity, 217
Polish, 215, m228–229
Potato Famine, 215
Puerto Rican, 218, 264
reasons, 215, 216
Russian, 215, m228–229
Scandinavian, m228–229
Scottish, 78, 112
Senegalese, 223
and skyscrapers, 213, 230–231
social impact, 234
Swedish, 69, 70, 112, 215
Syrian, m228–229
tenements, 217, 219
travel, 216
Turkish, 225, m228–229
work, 215, 217
Indentured servants, 113
Independence, defined, 122, 126
Treaty of Paris (1783), 136
See also Declaration of Independence.
Independence Day, 127, 171
Independence Hall, 158
Indian immigration, 218
Indigo, 99, 107, 111
Industrial Revolution, 191
Industrialization, 188
assembly lines, 191
communication, 195
effect of geography, 191–195
emergence of New York as an economic power, 192–194
Erie Canal, 181, 182, 192–193, m192–193
factories, 191, 201
Industrial Revolution, 191
railroads, m182, 194, 195, 237
steamboats, 194
Infographics Features
Dutch Style in New Amsterdam, 74–75
New York City Neighborhoods, 228–229
New York from Space, 18–19
Organizing Government, 258–259
Trade with England, 110–111
Values and Traditions, 170–171

Interdependence, 218
Interpret Historical Images, 172–173
Inventions, 106, 194, 195
Ireland, 78
Irish immigration, 183, 215, m228–229
cultural contributions, 224
Potato Famine, 184, 215
Iroquois, 30–31
five nations, 30
See also Haudenosaunee.
Italian immigration, 215, m228–229

J

James, Duke of York, 77, 106
Jamestown, 102, 116–117
Jay, John, 126, 139, 158
Jefferson, Thomas, 127, 128–129, 139, 148, 165
Jewish immigration, 72, 112, 216, 222, m228–229
Jobs, in colonial New York, 83, 113
Judges, 255, 259, 265
Judicial branch, 252, 255, 259, 275
Junior League of New York, 282
Juries, 77, 281
Jury duty, 281
Justices, 255, 264

K

Kieft, Willem, 62, 72
King, Martin Luther, Jr., 171
King of England, 114
Kingston, New York, 156

L

Labor movement, 234
Labor unions, 212, 213, 234
garment workers, 234
Mullany, Kate, 237
Randolph, Asa Philip, 237
Schneiderman, Rose, 236
strikes, 234, 236, 237
Laborers, 106
Lafayette Theater, 223
La Guardia, Fiorello, 253, 265
Lake Champlain, 61, 65, 126
Lake Erie, 13, 16, 18, 188, 192
Lake Ontario, 4, 13, 16, 19
Lake Placid, 14
Lamb, Pompey, 136
Land
conflicts over, 62
Native Americans and, 78, 136, 138
ownership among Lenape, 38
selling of, 78
Landform, 9, 14–15, 18–19
Languages, 70, 72, 224–225
Lansing, John, Jr., 157
Latitude, defined, 66
map, m66, m67
Laws
assemblies, 77, 106
British tax, 124, 125
Charter of Liberties, 77
in England, 77
enslaved Africans and, 114, 197

gradual emancipation, 197
House of Burgesses, 107
Mayflower Compact, 103
in the Netherlands, 70
in New Netherland, 70, 77
in New York colony, 77, 114
protecting rights, 77
public health, 232
safety, 232
self-government, 103
town meetings, 105
trade, 109
Lawyers, 139
Lead, 125
Legend, 21
Legislative branch, 252, 255, 259, 275
Lenape, 36–41
animal signs, 37
ceremonies, 40
clans, 37
crops, 38
division of labor, 39
elders, 37, 39
fishing, 38, 39
food, 38
government, 37
hunting, 38, 39
interaction with explorers, 65
land ownership, 38
leaders, 37, 39
legends, 40
longhouses, 38
sachems, 37, 39
slash-and-burn farming, 38
tools, 39
villages, 37, 38
Lexington, Massachusetts, 126
Libraries, 249
Lincoln, Abraham, 201
Line graphs
Population Growth, 1800s, 149
Population Growth Today, 149
Little Guyana, Queens, 222
Living document, 272, 276
Location
absolute, 66
latitude and longitude, 66
of the Middle Colonies, 100, m101
of Native Americans, 30, 36–37
of New England Colonies, 100, m101
of New York, 10
of the Southern Colonies, 100, m101
of the thirteen colonies, 100, m101
Long Island, 4, 15, 55
Battle of, 133
Longhouse, 30, 38
Longitude, defined, 66
map, m66, m67
Look Closely at Primary Sources Features
African Americans in New York City, 80–81
Civil War Photographs, 204–205
The Declaration of Independence, 128–129
Foundations of Our Government, 160–161
National Symbols, 284–285
Native American Artifacts, 32–33
Lords Canal, m71
Louisiana Purchase, 148

Lower East Side, Manhattan, 224
Loyalists, 132, 135–136
    Brant, Joseph, 135
    Cornplanter, 138
    leave New York City, 136
Ludington, Sybil, 134
Lumber, 105, 106, 111

Mackerel, 105
Madison, James, 158, 165
Main idea and details, 14, 36, 68, 76, 112, 156, 280
Maize, 27, 31
Make Decisions, 266–267
Make a Map, 34–35
Make a Timeline, 162–163
Manhattan, 17, 223, 224, 260
    American Revolution in, 133, 136
    colonial, 70, 74, 112
    growth of, 70, 78, 214–215, 217, 228, 230–231
    Lenape word for, 65
Manhattan Indians, 68
Manhattan Island, 68, 70
"Manna-hata", 65
Map and Globe Skills
    Make a Map, 34–35
    Review Map Skills, 20–21
    Use Latitude and Longitude, 66–67
Map scale, 21
Maps
    Albany, New York, mR44
    Buffalo, New York, mR44
    Cannon Route from Fort
        Ticonderoga, m126
    Dutch Settlement, 1611–1640, m62
    Eastern United States Resources, m49
    European Exploration Around New
        York, m52–53
    Henry Hudson's Voyage, m89
    Lake Champlain, m61
    Latitude Globe, m66
    Lenape Lands, m37
    Location of New York State:
        Continental United States, m12
    Location of New York State: North
        America, m12
    Location of New York State: Western
        Hemisphere, m12
    Longitude Globe, m66
    New Amsterdam in the 1600s, m71
    New Netherland, m69
    New York, m23
    New York American Revolution
        Battles, m133
    New York City Boroughs, mR45
    New York City in the 1740s, m80–81
    New York City Neighborhoods, 1920,
        m229
    New York Counties, m256
    New York Land Regions, m15
    New York: Latitude and Longitude,
        m85
    New York: Major Roads and Airports,
        mR43
    New York Native Americans, 1100,
        m30
    New York: Physical, mR41

New York: Political, mR40
New York: Precipitation, mR42
New York State, m20
New York: State Parks, mR43
New York: Temperature, mR42
New York's Lakes and Rivers, m16
North America, 1740s, m92
Northeast, m67
Northern Hemisphere, m12
Physical Features of New York State,
    m2
Population Density in New York
    Counties, m246
Railroads in New York, mid-1800,
    m182
Thirteen Colonies, m101
Traveling the Erie Canal, m192
Triangular Trade Routes, m108
Union and Confederate States, 1861,
    m201
United States of America, m12,
    m148–149
United States: Physical, mR38
United States: Political, mR36
Western Hemisphere, m12
Western Hemisphere: Physical, mR35
Western Hemisphere: Political, mR34
Westward Expansion, m148
World: Physical, mR32
World: Political, mR30
Martin Luther King Jr. Day, 171
Maryland, 100
Mass transportation, 232–233
Massachusetts, 102, 105, 125, 126
May, Cornelius, 62
Mayflower, 103
Mayflower Compact, 103, 160
Mayor, 253, 256, 261, 265
    Giuliani, Rudy, 282
Meal Market, 8
Melting pot, 214
Mercantilism, defined, 108
Merchants, 115
Messenger, The, 237
Metropolitan Museum of Art, 248
Mexican immigration, 223
Middle Colonies, 106
    agriculture, 100, 106
    cities, 106
    crops, 100, 106
    culture, 106
    daily life, 106, 113
    economy, 106
    farming, 100, 106
    Franklin, Benjamin, 106
    geography, 100
    government, 106
    inventions, 106
    James, Duke of York, 77, 106
    location, 100, m101
    New York City, 106
    Penn, William, 102
    Pennsylvania, 102, 106, 126, 134, 157
    Philadelphia, 93, 106, 126
    population, 106
    proprietors, 106
    Quakers, 102
    religion, 102
    science, 106
    settlement, 100, 102
    technology, 106

trade, 100, 106
transportation, 100
See also New York colony.
Middle Passage, 69
Migration, 202, 216, 223
    forced, 62, 69, 78, 107, 114, 136, 216
    of freed slaves, 203
    migrate, defined, 223
    to New York City, 216
    See also Movement.
Militias, 126, 134
Minuit, Peter, 68
Mohawk Indians, 30
    Brant, Joseph, 135
    Mohawk ironworkers, 43
Mohawk River, 16
Mohawk River Valley, 135
Monitor and clarify, 27, 189
Montreal, 65
Morse, Samuel, 195
Motley, Constance Baker, 265
Mott, Lucretia, 198–199
Mount Marcy, 15
Mountains, 15, 19
Movement
    of enslaved Africans, 69, 78, 107, 114
    forced, 62, 69, 78, 107, 114, 136, 216
    of Native Americans, 62, 78, 114, 136
Mullany, Kate, 237
Munsee clan, 37, 114
Murals, 226
Music, 224

Narrows, the, 64
Nassau, Fort, 62
National symbols, 284–285
    bald eagle, 285
    flag, 285
    Statue of Liberty, 284
Native Americans, 28–31, 32–33, 36–41,
    42–43
    Algonquians, 61
    in American Revolution, 132, 135, 136,
        138
    animals and, 29, 27
    artifacts, 32
    Big Tree Treaty, 190
    Brant, Joseph, 135
    climate and, 29, 31
    Cornplanter, 138
    environment and, 28–31, 38–40
    furs and, 61
    Harmon, Patience, 40
    Haudenosaunee, 132, 136, 138, 190
    Hurons, 61
    interaction with Dutch, 62, 68
    interaction with explorers, 61, 64, 65
    land and, 78, 136, 138
    Lenape, 36–41, 65
    location in New York State, 30, 36–37
    maps, 30
    Mohawks, 43, 135
    movement of, 78, 114, 136
    Munsee, 114
    natural resources and, 28–31, 38–40
    in New York colony, 114
    Parker, Ely S., 42
    past and present, 42

population, 78
Red Jacket, 190
reservations, 190
selling land, 190
Seneca, 30, 138, 190
settlers and, 78, 114
Shenandoah, Joanne, 43
trade, 61, 65
in war between Britain and France, 124
Natural resources, 39
fish, 101
forests, 101
furs, 61
Native Americans and, 28–31, 38–40
of New Amsterdam, 70
of New England Colonies, 101, 105
of North America, 108, 110
trade and, 110
Navies
British, 108, 133
French, 136
Navigation Acts, 109
Neighborhoods, ethnic, 223, 228–229
Netherlands, the, 112
Amsterdam, 71
colonies, 60, 62–63, 76
conflict with England, 76
explorers, 61
Hudson, Henry, 61
New Amsterdam, 52, 68–72, 74–75
daily life, 70
diversity, 69, 70, 72
Dutch influence in, 70, 73–74
Dutch Reformed Church, 70
Dutch West India Company, 68–69
education, 70
enslaved Africans in, 69
farming, 70
founders, 68–69
fur traders in, 70
growth of, 70, 72
languages, 70, 72
laws, 70
Minuit, Peter, 68
Native Americans and, 68, 71
natural resources, 70
Nieuw Haarlem, 70
renamed New York City, 77
settlement of, 68, 70
Stuyvesant, Peter, 58, 76, 77
surrender to English, 76
technology, 70
tolerance, 59, 72
under English rule, 76–79
windmills, 55, 70
New England Colonies, 105
agriculture, 101, 105
cities, 105
culture, 105
daily life, 105
economy, 98, 105
farming, 101, 105
fishing, 98, 105
geography, 101, 104
government, 105
location, 100, m101
Massachusetts Bay Colony, 105
natural resources, 101, 105
Pilgrims, 102, 103
Plymouth, 102

Puritans, 105
religion, 102, 105
resources, 105
science, 105
settlement, 101, 102
shipbuilding, 105
technology, 105
trade, 105
New Jersey, 134
New Netherland, 62–63, 68–69
courts in, 77
diversity, 72
economy, 69, 70
English settlers in, 69
enslaved Africans in, 69
French settlers in, 69
government, 62, 76, 77
governors, 58, 62, 68, 76, 77
growth of, 63, 68, 72
Native Americans and, 62, 68, 71
patroons, 69
renamed New York, 77
Rensselaerswyck, 69
settlement of, 62, 68
slavery, 69
Swedish settlers in, 69
tolerance, 59, 72
windmills, 55, 70
See also Dutch colonies *and* New Amsterdam.
New Paltz, New York, 69
New York Bay, 64
New York City, 247
African Americans, 80–81, 136, 223, m228–229
American Revolution in, 132, 133, 136
banking, 218
basketball team, 248
boroughs, 260
the Bronx, 17, 260
Brooklyn, 78, 112, 133, 186, 260
building codes, 232
city officials, 262
climate, 17
colonial, 77, 80–81
diversity, 78, 214–215, 218, 222–226
Draft Riots, 202
Dutch influence in, 70–m71, 73–74
economy, 218
education, 70, 151, 217, 271, 277
Erie Canal and, 192–193
ethnic neighborhoods, 223, 228–229
Federal Hall, 159
fire department, 233
geography, 17
government, 245, 258, 260–263
government services, 262
growth of, 93, 228, 214, 218, 228, 230–232
immigration, 214–219, 222–227, 228–235
interdependent with New York State, 218
labor unions in, 234, 236–237
land area of, 247
leaders, 262
Manhattan, 65, 70, 74, 112, 133, 136, 223, 224, 260
mass transportation, 232–233
as a melting pot, 214
merchants, 115

as national capital, 149, 157, 163
Native Americans in, 78
neighborhoods, 223, 228–229, 226
New York Harbor, 215
New York Public Library, 249
parks, 5, 265
population, 78, 80, 93, 111, 149
as a port, 218
public health laws, 232
Queens, 222, 260
sewer systems, 232
shipbuilding, 110–111
shipping, 193, 218
skyscrapers, 185, 213, 230–231
slave trade, 69, 78, 80–81
Staten Island, 15, 17, 260
subway, 232–233
"tea party", 125
tenements, 217, 219
water systems, 232, 233
working conditions in, 234
See also New Amsterdam.
New York colony, 77, 100
Africans in, 114
apprentices, 78, 80–81, 113
assembly, 77, 114
Charter of Liberties, 77
courts, 77
daily life, 113
diversity, 112
Dutch influence in, 70–m71, 73–74
economy, 78, 113
English rule in, 74, 76–78
farms, 78, 113
Floyd, William, 126
French influence in, 69, 78
government, 77, 106, 114
governors of, 77, 114
growth, 93, 112
James, the Duke of York, 77, 106
Jay, John, 126, 139
laws, 77, 114
Native Americans, 114
newspapers, 115
population, 78, 80, 93, 111
proprietors of, 77, 106
Richard Nicolls, 77
rights, 77, 114
settlement in, 78
taxes, 77
voting rights, 114
women, 114
workers, 113
See also New Netherland.
New York Harbor, 79
American Revolution and, 133
colonial, 79, 111
exploration of, 61
New York Public Library, 249
New York State, 275
abolitionists, 197
Adirondack Mountains, 10, 14, 15
American Revolution in, 132, 133, m133, 134, 135, 136
bodies of water, 16
capitol building, 275
in the Civil War, 202, 205
constitution, 150, 154, 156, 160, 162, 165, 254–255, 272
counties, m256
Dutch influence in, 70–m71, 73–74

emergence as an economic power, 191
English influence in, 77–78, 112–115
Erie Canal and, 192–193
exploration of, 61, 64–65
"Father of New York", 139
features, 18
forts, 62, 78, 126, *m126*, 136, 137, 138
French influence in, 69, 78
geography of, 14, 17
government, 139, 252, 245, 254–256, 258–259
growth, 191, 193
interdependent with New York City, 218
lakes and rivers, *m16*
land regions, *m15*
landforms, 14–15
location, 10–13
lowlands, 15
maps, *m15, m18–19, m20*
physical features, *m2–3*
population density, *m246–247*
public schools, 151, 272, 277
railroads and canals, 182–183
revolution in, 132–137
revolutionary leaders, 136
uplands, 15
Newspapers, 115, 125
Nicolls, Richard, 76
Nieuw Haarlem, 70
Niña, 60
North America, 58, *m92–93*, 103
competition for land in, 60, 76
exploration of, 60, 61, 64–65
fur trade in, 63
Native Americans in, 61
natural resources, 108
reasons for settlement, 102
North Star, The, 197

Oats, 106
O'Bail, John (Cornplanter), 138
Oglethorpe, James, 102
Oklahoma, 40
Old Forge, New York, 18
Old Hook Mill, 55, 57
Oneida Indians, 30
Onondaga Indians, 30
Oriskany, Battle of, 135
Oriskany Creek, 135

Pacific Ocean, 92
Paints, 125
Paper, 125
Park Row Building, 231
Parker, Ely S., 42
Patriot Day, 283
Patriotism, 273, 283
Patriots, defined, 123, 132
Allen, Ethan, 126
Arnold, Benedict, 126, 135
Clinton, George, 136, 139
Corbin, Margaret, 123, 137
Daughters of Liberty, 125
Floyd, William, 126
Fraunces, Samuel, 136

Gates, Horatio, 135
Herkimer, Nicholas, 136
Jay, John, 126, 139, 158
Jefferson, Thomas, 127, 128–129, 139, 148, 165
Lamb, Pompey, 136
Ludington, Sybil, 134
Schuyler, Philip, 126
Sons of Liberty, 125
Washington, George, 126, 133, 134, 136, 138
Patroons, 69
Peaches, 106
Pearl Street, 72
Penn, William, 102
Pennsylvania, 102, 106, 126, 134, 157
Philadelphia, Pennsylvania, 93, 106, 126
Photography, 204–205
Pie charts
New York City population, 222
Workers in New York, 1700s, 83
Pilgrims, 98, 102, 103
Pinckney, Eliza Lucas, 107
Pinta, 60
Plantations, 107, 201
Plateau, 15
Plymouth, 102
Point of view, defined, 130
Polish immigration, 215, *m228–229*
Political reasons for settlement, 102–103
Population
of African Americans, 78, 80
of cities, 106
density of New York State, *m246–247*
of Dutch colonies, 63
of English colonies, 63, 78, 80, 93, 106
growth, 70, 78, 214–215, 217, 228, 230–232
of New York City, 78, 80, 93, 111, 149
of New York colony, 78
of New York State, 149, 247
Ports, 110
Potatoes, 106
Practices, 170–171
Preamble (to the Constitution), 160
Predict and infer, 99, 213
Primary sources, defined, 220
Features, 32–33, 80–81, 128–129, 160–161, 204–205, 284–285
Prime meridian, 12, 66, *m66*
Princeton, Battle of, 134
Problem and Solution, 164
Proprietors, defined, 106
James, Duke of York, 77, 106
in the Middle Colonies, 106
in the Southern Colonies, 107
Protest, 125
Public advocate, 262
Public health laws, 232
Public schools, 151, 272, 277
Puerto Rican immigration, 218, 264
Puritans, 105

Quakers, 102
Quebec, 65
Queens, 222, 260
Question, 123, 253

Railroads, *m182*, 194, 195, 202, 237
Randolph, Asa Philip, 237
Ratification, 155, 158–159
Raw materials, 108, 110
Read a Circle Graph, 82–83
Read a Table, 278–279
Reading Skills
categorize, 76, 260
cause and effect, 124, 190, 214, 222
classify, 132
compare and contrast, 28, 104, 200, 274
draw conclusions, 60, 100, 230
generalize, 10
main idea and details, 14, 36, 68, 112, 156, 280
problem and solution, 164
sequence, 196
summarize, 254
Reading Social Studies
Cause and effect, 184–185
Compare and contrast, 94–95
Draw conclusions, 54–55
Generalize, 4–5
Main idea and details, 150–151
Summarize, 248–249
Reading Strategies
monitor and clarify, 27, 189
predict and infer, 9, 99, 213
question, 123, 253
summarize, 58, 155, 273
Reasons for immigration
better living conditions, 216–217
financial gain, 217
forced migration, 216
land acquisition, 215
religion, 216
wars, 216
work, 215–217
Red Jacket, 190
Regions, 11
of New York State, 15
of the thirteen colonies, 100–101
Religion
Church of England, 102
daily life and, 105
Dutch Reformed Church, 70
freedom of, 69, 77, 102
government and, 105, 114
Huguenots, 69
Pilgrims, 102
Puritans, 105
Quakers, 102
as reason for settlement, 102
Rensselaerswyck, 69
Report, defined, 116
Representatives, 122, 124
First Continental Congress, 122, 139
Reservations, 190
Reservoir, 232
Resolve Conflicts, 206–207
Resources, 105, 108
economy and, 98, 105
See also Natural resources.
Responsibility, 273, 278, 281
to obey the law, 281
to participate in government, 281
to serve on a jury, 281
Retreat, defined, 133

Review Maps Skills, 20–21
Revise, 274
Revolution, defined, 126
  See also American Revolution.
Revolutionary War. See American
  Revolution.
Rice, 107
Rights, 77, 158, 164, 275, 278, 281
  of African Americans, 77, 114
  assembly, 77
  Charter of Liberties, 77
  Declaration of Independence, 127,
    128–129, 160, 198
  in Dutch colonies, 77
  education, 281
  in English colonies, 77, 114, 115
  equal job opportunities, 281
  exercising, 115
  holding office, 114
  lack of inclusiveness in Constitution,
    166–167
  laws protecting, 77
  limited, 114, 125
  of Native Americans, 114
  in New Netherland, 77
  in New York colony, 77, 114
  property, 77, 114
  trial by jury, 77, 281
  voting, 114, 281
  of women, 77, 114
Rivers, 100, 101
  Connecticut, 62
  Delaware, 36, 62, 69, 134
  Genesee, 138
  Hudson, 61, 62, 65, 70, 100, 133, 134,
    135
  St. Lawrence, 62, 110
Roads, 195
Rochester, New York, 11, 191, 193, 197
Rocky Mountains, 29
Roebling, John A., 226
Roebling, Washington, 226
Roelantsen, Adam, 70
Rome, New York, 16, 192
Routes, defined, 60
  to Asia, 52, 60–61
  cannons from Fort Ticonderoga,
    m126
  exploration, m52–53
  trade, 108
Rule of law, 158, 160, 171
Russian immigration, 215, m228–229
Russwurm, John, 197
Rye, 105

S

Sachems, 37, 39
St. Lawrence River, 16, 61
St. Leger, Barry, 135
Sales tax, 263
Santa Maria, 60
Saratoga, Battle of, 123, 135
Saratoga National Historical Park,
  120–121
Satellite, 18
Scandianvian immigration, m228–229
Schneiderman, Rose, 236
Schoharie Valley, New York, 32
School, 70, 95, 105. See also Education
  and Public schools.

Schuyler, Philip, 126
Science, 105
Scotland, 78, 112
Seaports, 111
Secede, defined, 201
Second Continental Congress, 126, 128
Secondary source, 220
Self-government, defined, 103
Senate, 255, 259, 265, 275
Seneca Indians, 30, 138, 190
Seneca Falls Convention, 189, 198–199
Seneca Falls, New York, 198
Senegalese immigration, 223
September 11, 2001, 282
Sequence, 196
Servants, indentured, 113
Services, 113
Settlement
  Dutch, 62, m62, 63, 68, 70
  English, 100–101, 102
  geography and, 62, 100, 101
  in the Middle Colonies, 100, 102
  in New England Colonies, 101, 102
  in New York colony, 78
  reasons for, 102
  in the Southern Colonies, 101, 102
Seward Park, New York City, 282
Sewer systems, 232
Sheep, 105
Shenandoah, Joanne, 43
Shipbuilding, 98, 101, 105, 110–111, 113
Ships, 110–111, 113, 125
  in American Revolution, 133, 136
  carrying goods, 77, 100, 125
  of Christopher Columbus, 53, 60
  Clermont, 194
  exploration, 64
  Half Moon, 65
  improvements to, 105
  Mayflower, 103
  Niña, 60
  Pinta, 60
  river transportation, 70, 100
  Santa Maria, 60
  See also Shipbuilding.
Shipping, 106, 108, 109, 218
  Erie Canal and, 193
Shopkeepers, 106
Shops, 95, 113
Skillbuilders
  Identify Primary and Secondary
    Sources, 220–221
  Interpret Historical Images, 172–173
  Make Decisions, 266–267
  Make a Map, 34–35
  Make a Timeline, 162–163
  Read a Circle Graph, 82–83
  Read a Table, 278–279
  Resolve Conflicts, 206–207
  Review Maps Skills, 20–21
  Understand Point of View, 130–131
  Use Latitude and Longitude, 66–67
  Write a Report, 116–117
Skilled workers, 113
Skills, 113
Skyscrapers, 185, 213, 230–231
Slash-and-burn farming, 38
Slavery, 69, 166, 200
  abolitionists, 197, 200
  in the Constitution, 203
  Dutch West India Company, 68–69

emancipation, 196–197, 203
  in English colonies, 80–81, 107, 113
  Fields, the, 81
  Meal Market, 81
  Middle Passage, 69
  in New Netherland, 69
  in New York, 80–81, 113, 196–197
  in Southern Colonies, 107
  trade, 69, 81
  See also Enslaved Africans.
Smallpox, 62
Social impact of immigration, 234
Sons of Liberty, 125, 136
Southern Colonies, 107
  agriculture, 99, 107
  cash crops, 99, 107
  culture, 107
  daily life, 107
  economy, 107
  enslaved Africans, 107
  fall line, 101
  farming, 99, 101, 107
  geography, 101
  Georgia, 102
  government, 107
  House of Burgesses, 107
  Jamestown, 102, 116–117
  location, 100, m101
  Pinckney, Eliza Lucas, 107
  plantations, 107
  proprietors, 107
  settlement, 101, 102
  science, 107
  slavery, 107
  technology, 107
  transportation, 101
  Virginia, 107
Spain, 60
Special districts, 257
Spices, 60, 111
Spinning wool, 113
Squash, 31, 38
Stamp Act, 125
Stanton, Elizabeth Cady, 198–199
Staten Island, 15, 17, 260
States' rights, 200
Statue of Liberty, 210, 284
Steamboats, 194
Stevens, John, 192
Stevens, Robert, 194
Stony Point, Fort, 136
Strengthening democracy, 168–169
Strikes, 234, 236, 237
Study Skills (chapter)
  Anticipation Guide, 25
  Connect Ideas, 121
  Make an Outline, 271
  Organize Information, 187
  Pose Questions, 57
  Preview and Question, 7
  Skim and Scan, 251
  Use a K-W-L Chart, 97
  Use Visuals, 153
  Vocabulary, 211
Study Skills (skillbuilders)
  Identify Primary and Secondary
    Sources, 220–221
  Write a Report, 116–117
Stuyvesant, Peter, 58, 76, 77
Subway, 183, 232–233

Suffrage

Suffrage, 189, 198
   Anthony, Susan B., 189, 198–199
   Declaration of Sentiments, 198
   Mott, Lucretia, 198–199
   Seneca Falls Convention, 189, 198–199
   Stanton, Elizabeth Cady, 198–199
Sugar Act, 125
Summarize, 58, 155, 248–249, 254, 273
Supreme Court, 264
Surrender, defined, 123, 135
   at Saratoga, 123, 135
   at Yorktown, 93, 136, 168
Sweden, 112
Swedish immigration, 215
Symbols, 284
Syracuse, New York, 55
Syrian immigration, *m228–229*

Tables
   Amendments to the New York State
      Constitution, 278
   Citizens Take Responsibility in New
      York City, 287
   Federal Holidays, 283
   Federal System of Government, 258
   Middle Colonies, 106
   National and State Governments, 258
   New England Colonies, 105
   New York by the Numbers, 19
   New York's Three Branches of
      Government, 255
   Read a Table, 278–279
   Southern Colonies, 107
   Traded Goods, 111
   Values, Practices, Traditions, 171
Tappan, Arthur, 197
Tappan, Lewis, 197
Taxes, defined, 77, 263
   British laws, 124, 125
   calendars, 125
   colonial, 77, 124
   glass, 125
   lead, 125
   in New York colony, 77
   in New York State, 263
   newspapers, 125
   paints, 125
   paper, 125
   protests of, 77, 125
   sales, 263
   Stamp Act, 125
   Sugar Act, 125
   Tea Act, 125
   Townsend Acts, 125
Tea, 111, 125
   Tea Act, 125
"Tea parties", 125
Technology, 70
   elevators, 231
   in the Middle Colonies, 106
   in New Amsterdam, 70

   in New England Colonies, 105
   in the Southern Colonies, 107
   skyscrapers, 231
   windmills, 55, 70
Telegraph, 195
Tenements, 217, 219
Thirteen colonies, 100–101
   founding, 100–101
   location, 100–101, *m101*
   settlement, 100–101
   See also Middle Colonies; New
      England Colonies; Southern
      Colonies.
"Three Sisters", 31
Ticonderoga, Fort, 126, *m126*
Timelines, 76–77, 128–129, 162
Tobacco, 107, 109, 111
Tolerance, 59, 72
Tonawanda Reservation, 42
Tools, 39, 108, 111, 113
Town meetings, 105
Townshend Acts, 125
Trade, 157, 193, 218
   centers of, 106, 111
   Dutch West India Company and, 69
   between England and the colonies,
      108–109, 110–111, 113, 126
   English colonies, 108–109
   enslaved Africans, 69
   between Europe and Asia, 60
   French posts, 65
   furs, 61, 62, 63, 68, 69, 70, 111
   laws, 109
   mercantilism, 108
   in the Middle Colonies, 106
   with Native Americans, 61, 65
   networks, 108
   in New Amsterdam, 69, 70
   in New England Colonies, 105
   New York City, 110–111, 157, 193
   in the Southern Colonies, 107
   triangular, 108, *m108*
Traders, 113
Trading posts, 65
Tradition, 29, 170
Transportation, 69, 70, 100, 101
   Erie Canal, 181, 182, 192–193,
      m192–193
   Hudson River, 194
   in New Amsterdam, 74
   railroads, *m182*, 192, 194, 202, 237
   steamboats, 194
   subway, 183, 232–233
   turnpikes, 188, 194
Treaties, 136, 138, 139, 190
Treaty of Paris (1783), 136, 139
Trenton, Battle of, 134
Trial, 115
   by jury, 77
   as a right, 77
   Zenger trial, 115, 164
Triangular trade, 108, *m108*
Troy, New York, 18, 237
Truth, Sojourner, 197

Tubman, Harriet, 200
Turbines, 55
Turkish immigration, 225, *m228–229*
Turnpike, 194

Unalachtigo clan, 37
Unami clan, 37
Underground Railroad, 197
Understand Point of View, 130–131
Union, 201–203, 207
United States
   Constitution, 150, 154, 157–159, 160,
      162, 164, 165–167, 168, 254
   expansion, *m148–149*
   flag, 285
   government, 258, 264, 265
   Independence Day, 127, 171
   symbols, 284–285
United States Military Academy, 137
Use Latitude and Longitude, 66–67
Utica, New York, 193

Values, 170–171
Verrazano, Giovanni da, *m52–53*, 61, 64
Verrazano-Narrows Bridge, 64
Veto, 255, 259
Virginia, 93, 102, 107, 136, 165
Volunteer, 189, 203
Voting, 105, 114, 254, 275

Wall Street, *m71*
Walum Olum, 37
Washington, Fort, 137
Washington, George, 126, 133, 134, 136,
   138, 159, 161, 163, 168
Water systems, 232, 233
Waterfalls, 101
Waterpumps, 80
Waterways, 74, 101
Weeksville, New York, 197
West Indies, 108
West Point, 137
Westward expansion, *m148–149*
Wetlands, 101
Whales, 101, 105, 111
Wheat, 105, 106
Wigwams, 26, 28
Wind farms, 55
Wind power, 55, 70
Wind turbines, 55
Windmills, 70
Women
   Adams, Abigail, 166
   Alexander, Mary Provoost, 115
   in American Revolution, 123, 134, 137
   Anthony, Susan B., 189, 198–199

Index

Baker, S. Josephine, 232
in Civil War, 189, 203
Corbin, Margaret, 123, 137
daily life of girls, 95, 105, 106, 107, 113
Daughters of Liberty, 125
Ellerin, Betty W., 264
Harmon, Patience, 40
lack of inclusiveness in Constitution, 166–167
Ludington, Sybil, 134
Motley, Constance Baker, 265
Mott, Lucretia, 198–199
Mullany, Kate, 237
in New Netherland, 77
in New York colony, 77, 113
property rights of, 77

Schneiderman, Rose, 236
Shenandoah, Joanne, 43
Stanton, Elizabeth Cady, 198–199
suffrage, 167, 198–199
Truth, Sojourner, 197
Tubman, Harriet, 200
Wood, 105, 106, 108
Wool, 113, 193
Woolworth Building, 231
Workers, 113
dentists, 113
enslaved Africans, 69, 80–81, 113
printers, 113
skilled, 113
Write a Report, 116–117
World Trade Center, 282

Yates, Robert, 157
Yorktown, Battle of, 93, 136, 168

Zenger, John Peter, 115, 164
Zenger Trial, 115, 164

Acknowledgments

For each of the selections listed below, grateful aknowledgment is made for permission to exerpt and/or reprint original or copyrighted material, as follows:

Illustration Credits
86, 142, 177 Will Williams; **259** Argosy; **22, 44, 84, 238, 268** Steve McEntee; **31** Bill Melvin; **44, 208** Jun Park; **74–75** Susan Moore; **38–39** Eric Sturdevant; **118** Inklink.

Map Credits
2, 3, 37, 229, R45 Spatial Graphics Inc.
All other maps by Maps.com

Photography Credits
Placement Key: (t) top, (b) bottom, (c) center, (l) left, (r) right, (bg) background, (fg) foreground and (i) inset.

Cover © Jose Fuste Raga/CORBIS; **xvi** (t) Laura Dwight; **xvii** (tl) Delpho/Photolibrary.com; **xvii** (tr) Superstock; **xvii** (tcr) Piotr Redlinski/CORBIS; **xvii** (bl) Craig Lovell/Eagle Visions Photography/Alamy; **xvii** (cr) Uschi Gerschner/ digital Railroad; **xviii** Michael Ventura/PhotoEdit; **1** JTB Photo/Digital Railroad; **2** (br) Anne Labastille/Bruce Coleman; **3** (c) Claudia Parks/Bruce Coleman, Inc.; **3** (br) Shiva Twin/Getty Images; **6** (cr) Ted Spiegel/The Image Works; **8** (cl) Crackshots/CORBIS; **9** (cl) Peter Adams Photography/Alamy; **9** (cr) Theo Allofs/CORBIS; **10** (b) James L. Amos/CORBIS; **11** (tr) Bettmann/CORBIS; **13** (c) Maya Barnes Johansen/The Image Works; **14** (br) Barry Winiker/PhotoLibrary; **15** (tr) Jane Sapinsky/CORBIS; **16** (br) Shiva Twin/Getty Images; **17** (tr) aerialarchives. com/Alamy; **18** Jacques Descloitres, MODIS Land Rapid Response Team, NASA/GSFC/Satellite: Terra/Sensor: MODIS/Image Date: 11-06-2001/VE Record ID: 10739.10; **18** (bl) USGS EROS Data Center Satellite Systems Branch/ NASA; **24** Lee Snider/Photo Images/CORBIS; **26** (cl) Roman Soumar/CORBIS; **26** (cr) J Marshall - Tribaleye Images/Alamy; **27** (cl) Courtesy of The Woodland Cultural Center; **28** (br) Roman Soumar/CORBIS; **29** (tl) The Mariners' Museum/CORBIS; **29** (tr) Marilyn Angel Wynn/ Nativestock Pictures; **32** (br) Sean Rafferty; Ph.D./ University at Albany; SUNY Anthropology Dept.; **32** Philip Scalia/Digital Railroad; **33** (t) Sean Rafferty; Ph. D./University at Albany; SUNY Anthropology Dept.;

33 (cl) Sean Rafferty; Ph.D./University at Albany; SUNY Anthropology Dept.; **33** (bl) Sean Rafferty; Ph.D./University at Albany; SUNY Anthropology Dept.; **34** (cr) Sean Rafferty; Ph.D./University at Albany; SUNY Anthropology Dept.; **35** Houghton Mifflin Boston; **36** (br) Marilyn Angel Wynn/Nativestock; **36** (bl) Marilyn Angel Wynn/ Nativestock; **40** (br) Marilyn Angel Wynn/Nativestock; **41** (c) Marilyn Angel Wynn/Nativestock; **42** (br) National Archives photo #111-B-5272; **42** (br) PhotoDisc; **43** (tr) Joe Raedle/Newsmakers/Getty; **43** (bl) Rick Maiman/AP; **50** Houghton Mifflin Boston; **51** Mikael Utterström/Alamy; **52** (bl) Peter Bennett/Alamy; **52** (br) The Granger Collection, New York; **53** (tr) Bettmann/CORBIS; **55** (br) Peter Bennett/Alamy; **56** Peter Bennett/Alamy; **58** (cl) The Granger Collection, New York; **58** (cr) The Granger Collection, New York; **59** (cl) New York Public Library; Art Resource NY; **59** (cr) The Granger Collection; New York; **60** (tr) Explorer/Courau/Mary Evans Picture Library; **61** (tl) Bibliotheque nationale du Quebec; **61** (tr) America's Historic Lakes; **62** (tl) Len Tantillo; **63** (tr) Robert Holmes/ CORBIS; **64** (bl) The Granger Collection, New York; **65** (tr) Stock Montage/Getty; **65** (bl) The Granger Collection, New York; **68** (b) The Granger Collection, New York; **71** Art Archive; **72** (bl) Collection of the New-York Historical Society; USA; The Bridgeman Art Gallery; **73** (c) Hans Georg Roth/CORBIS; **74** (bl) MLI Image Group/Alamy; **76** (bl) North Wind/North Wind Picture Archives; **77** (bl) Miniature of James II as the Duke of York, 1661 (gouache & w/c on vellum), Cooper, Samuel (1609-72)/Victoria & Albert Museum, London, UK/The Bridgeman Art Library; **79** (cl) Superstock; **79** (cr) Dennis Hallinan/Alamy; **81** New York Historical Society Library; **90** Houghton Mifflin Boston; **91** Philip Scalia/Ambient Images; **92** (bl) Courtesy of Oakland Museum of California; **93** (cl) Courtesy of The Library of Virginia; **93** (br) Mark Segal/Panoramic Images; **95** (br) Colonial Williamsburg Foundation; **96** (brt) Photo/ Alamy; **98** (cl) Courtesy of the Pilgrim Society; Plymouth; Massachusetts; **100** (b) Robert Estall/CORBIS; **102** (tl) Jeff Greenberg/PhotoEdit; **103** (cr) Courtesy of the Pilgrim Society; Plymouth; Massachusetts; **104** (b) Robert Y. Ono/ CORBIS; **106** (b) Michael Sheldon/Art Resource, NY; **107** (b) Hulton Archive/Getty Images; **109** (tr) Burke/ Triolo/Alamy; **110** The Picture Collection of the New York Public Library; **112** (b) Granger Collection; **114** (tl) North

Wind Picture Archives; **115** (cr) MPI/Stringer/Hulton Archive/Getty Images; **117** (t) Sidney King, National Park Service, Colonial National Historic Park, Jamestown Collection; **120** Susan Gable; **122** (cl) The Granger Collection, New York; **122** (cr) Vladimir Pcholkin/Getty Images; **123** (cl) United States Military Academy; **123** (cr) John Trumbull/The Architect of the Capitol; Photography Branch; Washington D.C.; **124** (br) The Granger Collection; New York; **125** (tl) North Wind/North Wind Picture Archives; **125** (tr) North Wind/North Wind Picture Archives; **126** (br) Tom Lovell; The Noble Train of Artillery; Fort Ticonderoga Museum; **127** (tr) Kurz & Allison/Library of Congress; **128** (cr) Bettmann/CORBIS; **129** (c) Library of Congress; **129** (bl) National Museum of American History; Smithsonian Institution; Behring Center; **130** Houghton Mifflin Boston; **130** Hougton Mifflin Boston; **132** (br) William Walcutt/Williams Center for the Arts; Lafayette College; **134** (cl) Putnam Co. Historians office; **134** (b) Susan Gable; **136** (bl) Peter Bennett/Ambient Images; **137** (cl) United States Military Academy; **138** (br) Ron Shoup; **139** (tl) Bettmann/CORBIS; **146** Houghton Mifflin Boston; **147** Bill Bachmann/Mira; **148** (bl) John Ford Clymer, "Up the Jefferson", Courtesy Mrs. John F. Clymer and the Clymer Museum; **149** (b) Collection of the New York Historical Society/Bridgeman Art Library; **152** Collection of the New-York Historical Society/ Bridgeman Art Library; **154** (cl) Courtesy New York State Archives; **154** (cr) The Granger Collection; New York; **155** (cl) National Portrait Gallery; Smithsonian Institution/ Art Resource; NY; **156** (br) National Portrait Gallery; Smithsonian Institution/Art Resource; NY; **157** (t) North Wind/North Wind Picture Archives; **158** (bl) CORBIS; **158** (br) The Pierpont Morgan Library/Art Resource; NY; **159** (cr) National Museum of American History, Smithsonian Institution, Behring Center; **160** Superstock; **164** (bl) The Granger Collection; New York; **165** (br) National Archives; **166** (tr) Bettmann/CORBIS; **166** (br) Hulton Archive/Getty Images; **167** (cr) Bettmann/CORBIS; **168** (br) Joseph Sohm/Visions of America/CORBIS; **169** (tr) Schomburg Center/Art Resource, NY; **169** (bl) Wisconsin Historical Society; **170** Richard Levine/Alamy; **171** (tr) mylife photos/Alamy; **171** (cr) Francis M. Roberts/Ambient Images; **171** (br) Michael Ventura/Alamy; **172** (c) Wally McNamee/CORBIS; **173** Hougton Mifflin Boston;

179 (tr) Bettmann/CORBIS; 181 Megapress/Alamy; 182 (br) Bettmann/CORBIS; 183 (bl) Ramin Talaie/CORBIS; 186 Granger Collection; 188 (cl) Courtesy Erie Canal Museum; Syracuse; NY; 188 (cr) Bruce Castle Museum Illustration by C B Newhous/Mary Evans Picture Library; 189 (cl) CORBIS; 189 (cr) CORBIS; 190 (br) Marc Charmet/The Art Archive; 191 (tr) Courtesy Erie Canal Museum; Syracuse; NY; 192 (cr) Lee Snider/Photo Images/CORBIS; 193 (cl) Courtesy Erie Canal Museum; Syracuse; NY; 193 (tc) Courtesy Erie Canal Museum; Syracuse; NY; 194 (cl) Barney Burstein/CORBIS; 194 (br) Bettmann/CORBIS; 195 (cr) CORBIS; 197 (bl) The Art Archive/Picture Desk; 197 (b) Library of Congress; Serial and Government Publications Division; 198 (b) Philip Scalia/Alamy; 199 (cr) Photo by Time Life Pictures/Timepix/Getty Images; 200 (br) Time & Life Pictures/Getty Images; 202 (bl) C. O. Bostwick/CORBIS; 202 (br) Philip de Bay/Historical Picture Archive/CORBIS; 203 (cr) Tria Giovan/CORBIS; 204 Bettmann/CORBIS; 205 (tc) Civil War Photograph Collection, Library of Congress; 207 Hougton Mifflin Boston; 210 Gala/Superstock; 212 (cl) Bettmann/CORBIS; 212 (cr) Mitch Jacobson/Associated Press; 213 (cl) Lake County Museum/CORBIS; 213 (cr) Library of Congress; Prints and Photographs Division; 214 (bl) Brown Brothers; 216 (bl) Image Asset Management/Superstock; 217 (bl) Bettmann/CORBIS; 217 (br) Library of Congress; 218 (bl) Superstock; 218 (br) Peter Bennett/Alamy; 219 (c) Lewis Wickes Hine/CORBIS; 220 (br) Steve Vidler/Superstock; 222 (t) John Springer Collection/CORBIS; 222 (b) Picture History; 224 (br) Kathy Willens/AP; 224 age fotostock/Superstock; 225 (bl) Richard Levine/Alamy; 225 (tl) Ingram Publishing/Superstock; 225 (cr) Richard Levine/Alamy; 226 (b) Tetra Images/Superstock; 227 (cr) Craig Lovell/Alamy; 229 (bl) Picture History; 230 Joseph Sohm/Visions of America/CORBIS; 233 (tl) Library of Congress; 233 (tr) Viviane Moos/CORBIS; 233 (br) Pictures Colour Library/Alamy; 233 (bl) Bettmann/CORBIS; 234 (br) Schenectady Museum; Hall of Electrical History Foundation/CORBIS; 234 (bl) Lewis Wickes Hine; 1874-1940; photographer; Library of Congress; 235 (cl) Library of Congress; 235 (cr) age fotostock/Superstock; 236 (bl) Bettmann/CORBIS; 237 (tr) North Wind/North Wind Picture Archives; 237 (bl) Culver Pictures; 244 Houghton Mifflin Boston; 245 Gary D. Gold/Mira.com/drr.net; 246 (br) George Glod/SuperStock; 247 (tc) Visions of America; LLC/Alamy; 250 Peter Bennett/Ambient Images; 252 (cl) Tim Roske/Associated Press; 252 (cr) Tim Roske/Associated Press; 253 (cr) Bettmann/CORBIS; 253 (cl) Stan Honda/AFP/Getty Images; 254 (br) Frances Roberts/Alamy; 255 (c) Stan Honda/AFP/Getty; (l) (r) Tim Roske/Associated Press; 257 (tr) Monika Graff/The Image Works; 260 (b) Aerialarchives.com/Alamy; 261 (t) age fotostock/Superstock; 262 (br) Jason DeCrow/AP; 263 (cr) Houghton Mifflin Harcourt; 264 (bl) Courtesy Betty W. Ellerin; 264 (cr) Tina Fineberg/AP; 265 (bl) Eddie Adams/AP; 265 (tr) Bettmann/CORBIS; 267 Hougton Mifflin Boston; 270 Richard Levine/Alamy; 272 (cl) Courtesy New York State Archives; 272 (r) Laura Dwight; 273 (cl) Will Hart/PhotoEdit; 273 (cr) Ezra Shaw/Getty Images; 274 (br) Courtesy New York State Archives; 275 (t) Visions of America; LLC/Alamy; 276 (bl) Bob Daemmrich/The Image Works; 277 (cr) Laura Dwight; 279 (br) Underwood & Underwood/CORBIS; 280 (br) Syracuse Newspapers/David Lassman/The Image Works; 281 (tl) Bob Daemmrich/PhotoEdit; 282 (bl) Bernd Obermann/CORBIS; 284 (r) CORBIS; 285 (tr) Getty; 285 (cl) Photodisc/Getty.

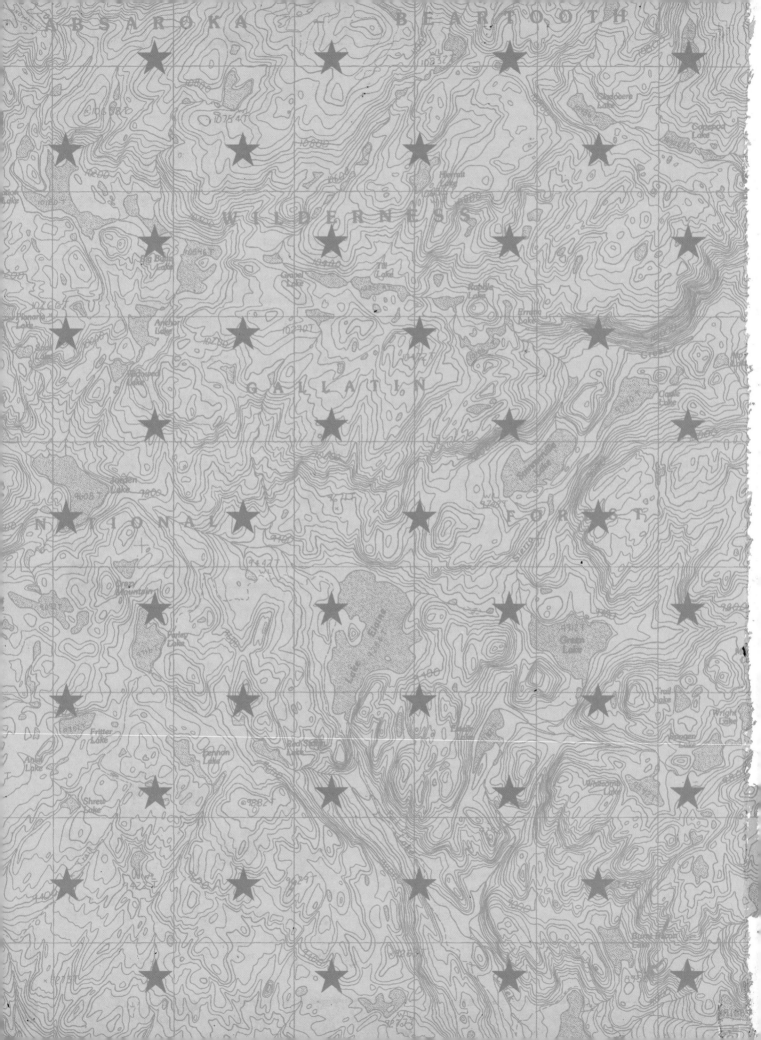